BEST SPORTS STORIES 1986

Edited and Published by
The Sporting News

President and Chief Executive Officer
RICHARD WATERS

Editor
TOM BARNIDGE

Director of Books and Periodicals
RON SMITH

Published in the United States by THE SPORTING NEWS Publishing Co., 1212 North Lindbergh Boulevard, St. Louis, Missouri 63132.

Library of Congress Catalog Card Number: 45-35124

ISSN: 0067-6292
ISBN: 0-89204-222-2
10 9 8 7 6 5 4 3 2 1

First Edition

Table of Contents

The Prize-Winning Stories

Other Stories

The Prize-Winning Photographs

BEST ACTION PHOTOGRAPH

BEST FEATURE PHOTOGRAPH

Other Photographs

**The Prize-Winning Color Photograph
Andujar's Rage**

by **Gary Weber**, a contract photographer for **Agence France Presse**. The winning color photograph, which appears on the front cover, shows St. Louis Cardinals pitcher Joaquin Andujar being restrained by teammates in the seventh game of the 1985 World Series. Andujar was ejected from the game and the Kansas City Royals pounded the Cardinals, 11-0. Copyright © 1985, Gary Weber.

**Back-Cover Photograph
Celebration**

by **Joe Kennedy** of the Los Angeles Times. Two of Kansas City's brightest stars, third baseman George Brett and pitcher Bret Saberhagen, were shining after Game 7 of the 1985 World Series when the Royals began their reign as world champions. Copyright © 1985, the Los Angeles Times.

PREFACE

The 1985 baseball season will be remembered as both the best and worst of times. On the negative side, baseball was forced to bow its head in shame, its image tarnished after player testimony in a Pittsburgh trial revealed widespread drug use in the game. On the positive side, Pete Rose ended the granddaddy of all chases by breaking Ty Cobb's all-time career hit record, Tom Seaver, Phil Niekro, Nolan Ryan and Rod Carew all reached impressive career milestones, the St. Louis Cardinals won the National League pennant with one dramatic flick of Jack Clark's bat and the comeback kids from Kansas City became the champions of baseball.

There were some interesting and surprising developments in other sports, too. The Los Angeles Lakers finally snapped the Celtics jinx and captured the National Basketball Association championship, Cinderella Villanova defeated big, bad Georgetown to complete its romp to a national championship in college basketball, the Chicago Bears were near perfect in their run to a Super Bowl title and Oklahoma methodically plowed its way to a college football championship while Grambling Coach Eddie Robinson was in the process of becoming the winningest college football coach of all time.

Wherever the action, *they* were there. "They" refers to the men and women who put as much effort into their pursuit of the perfect story or picture as athletes put into their search for excellence. The competition is fierce and the results gratifying. Those who chronicled the 1985 sports world for newspapers and magazines throughout the country continued to move toward the lofty goal of perfection, taking their readers behind the scenes for insight and perspective on the personalities and events that made the year memorable.

The Sporting News is proud to present a small sprinkling of those memories in the 42nd edition of *Best Sports Stories,* the anthology that honors the year's top writers and photographers. TSN is editing and publishing its fourth edition of the anthology, which traces its roots to 1944 and the efforts of Irving Marsh and Edward Ehre. The contest to select winners and contributors attracted hundreds of newspaper and magazine entries. It was open to writers and photographers throughout the country and accepted only stories and pictures that were published in 1985. Serving as judges for the fourth straight year were five teachers from the University of Missouri, home of one of the world's top-rated journalism education programs. They are:

Brian Brooks, the *St. Louis Post-Dispatch* Distinguished Professor of Journalism at the University of Missouri and managing editor of the *Columbia Missourian,* a student and faculty-run newspaper that serves the city of Columbia, Mo.

George Kennedy, an associate professor in the news-editorial sequence in the University of Missouri's School of Journalism.

Ken Kobre, an associate professor in the school's photojournalism sequence.

Daryl Moen, a professor in the School of Journalism's news-editorial sequence.

George Pica, an assistant professor and director of the J.C. Penney-Missouri Awards Program.

These five judges know better than anybody how agonizing it can be to sort through hundreds of well-written and creative stories and single out four for special recognition. Likewise, the selection process for three pictures. But, after painstakingly considering the merits of each entry, the judges chose the following winners, each of whom receives $500:

WRITING

Reporting	Jeffrey Marx, Michael York	Lexington (Ky.) Herald-Leader
Feature	Mike McKenzie	Kansas City Star and Times
Commentary	Phil Hersh	Chicago Tribune
Magazine	Mike Trimble	Arkansas Times

PHOTOGRAPHY

Color	Gary Weber	Agence France Presse
B&W Action	Louis DeLuca	Dallas Times Herald
B&W Feature	Jeff Shaw	Dallas Times Herald

It also was difficult for the judges to weed down the selection list to the choice few that would appear in this book. By no means are the stories and photos that follow the winning selections losers. They are, rather, a tribute to the sports journalism profession, which seems to get stronger every year. All of the *Best Sports Stories* contributors are providing an entertaining look at the 1985 sports year, as seen through the eyes and lenses of some of the country's top journalists.

Best Action Photo
Loose-Ball Scramble

by Louis DeLuca of the Dallas Times Herald. The viewer is on the floor, actually feeling the intensity of the moment as Mark Aguirre (above) of the Dallas Mavericks and Maurice Cheeks of the Phila-delphia 76ers struggle for a loose ball during a National Basketball Association game. That's what photography is all about. Bring the subjects to life and make the viewer part of the gripping action. This picture succeeds in those goals. Copyright © 1985, Louis DeLuca, Dallas Times Herald.

Best Feature Photo
Devastated

by Jeff Shaw of the Dallas Times Herald. At one end of the court
the celebration begins. At the other — pure agony. The essence of
sports is captured by this alert photographer who manages to get
the conflicting emotions of victory and defeat into one candid picture after a semifinal game in the Texas girls state high school
basketball tournament. Copyright © 1985, Jeff Shaw, Dallas
Times Herald.

Best Commentary Story

Baseball Is a Dream That Can't Go Away

BASEBALL

By *PHIL HERSH*

From the Chicago Tribune
Copyright © 1985, Chicago Tribune

The field where the boy played pickup baseball games everyday was called, in simple elegance, Big Hill. The hill began about 40 feet behind third base and rose, with almost no incline, to the road that ran along its crest. The strong righthanded batters in the neighborhood began to hit balls onto the road when they were 10 years old, but they never seemed to hit passing cars.

The boy was righthanded, too, but he wasn't very strong. It wasn't until he was 12 that he reached the heights nearly everyone he played with had already attained. The first ball he hit onto the road smacked against the side window of a car, which immediately stopped. The driver ran down Big Hill and grabbed the boy and a friend and dragged them to the police station. A police officer asked the boy what had happened and he said, "I hit a home run." He would never forget how that sounded.

★   ★   ★

Once again, the joyous noise of baseball was briefly silenced. Once again, baseball has not only suffered that foolishness but has beaten it with a resounding grand slam.

You could see the game's triumph in the people lined up at the "future games" ticket window Thursday morning at Comiskey Park. There was suddenly no reason for doubt about the immediate future of the game, but there never was, really. You could see that in the eyes of a 6-year-old boy, one of the few people in the ball park a couple of hours before the irregularly scheduled doubleheader was to begin.

The boy was sitting next to the White Sox dugout and watching batting practice, the only practice in sports anyone but a coach does watch. He was wearing a tiny uniform jersey that said "Fisk 72" on its back. When the large man wearing a uniform that said "Fisk 72" on its back emerged from the dugout, the boy's mouth opened and his eyes got wide.

"The essence of the professional game in the United States of America," wrote Robert Creamer, author of the best biography of Babe Ruth, "is a small boy looking with absolute rapture at a grown man."

That essence hadn't been spoiled by Black Sox scandals, white drug scandals, artificial stadiums, unnatural turf, unreal salaries or surreal uniforms. It wasn't spoiled by a two-day strike in which rich old men failed to regain control of the game from rich young men who once were indentured servants. It would not have been spoiled even if the strike lasted far longer.

The game persists, so solidly woven underneath the fabric of American society that it can retain the romantic quality of the 19th Century while the country hurtles pell-mell into the 21st. The men who play the game remain dream weavers.

Baseball is the only game you can see on the radio.

Baseball is the only game you can see yourself playing.

"Any schnook can play it, and they do play it, at all levels, whether it is stickball in the streets or rockball in the country," says Carlton Fisk, the White Sox catcher.

"Because everybody has or can or could play it, they live their dreams through ball players. Baseball is the only sport they do that in. Oh, I'm sure people go one-on-one in their minds, Larry Bird against Doctor J, but most don't really imagine themselves in the situation. Basketball is a game for exceptional physical specimens. Baseball is for everyday people."

What better example of that could there be than Pete Rose, who is too short, too slow, too old and too much in love with the game to let any of that stop him from becoming one of its immortals? His is the apotheosis of everyman, chronicled daily in type so small that it would reduce other news to insignificance. Baseball is a game that thrives on statistical minutiae; putting it in bigger type would be aggrandizement as ridiculous as the Roman numerals tacked onto the end of the Super Bowl.

"It is on the radio and in the newspapers everyday, the only game you can follow on that basis, from whatever arm's length you choose," says White Sox pitcher Tom Seaver. "It is always there."

It is *every* day. That is why people take it so badly when it is interrupted. Suddenly, baseball is gone, and the dream is a nightmare. Fans become angry at the players, but they are only a convenient target because of their large salaries. What the people are really mad about is the change in the rhythms of their lives.

"Some people respond like jilted lovers," Seaver says. "The first reaction is out of hate or revenge. If they still have a love for it, which a fan does for baseball more than for its players, they will miss it."

Baseball officially goes from April to October, which is more than half of every year, and unofficially the rest of the year. Think about that: What else, other than family or job, can occupy someone's attention for such an extended period of time? The game becomes a habit; the ritualization of such habits, as Sinclair Lewis said of George Babbitt's daily choice of clothes, is "of eternal importance, like baseball."

It disappeared for a week in 1972, almost two months in 1981 and a couple of days this past week. It was missed far more each one of those days than football was during its nine-game strike three years ago. Football is a passing fancy. Baseball is the only game whose season knows none.

"The gods decree a heavyweight title match only once in a while and a national election only every four years, but there is a World Series with every revolution of the earth around the sun," wrote French-born historian Jacques Barzun. "And in between, what varied pleasures long drawn out!"

★   ★   ★

The build-up to the biggest game in professional football, the Super Bowl, is unnaturally long. At least a week goes by between ordinary games. That is one of the reasons why football writers have the worst—or at least the most difficult—assignment on a daily newspaper. All week long, they have to write about nothing. The day of the game, they have to write about something even the coach can't analyze until he has seen the films.

"Baseball is a game of complex simpleness, or simple complexity," Fisk says. "People can get involved with its workings and strategies more than any other sport."

As a strategist, a baseball manager acts his role before an audience of educated critics. At football games, only those aliens born with headphones growing out of their ears can argue that a trap play wouldn't work against a hexadexamexaflexa defense. Nearly everyone in a ball park can debate the merits of a suicide squeeze.

"It starts out being a very easy game to explain, and then the fans who get into the game realize how much more is going on," says White Sox Manager Tony LaRussa.

The fourth game of last year's National League playoffs will be remembered always for its dramatic ending—Steve Garvey's two-run homer in the ninth. But its purest baseball moment occurred three innings earlier, when the game was tied and the Padres' Kevin McReynolds was on first base with one out.

The batter, Carmelo Martinez, hit a ground ball that looked like a live grenade, but Cubs shortstop Larry Bowa fielded it and threw to second baseman Ryne Sandberg. As Sandberg crossed second, he was upended by the powerful McReynolds, whose clean, hard slide drove Sandberg's throw to first off-line. First baseman Leon Durham instantly moved in the throw's direction, grabbed it and reached back to tag Martinez.

Double play. End of inning. And so much more—a perfect distillation of professionals at their best, everyone doing his job well. Martinez had hit the ball hard, but it was the ground ball pitcher Warren Brusstar had tried to make happen; Bowa had fielded the ball cleanly, but not fast enough to save Sandberg from peril; McReynolds had slid the way a man must to break up a double play, but Durham's instinctive reaction had prevented it. This description lasted longer than the play. It was only an instant, its result plain and simple, its individual components clearly visible, the chain connecting them beautiful in its intricacy.

"Baseball is a kind of collective chess with arms and legs under play in sunlight," wrote Barzun, who taught for 50 years at Columbia University.

Baseball has satisfied the intellectual and the mindless, the yuppie and the hippie, the writer and the reader. The president of Yale, a scholar of romance languages, has thought out loud that becoming American League president would be a lateral move. More distinguished authors have tried their hand at describing this game—some with needless pomp, others with remarkable circumstance—than any other. What better modern stories have been written than Gay Talese's profile of Joe DiMaggio or John Updike's description of Ted Williams' last game, the latter filled with distracting but necessary statistical footnotes?

"Say this much for big league baseball," wrote American historian Bruce Catton, "it is beyond question the greatest conversation piece ever invented in America."

It is the link between fathers and sons—and now, thankfully, fathers and daughters—because they are talking about the same game. Its true marvel is that the same 6-4-3 double play involving the Cubs, who have been a team since 1876, and Padres, who did not exist until 1969, could have been made 24 or 50 or 100 years ago, by men whose gloves were tatterdemalion, whose fields were unfenced, whose strength and size were less than that of most high school ball players today.

The critical dimension that Alexander Cartwright conceived for his New York Knickerbockers in 1846, that the distance from home to second and first to third should be "42 paces" or 126 feet, has changed only 15 inches in 139 years. The pitcher's mound has not moved since 1893. The grounder to deep short still produces a bang-bang play at first base, whether the runner is Ty Cobb or Rickey Henderson, the shortstop Honus Wagner or Alan Trammell. Walter Johnson's fastball and Dwight Gooden's fastball ride the same express train to home plate.

"It is the unchanged item in a changing world, the one stable factor in a lot of people's lives," Fisk says.

To say baseball, as an enterprise, is the same as it was 30 years ago is impossible. It has moved west, expanded twice, become a bastard son of the entertainment industry. And yet the game, as a game, is comfortingly constant. Sure, the strike zone was shrunk in 1969 and the designated hitter added in 1973, both out of a well-intentioned desire to add scoring, but those are not important. It is not the number of runs scored, but how they are scored and prevented, that is the fundamental interest of baseball.

★   ★   ★

"On a fair and beautiful October day about 1820, two distinguished Maine citizens each selected a team of neighborhood men to play a match game of 50 scores," the Bangor Whig reported. "A referee was selected and empowered to decide all questions. With the score 45 to 40 darkness intervened, and the outcome was decided by pitching pennies."

Even inflation can't account for the outcome of the mind games baseball's management and players now choose to play with each other every five years. The hundreds of millions of dollars involved have apparently become a pox on both their houses. Working men once sympathized with players who fought pitched salary battles against the robber barons who ran the game. Now they find themselves on the side of owners with whom they have never had anything in common, people for whom the game is merely a ledger item. "The rich are different from you and me," Hemingway told Fitzgerald, but we needed to harbor the illusion that ball players weren't, that they were doing what we always wanted to, enjoying a life where work was child's play.

"The one thing that you have to understand," Seaver says, "is that this game is still a way we make a living and pay for our children's education and the rest. Ideally, you would like to keep that all behind the scenes, but the financial aspects of baseball are there.

"We don't go on the field thinking about how much money we're making by playing. When we sit around as a group and discuss aspects of our industry and how that affects us, we're simply wearing a different hat."

We don't want to hear that coming from Tom Seaver. We want to hear him talk of the joys of the old ball parks, which he does with eloquence. We want to see him only in a baseball cap, jumping into Fisk's arms after winning his 300th game last Sunday. That Seaver sensibly thinks of his bottom line as well as his pitching line seems a sacrilege.

We accept heroes with feet of clay; Babe Ruth was a womanizer, a glutton and a boozer, and that has oddly enhanced his deserved reputation as baseball's greatest player. Why, then, do we find it harder to accept heroes whose solid feet are firmly grounded?

Illusions die hard. We want this to be a simpler world, one with no grays, and we want baseball to embody it. A baseball writer whose boyhood hero was Henry Aaron wanted to crawl into a hole the night that Aaron called the press box in the middle of a game to harangue the official scorer about a call that deprived him of a base hit. That churlish behavior had demeaned only Aaron, not the game;

it would not stop another child from looking in rapture at another player, unknowing that the image might later be shattered by a personal scandal or a collective strike to preserve salaries some would call already outrageous.

The paradox is that those salaries are helping baseball, by helping it draw the best athletes. How ironically satisfying that must seem to Bill Veeck, who worried about what once were declining numbers of good black athletes in the sport. Ten years ago, a remarkable athlete like Tennessee's Condredge Holloway would choose, without question, to pursue a football career in Canada rather than a baseball career in the United States. This year, Auburn's Bo Jackson, a Heisman Trophy candidate and hard-hitting outfielder, knows he might get richer and have a longer—and less perilous—career in baseball.

Making money, after all, is as American as apple pie. Why else would a television program that lets the rich and famous flaunt their lifestyles be watched so widely by people who are neither, except in their dreams?

★   ★   ★

"Whoever wants to understand the heart and mind of America had better learn about baseball, its rules and realities," Barzun wrote.

In 1907 the Spalding Commission resolved a dispute over the origins of baseball in favor of the jingoistic and mythical theory that Abner Doubleday, a West Point graduate and military hero, had invented it. The committee also decided, with equal disregard for facts, that "Base Ball had its origin in the United States." So what if, as baseball historian Fred Lieb pointed out, the New York Times' long obituary for Doubleday in 1893 did not contain the word "baseball"? To say, officially or officiously, that baseball is American does no harm to a game which, although it had English roots, has grown into more than just an national pastime.

Baseball is the game that brought a rainbow of joy after the racial storms that devastated Detroit in 1968 and New York the following year. The reality of those cities and this country's worst problems did not change, of course, but at the darkest moments even a brief shift in mood is important. It is like the walk down the darkened tunnels of an old ball park. Beyond them is a world where mean and chaotic streets suddenly are transformed into a pastoral landscape, where the sun or the sodium vapor bulbs make the grass as green as grass should always be. The light at the end of those tunnels is magical, and the first sight of it can never be stricken from our minds.

Judge's Comments

Essayists probably have been writing odes to baseball since not long after the 1820 game Phil Hersh mentions in this year's winning commentary. The best contemporary sports writers—Thomas Boswell, Roger Kahn and Roger Angell, for instance—have built their reputations largely on accounts and analyses of the game that remains the nation's pastime and the writer's passion.

It may be true, as Dan Jenkins wrote in a commentary that didn't quite make it into this year's collection, that "these lyrical outbursts" are attributable to the influence of daddies and book critics. Phil Hersh's conclusion probably does more, however, to explain the game's attraction for the best of us.

He writes of baseball's impact on America's psyche. *"It is like the walk down the darkened tunnels of an old ball park. Beyond them is a world where mean and chaotic streets suddenly are transformed into a pastoral landscape, where the sun or the sodium vapor bulbs make the grass as green as grass should always be. The light at the end of those tunnels is magical, and the first sight of it can never be stricken from our minds."*

The other finalist essays in this year's competition evoke moods ranging from nostalgia to outrage. They portray people as different as Bobby Knight and Buddy Biancalana. They cover topics as sharply focused as one coach's handling of one troubled player and as broad as the impact on sport of artificial playing surfaces.

All have in common, though, fine craftsmanship and an appreciation of the requirements of the essay—that it have a point, sharply made and solidly supported; that it be consistent in voice and tone; that it honor the conventions of the language; and that it stir the reader to intellectual or emotional reaction.

Best Feature Story

Eddie Robinson

COLLEGE FOOTBALL

By _MIKE McKENZIE_

From the Kansas City Times
Copyright © 1985, Kansas City Star Co.

Time seems to have stood still in a tiny college community bounded by bountiful cropland in northernmost Louisiana, an area populated mostly by black persons and tucked five miles further rural than Ruston, the nearest town.

No tall buildings. No traffic jams. People walking to and fro, lolling about red-brick campus buildings, yakking in cafe and barbershop hangouts on the two blocks of Main Street. Life in a no-hurry lane.

Many things have never changed in Grambling town, the old-timers say.

One thing has, drastically, dramatically, making Grambling, in all its sleepiness and plain wrapping, known throughout the world.

Football has changed at Grambling State University since a certain Edward G. Robinson appeared during World War II. Robinson wrought change that was difficult to believe, given the circumstances of rural South, small school and black heritage.

The Grambling Tigers defeated Prairie View A & M, 27-7, Saturday night, the 324th victory for Robinson, an NCAA coaching record. Grambling belongs now to all time.

Football added dash to a mere dot of a place which has but 4,200 students and fewer residents. And the change began one summer day in 1941.

Dan Washington remembers the day. So does Fidelia Johnson, known to all about her as Mamma Fi. Their lives are in overtime, entwined tightly to the life of the university, and their memories house a history that came full flower Saturday night.

In that memorable genesis so long ago, a boyish football quarterback and graduate of English from Leland College in Baton Rouge came to be interviewed. Washington, the trainer for the college's athletic teams since 1940, laughed heartily at the original picture of Robinson in his mind.

"He came in wearing a white, linen zoot suit," Washington said. "The kind—I had one, too—where you'd wear a long, gold chain that made people think you owned a watch.

"He had on those big ol' long-pointed shoes. Looked so young. Was young (22 at that time). I wondered. But he got the job. Good thing for us he did."

Robinson got the job as football coach. And basketball coach. And director for the drill team. He assumed other duties: he tended the playing fields, wrote articles on the games for newspapers, made sandwiches for after-game meals and served as surrogate father to hundreds of young men.

Mrs. Johnson is the daughter of the founder of Grambling, Charles P. Adams. She coached the women's basketball team when Robinson showed up.

"He looked awful young," she said, resting her 80 years in an overstuffed chair in the living room of her home two blocks off campus, her arthritic legs covered by a hand-woven afghan.

"I said to the prez (school president Ralph Waldo Emerson Jones), 'You sure he's a coach?' He said yeah, and I said, 'If you say so, we'll give it a try.'

"Prez was right."

Grambling has had the same football coach for 44 years. When he started, the college was called a Negro school—Louisiana Negro Normal College—and his players were called, in proper terms, colored. He started drawing crude plays in nickel notebooks, including a favorite called "Gone with the Wind."

It's the profession Robinson longed for from the time he was 8, and it has been his only job since he gave up 25 cents an hour in a feed mill and $4 a week for making pre-dawn rounds on a mule-drawn ice wagon.

His coaching legacy draws measure these days against a pair of Bears.

Victory No. 324 is one more than the late Paul (Bear) Bryant amassed at four major-sized universities. Three more victories will send Robinson past George (Papa Bear) Halas, the former Chicago Bears owner-coach whose 326 victories are the most by a football coach above the high-school level.

Robinson has pointed minor Grambling to major playgrounds from Yankee Stadium to Japan, to major television exposure and to major impact on the professional game beyond his school's country climes. At latest count by Grambling sports information director Henry Hawkins, there have been 219 Grambling players who performed in the National Football League, Canadian Football League, World Football League and the United States Football League.

Tank Younger became the first black drafted into the NFL from a small black college. Willie Davis and Willie Brown entered the

NFL Hall of Fame. Doug Williams became the first black quarterback to be drafted in the NFL's first round. Kansas City has known the Grambling touch through All-Pro performers Ernie Ladd and Buck Buchanan, and presently with defensive back Albert Lewis.

"I have been around long enough to smell a lot of roses," Robinson said. "President Jones turned me loose and didn't slow me down."

Robinson, the son of a sharecropper and housemaid, adheres to a strong work ethic with his players. They are required to be on time, attend class and church, exhibit good manners and clean appearance.

He is quick to point out with a beaming smile that a former player recently was promoted to vice president of the largest bank in New Orleans, and how the president of Grambling, Joseph B. Johnson, "came through our athletic program (basketball), and that's something to be proud of.

"This job is not just all about football. And no coach in America can out-American Eddie Robinson. A youngster has to know there are rights and obligations to being American, and understand the system and know what you are all about."

★   ★   ★

The Grambling football scene on a recent Thursday said more than any discourse on the Robinson method.

This was two days before kickoff. No ordinary kickoff, either. Bryant's record could be tied. CBS-TV and ABC-TV had film crews in town. Reporters from newspapers in four large cities prowled about. An opponent loomed from a major conference—Oregon State from the Pacific-10.

At 7 a.m., Robinson stood at one end of a hallway in the dormitory housing his athletes. He carried a cowbell. At the other end an assistant coach had a whistle. They started toward one another, moving room to room, and football players two-by-two greeted another day in a clanging, shrill way. It's a daily Robinson ritual.

"We have to help take care of them," Robinson said. "A lot of them come here who haven't had a lot of love at home."

The players must go to breakfast. Then they must attend class. If they don't they pay.

At the end of practice Robinson called the names of a couple of dozen players. They had to go to the bleachers and run from bottom to top and back 20 times. They had missed breakfast. Later, he took their meal tickets away for the next day's free supper.

"If they don't get the grades, they don't do you any good or anybody else. And when they get the grades it makes their parents feel happy."

The practice that day—remember, just two days before the game—lasted three hours and 45 minutes.

He had another practice scheduled from 10 p.m. until 1 a.m. if the team didn't perform to expectations. Robinson held just such a practice two nights before the opening game against Alcorn State, the preseason favorite in the Southwestern Athletic Conference. Grambling won, 30-20.

Thursday practice was alive with activity, and also with scattered laughter among coaches and players. James Polk, a mountain of a youth at 6-feet-9 and 320 pounds, kept yelling, "Thunder!" (Thunder is what Grambling calls its defense.) "Thunder, the barbarian!" And he laughed heartily at stories told between drills by Ernest Sterling, an assistant coach, and a former player who dropped by.

"We attend to business," Robinson said, "but we want them to have fun, too." During practice he wore a frown frequently, and he barked at individuals when they didn't toe the right line. He ran pass routes, acted out blocking schemes. And he called off the moonlight practice.

The next day, Friday, the day before kickoff, the team practiced three hours. Assistant coach Fred (Bossman) Collins remembered a time when he told Robinson he'd read some material about shorter practices becoming the trend.

"Hold that point," Robinson said, and disappeared in his office. He returned with a record book and said, "It says here, 'Winningest team of the '70s, Grambling, average nine wins a year.' Fred, we're the trend."

★   ★   ★

Robinson prefers a low-keyed lifestyle. He said he isn't sure exactly what his salary is now, but his wife knows ($53,000), and his business representative, Collie J. Nicholson, said Robinson makes "far more than his salary" on contracts to represent Coca-Cola and Southwestern Bell.

He walks home to lunch everyday. He lives a few blocks off campus in a large, but not fancy red-brick home with his wife of 44 years, Doris. They drive a 4-year-old car.

At home Robinson spends much of his time in a small, narrow room at one end of the house that he calls "my den I can't get into"—a museum in its own right. Bookshelves bulge with pamphlets and notebooks, textbooks, biographies, novels and speech-making materials. He has kept every practice schedule he has drawn up for 44 years, every bound volume of minutes from national coaches meetings and clinics.

Ever present at Robinson's side is a brown doctor's-style bag. Inside is a kaleidoscope of paperwork. "I've always had one, and I'll carry about anything in it," Robinson said. "In other years I had scissors and clippers and a straight razor in there, so when a boy came in on the bus, if he wasn't cut clean, I could reach in and trim him up."

Proudly, Robinson pulled several magazines from a rack and thumbed to photos of himself with several prominent people. A couple showed him and Gerald Ford. "I like to look over the President's shoulder and let 'em know I was there, too," Robinson said, laughing.

★   ★   ★

In the beginning he could not have dreamed he would dine with Presidents, perform before emperors, win with the Bears and Pop Warner and Amos Alonzo Stagg.

"I think Grambling has helped connect me with what is good in American society," Robinson said.

People speak of Robinson's vision, his daring to tread where others did not. Fred Hobdy, Grambling's basketball coach, said, "The man has climbed many mountains." An assistant coach, Ed Stevens, who is white and has been on the staff 17 years, said, "A million others wouldn't take the steps Coach Rob took, and wouldn't be taking them now if Grambling hadn't. He had imagination."

He also had fortitude. Robinson, when pressed, will recall situations such as the time the team bus broke down and, when it was towed, a man wielding a wrench yelled, "Get that nigger bus out of here."

Robinson would pack sandwiches and apples for his team to eat on the way home from games, stopping "Bluebird," the bus, usually in a churchyard. They could not get served in cafes along the way home from places they played all across Dixie.

"You can call me a black coach if you want, but I'm an American coach," he said. "Some people want to cry over the way it was. You can't unring a bell. Some people build roads, some ride on them. When you get to the 1-yard line, color doesn't matter. If you say somebody's going to stop you from doing something because of your color, that's a lie.

"I know how people loved Warner and Stagg and the Bear. I just want them to love me, too, for whatever I've done. I always wanted my piece of the pie, that's all.

"Sure, you'd like to know if you could have won at another place. But how else can you judge me except on what I accomplished?

"This record doesn't belong just to me. It belongs to many coaches, hundreds of players. But you know how we do it in America, somebody's got to be the hero."

Judge's Comments

In a category with hundreds of superior entries, it's tough to pick a winner. Mike McKenzie gets the nod with his superb account of the rise of Grambling's Eddie Robinson from a job in a feed mill and an ice wagon route to the top of collegiate coaching.

Much was written about Robinson in 1985, when he passed Paul (Bear) Bryant to become the all-time leader in collegiate football coaching victories. McKenzie's account stands out not only because of the writing, which is excellent, but also because of the reporting, which is superb. McKenzie has the observational skills of a master detective, and those skills serve a reporter well. His ability to describe is what makes this article stand out.

Moreover, this is not an article about a football coach, but one about a human being. And an extraordinary one at that.

McKenzie's ability to show the reader what makes Eddie Robinson tick without resorting to editorialized puffery is both commendable and unusual. This is not an essay; it is a story in the very best sense of the word.

Best Reporting Story

Boosters' Gifts Lined Kentucky Players' Pockets

BASKETBALL

By *JEFFREY MARX* and *MICHAEL YORK*

From the Lexington Herald-Leader
Copyright © 1985, Lexington Herald-Leader

For years, ordinary fans have rewarded University of Kentucky basketball players with a loyalty that is nationally known. What is less known is that a small group of boosters has been giving the players something extra: a steady stream of cash.

The cash has come in various amounts—as little as $20 and as much as $4,000 or more—and it has come often.

UK players have received what they call "hundred-dollar handshakes" in the Rupp Arena locker room after games. They have visited the offices and homes of boosters to receive gifts of up to $500 at a time. They have sold their free season tickets for $1,000 each or more, and they have pocketed excessive payments for public appearances and speeches.

The payments and other benefits directly violated the rules of the National Collegiate Athletic Association.

The *Lexington Herald-Leader* interviewed 33 former Wildcats who played during the 13 years. Thirty-one said they knew of improper activities while they were playing, and 26 said they participated.

Typical of the handouts described by those players were the following:

• Forward Fred Cowan (1977-81) said eastern Kentucky coal operator Maynard Hogg gave him "a couple hundred dollars . . . anytime I wanted it."

"I don't want to get into details, because you know and I know it was illegal," Cowan said, referring to violations of NCAA rules.

Hogg said the money represented deferred payments from Cowan's summer job with Hogg's coal company.

• Forward Scott Courts, who left UK after his freshman year, 1977-78, said that Lexington developer Donald Webb was his "sugar daddy" and gave him "a couple" of gifts, the largest of which was $500.

Webb refused to be interviewed for this article.

• Guard Dirk Minniefield (1979-83) said he shook the hand of booster Elmer Prewitt, a Corbin physician, in the locker room "a couple of times" and found himself holding a $50 bill. Three other players said they got up to $100 at a time in handshakes from Prewitt.

"A couple" of current players received money from Prewitt in the locker room last season, said another player, who watched but asked not to be identified.

Prewitt said he never gave money to players.

Other former players got the special handshakes from other boosters.

"I'm not saying I never got one, but I didn't get many," said All-America guard Kyle Macy (1977-80).

• Guard Jay Shidler (1976-80) said he made $8,400 as a Wildcat by selling his complimentary tickets to Cecil Dunn, who is former coach Joe B. Hall's lawyer. Dunn refused to comment.

Selling tickets for more than their face value without the permission of the university is a violation under Kentucky's ticket-scalping law and is punishable by a fine.

The Fayette County attorney's office, in which Dunn is an assistant, is responsible for prosecuting such violations.

• Macy said he made eight to a dozen speeches each spring for up to $150 apiece. "The title put on it was expenses, but really it was just a payment," he said.

Other players, including All-America center Sam Bowie (1979-84), said they received up to $500 apiece for speeches and other public appearances.

• Former players said they got other gifts, including clothing, tires and free meals, usually from boosters close to the program but also from ordinary fans they hardly knew. A favorite place for free meals was Cliff Hagan's Ribeye, co-owned by UK athletic director Cliff Hagan. Hagan said he knew nothing about the practice.

Because players were so well known and so many boosters were eager to help, handouts were likely to occur almost anywhere. Players said boosters stopped them on the street to give them money, put it in Christmas cards and handed it out in business offices.

"As I progressed the four years . . . it became a game of who could get what," said forward Chuck Verderber (1978-82).

"It wasn't so much the players' problem, it was the people who surrounded the program," he said. "It became real greedy, I felt. It got to be ridiculous. I was glad I got out."

However, Verderber acknowledged that he, too, received money. Asked to estimate how much, he said:

"It's not five bucks and it isn't $50,000. That's all I can say. I don't know because I didn't keep track of it."

Many former players said they felt no remorse over breaking the rules, which they described as unfair.

"It was just like there are no rules, and we're not doing anything wrong," Shidler said.

Cowan, Courts, Minniefield, Macy, Shidler, Bowie and Verderber were among 15 former UK players who said they took cash, received excessive speaking fees or sold their tickets in violation of the rules. The others were Dwight Anderson, Bret Bearup, Tom Heitz, Bo Lanter, James Lee, Troy McKinley, Mike Phillips and Tim Stephens. Additional players said they got free meals. Others said they got improper gifts but refused to say what they were for the record.

The NCAA believes that student-athletes should be students first and that allowing them to take money could cost them their amateur status.

NCAA rules limit students on athletic scholarships to receiving tuition and fees, room and board, required books for courses and four passes to games.

Players may not work during the school year, and if they make speeches, they may receive payment only for their actual expenses. No player is allowed to sell his passes to games.

The people primarily responsible for making sure NCAA rules were followed at UK were head coach Joe B. Hall, Hagan and President Otis Singletary. Singletary heads an NCAA Division I group charged with finding ways to tighten enforcement of the rules.

Singletary and Hagan said in separate interviews that they were unaware of any cash handouts to players or other violations of the rules. After speaking with the *Herald-Leader* on October 9, Singletary told university general counsel John Darsie to begin an investigation, Darsie said. Darsie refused to comment on the investigation last week.

Jack Blanton, UK's vice chancellor for administration, said, however: "Probably we'll never know the full story."

Blanton, who is Hagan's direct supervisor, said he was not directly involved in the investigation.

Hall, who announced his retirement in March, refused to answer questions for this article. He issued a statement saying that he was "unaware of any NCAA rules being violated" and that he took measures to make sure the players followed the rules.

Interviews disclosed that violations occurred the entire time that Hall was coach and continued even after UK was put on probation in late 1976 for infractions in the football and basketball programs.

The *Herald-Leader* attempted to determine how the NCAA rules are being enforced by Hall's successor, Eddie Sutton. But Sutton declined a request for an interview and instructed his players not to talk with the newspaper for this article.

Hagan, however, said that Sutton would no longer allow boosters into the locker room after games. Hagan said other changes, such as altering the school's policy on player speaking engagements, were under consideration.

The interviews with former players disclosed only payments to players once they were in school. None said UK made improper recruiting offers, as have been reported at a number of schools.

Former UK players differed widely when asked how much emphasis Hall put on following the rules.

Bowie said Hall "constantly" reminded his players that taking money or selling tickets was against NCAA rules.

"He said the first time he ever found out who was getting what, that they would be dismissed from the team," Bowie said.

Macy got a different impression and said that Hall neither encouraged nor discouraged payments to players.

"I'd say he was probably neutral on that," Macy said. "I just think he kind of looked the other way. Whether he even knew what was going on, I don't know."

Hagan said that among the steps Hall took was to send players a letter every year explaining the NCAA rules to them.

But many of the players said they thought the rules were unrealistic.

Forward Kevin Grevey (1972-75), an All-America and UK's No. 3 all-time leading scorer, said that a basketball player who had worked hard for years to get to college should be able to take whatever he wanted once he got there.

"If someone offered him a car, he ought to be able to take the car or money," said Grevey, who said he never took any cash handouts. "Rules are rules, and they have to be followed, but I personally say, the more the merrier. If a kid can get this or get that, take it."

Guard Jim Master (1980-84) said: "There is cheating going on, definitely, but it's going on everywhere. You can't stop it. It's not like you got a television camera on you the whole time."

"The approach I take," Master said, is "who really cares? I don't think there is anything wrong with it, as long as it doesn't stem from the coaches themselves." Master said he did not take cash handouts himself, however.

For Cowan, accepting money and gifts was just a practical matter.

"It's impossible to go by the rules . . . when you can save some money," Cowan said. "I'm not saying that it's right, either, to go out and get everything free. But that's the way it works in Kentucky more or less."

Others found the atmosphere, at times, disturbing.

"Probably my biggest concern was . . . seeing the players' attitudes," Macy said. "If a player gets to where he's starting to expect stuff (to be) given to him, that's going to lead to problems."

Reserve forward Tom Heitz (1979-1984) said the people who gave money to players generally fell into one of two categories:

"friends of the program" or "people that are just trying to impress you by giving you some cash."

"Some people are insecure with themselves, and they think, well, maybe if they can't win your friendship by just being a nice person, maybe they'll put a little cash in your hand," Heitz said.

"Too many players get controlled by the money, and they just become pawns," said Heitz, who acknowledged that he received small amounts of money from boosters, sometimes in the locker room after games. "Nobody was going to control me with money or own me.

"I'm not saying all the alumni are bad, because a lot of them are just great people."

Guard Dwane Casey (1975-79) was one player who said he knew of no violations. "If that makes me look like an oddball, I guess it has to," he said.

Casey, now an assistant coach at Western Kentucky University, also defended the UK coaching staff:

"There's no way that a coaching staff could go patrolling the numerous alumni in the Kentucky situation . . . . I know you think I'm crazy for me to sit here and say that they're squeaky clean or something like that. You can't say that, because the coaching staff can't control what alumni do."

Hogg was one of the few boosters willing to discuss why he helped a player out.

"I'm a Big Blue fan from the word go. I love Kentucky," said Hogg, who is from Fleming-Neon in Letcher County.

Hogg said that former assistant coach Dickie Parsons introduced him to Cowan and said: " 'If you want to help some poor boy that really needs help this summer, you ought to give that boy a job.' "

Hogg said he felt good about his relationship with Cowan.

"I would help him today if he was in a hard place," Hogg said.

Troy McKinley (1981-85) identified real estate developer Dick Sutherland as another booster who handed out money. Bret Bearup (1980-85) confirmed what McKinley said.

Sutherland said he wouldn't comment on that, but he did acknowledge that he was close to some players.

"Those relationships with those players were no different than my relationship with my children," Sutherland said. "Those players cannot be expected to exist in a vacuum here and have no friends."

Here are some details on what the former UK players said happened:

★   ★   ★

Some players said they had a special "sponsor" or "sugar daddy" who would provide help when needed.

• Scott Courts said that during his first day at UK he met the businessman who would become his sugar daddy.

Courts and Hall were outside Memorial Coliseum when Donald Webb drove by.

Courts said that Webb stopped and stepped out of his car to greet Hall. Courts said Hall told him: " 'This is going to be your best friend on the campus,' or something like that."

Webb then took Courts for a brief tour of Lexington. At the time, Courts said, he didn't know that Webb would become "my sugar daddy."

Courts said he first went to Webb for money on the advice of Leonard Hamilton, then an assistant coach. Courts said that during a break in a summer pickup game at Alumni Gym, Hamilton checked with him to make sure he had everything he needed.

According to Courts, Hamilton leaned over and said something like: "Hey buddy, if you ever have any money problems or anything, well, Don Webb might be able to take care of you. . . . Don't be advertising this now, but if you have a problem or something don't worry about it. Come and see me or see Don Webb."

Courts said that he visited Webb "a couple times" for money and that $500 was the most he received at one time. "It wasn't like there was always money under my door from Don Webb," Courts said. "He helped out when I ran short.

"I'd just say I needed a little help. And he'd say, "How much do you need? . . . What do you need it for? Don't spend it all at one place.' "

Courts said that he kept a little bottle in his dormitory room filled with money from Webb and from selling his four season tickets—for which he said he received about $2,250. The money went toward a stereo, records, clothes and other expenses.

"Thank God for those alums," Courts said.

Courts, now an investment counselor in Denver, said that Webb spoke of setting him up in business after graduation.

"I really felt he had sincere . . . reasons for doing what he was doing," Courts said.

Both Webb and Hamilton, now UK's associate basketball coach, refused to be interviewed for this article.

• Fred Cowan said he met coal operator Maynard Hogg in a Lexington restaurant after a game. Cowan was then a freshman.

He said that he was grateful to Hogg for helping him get through UK and that it would be "foolish" to even think about trying to repay him.

"When I did receive money from Maynard, it wasn't nothing like I was on a regular pay basis. He was helping me out," Cowan said.

"I didn't want him to feel like I was using him."

Hogg characterized the payments as deferred wages and benefits he owed Cowan for his summer work at Hogg's mine. He said that while Cowan wasn't a member of the United Mine Workers Union, he paid him as if he were and that meant Cowan had built up the extra pay.

NCAA rules state that players may be given deferred payments for summer work only if all other employees are treated the same way.

• Dirk Minniefield, who is now playing for the Cleveland Cavaliers of the National Basketball Association, said he received delayed payments when he worked for Laban Jackson at International Spike Inc.

"I would get paid my salary half at Christmas and half during the summer," Minniefield said.

And if Minniefield found himself running short between the summer and Christmas, he said he could get some of the money early.

Jackson said he paid Minniefield during the summer but not at other times of the year.

A number of boosters like to give a player a $50 or $100 bill in a locker room handshake. Dr. Elmer Prewitt of Corbin was one of them, Minniefield and others said.

Minniefield said that Prewitt gave him $50 "a couple of times."

"In my case, he would maybe say something like, 'Buy your kids something, take your wife to dinner,' or something like that," Minniefield said.

Shidler said that in four years, Prewitt gave him money in the locker room "probably half a dozen times." Each time, Shidler received either a $50 or a $100 bill, folded up and passed from Prewitt's hand to his own during a handshake, Shidler said.

Shidler said that Prewitt sometimes followed him into an equipment room off the main locker room, where a cooler of drinks sat after games, so Prewitt could hand him the money without anyone seeing.

"He was discreet," Shidler said. Prewitt wasn't "just like waving $100 bills in my face or something. He knew he had to be careful about it."

Three other players who asked not to be identified said that Prewitt sometimes handed out money in the locker room in amounts ranging from $20 to $100. Two of them said they got some of the money.

Prewitt said that he had been a friend of Hall's for more than 20 years and that he had often visited the UK locker room after games. But he said he never gave money to players.

"That's against the rules. I'm too smart for that," Prewitt said. "My support has been in counseling and this sort of thing. I don't deal in money."

Minniefield said that it would be wrong "just to point out one person" who handed out money in the locker room, because others did the same thing.

He said, for example, that Jimmy Robertson, who runs a Lexington construction company, once gave him $50 in the UK locker room.

Robertson declined to comment.

Kyle Macy also said he got special handshakes, but he would not identify the person or people who gave him money. He said that one handshake he remembered came in a hotel room after the NCAA championship game in 1978, when a booster gave him and Rick Robey $50 each.

Robey, an All-America forward-center (1974-78), told the *Herald-Leader* that he never accepted money from a booster.

Macy said that hundred-dollar handshakes "went on a lot" but that he didn't get many because he didn't go looking for them.

"I guess maybe it's always a nice thing thinking that if you ever needed help that you could get it," Macy said. "I guess I wasn't looking for it, so I wasn't really around it that much."

Tom Heitz, who acknowledged that he also got money in the locker room, said players took the gifts for granted.

"You just knew it goes on everywhere and just kind of expected it, I guess," said Heitz, now a commodities trader in Chicago.

The cash could pop up anywhere. Heitz said, for example, that a booster gave him a Christmas card containing $100.

"I don't think we (had) anybody getting a salary every week or anything like that, not to my knowledge at least," Heitz said. "But everybody would get money once in a while, and what are you going to do, say, 'Oh, I'm not going to take it?' "

The benefits were not always distributed equally, as an incident in which a player did not receive money illustrates.

Reserve guard-forward Troy McKinley said he was ignored when a booster delivered Christmas cards—with money enclosed—to a carload of players leaving Rupp Arena after a practice session during Christmas break 1983.

McKinley and forward-center Bret Bearup, who was also in the car, said that real estate developer Dick Sutherland gave Bearup $50 in his envelope and gave Jim Master and Dicky Beal $100 each in theirs.

McKinley, then a bench warmer, unlike the others, said he did not even get a card.

He said that being left out didn't bother him because he was "kind of used to it."

"If you come in the program, you don't play a lot, you find out a lot of stuff that you get missed out on," McKinley said.

Beal said that he did not remember the incident but that if McKinley and Bearup confirmed it "I guess it's true, but I don't know."

Master, now a salesman for Valvoline Oil, twice said that he would neither confirm nor deny that the incident took place. Then he said that he would deny it.

Sutherland said he would not discuss the incident. "It's highly personal, and I'm not going to comment on that at all."

His relationships with players "had nothing to do with the university," Sutherland said. "UK didn't aim them at me or aim me at them . . . and if Dr. Singletary and Cliff Hagan were asking me these very questions, I would not answer them."

Dwight Anderson (1978-79) said that because so many boosters were willing to pitch in, a popular UK player was in a position to get a lot of money. "The sky is the limit," he said.

Chuck Verderber, now a UK dental student, said that the boosters who gave him money were doing so as friends, because they cared about him, and not just because he dribbled and dunked more than the average undergraduate.

For example, one gave him money to buy a new set of tires before a vacation, he said.

"If people wanted to help me, I didn't want it to be a big deal," Verderber said. He added that he never turned down money when a booster offered it. "Would you?" he asked. "No. Hell no. Why?"

And Verderber said that he did not pursue money the way some of his teammates did. For a few players, "their whole motivation was to go out and get money from people and be with those people just for the fact that they were going to get something in return."

Mike Ballenger (1981-82), who now plays at Western Kentucky, said that he learned about the generous boosters from older teammates.

Ballenger said that the message he heard was: If you need help, ask the boosters with whom you feel comfortable. "I don't know who was making what," he said of his teammates, "but they were making a lot of money."

One prominent starter within the last few years estimated for the *Herald-Leader* how much that was: about $10,000 during his time at UK.

He also provided details but agreed to do so only if his identity and the identities of those who paid him were not disclosed.

The player said he got these payments that violated NCAA rules:

• Bonuses totaling $2,500 at the end of summer jobs from his employer, who has been close to the program.

• Several visits to a booster in his Lexington office, where he received about $1,000 in payments of at least $100 at a time.

• Speaking engagements and public appearances that brought as much as $500 each and a total of about $3,000.

• The sale of complimentary tickets on a game-by-game basis, which brought about $3,000.

• Random cash gifts, sometimes in the Rupp Arena locker room, totaling about $500.

Some players said they chose not to accept cash handouts.

Rick Robey, who now plays with the Phoenix Suns, said he never took money but was sure that other players did.

"Heck, if I gave you $500, down the road you would always feel kind of obligated to me, wouldn't you?" he said. "That's where I think some guys, if they did take money, made mistakes. I don't think you should ever get yourself in that situation, where you ever owe anybody anything."

Charles Hurt (1979-83), a forward now playing professional

basketball in Japan, offered another reason not to accept money: Some of the rich boosters cared more about wins and losses than the players' well-being.

"I tried to look at people a little different, you know, than just because they had money," he said. "If they were phony, I don't have to be associated with them.

"Those guys, if you played good, they were OK. If you didn't play good, it was like the end of the world."

Sam Bowie said that he decided to stay away from cash handouts other than speaking fees while playing at UK because he did not want to jeopardize his reputation and his chances for a professional career.

Bowie, who now plays with the Portland Trail Blazers, said that no one was known as his sponsor, and he would not discuss the specifics of what he knew other players received. Bowie did acknowledge that he knew "all the sponsors in Kentucky, as well as the guys that were probably designated to those sponsors."

And he said that he would socialize with some of the sponsors even if he didn't take money from them. He roomed with Cowan and said he knew Cowan's friend Hogg "quite well."

Bowie said he visited Hogg's home "quite a few times." But Hogg never gave him any money, he said.

If a player received money after a game, Bowie said, it would come from "that same booster or sponsor that was taking care of the player throughout the year."

"It wasn't like they were just giving money away after a game," he said.

Even the players who didn't want to say whether they personally received anything confirmed that the Wildcats routinely broke the rules.

Former guard Beal (1980-84) said he did not want to talk about any money or benefits he received as a Kentucky player. "I don't want to say anything to get anybody in trouble."

But he did say: "There's not too many people on the team that was ever hurting. I don't care if you played or never saw any action, I'm sure that you were never hurting for anything. That's just how it is."

Macy, who recently joined the Chicago Bulls, was another player who said he didn't want to get anyone in trouble.

"I wouldn't want to say anything that would hurt the program because it's been great to me and I enjoyed my time there.

"On the other hand, you're going to be honest about stuff, and maybe that will help get things cleaned up," he said.

★   ★   ★

Speeches and public appearances provide a ready source of income for some players.

A player would often talk about the values of hard work, a positive outlook and a solid education. Then the player would usually accept some money—sometimes only to cover expenses, as allowed under NCAA rules, but often more.

"You weren't making tons on that, but if you did enough of them, you were going to build up pretty good," Macy said.

Minniefield, who made money from speeches, said they could be a good source of income over the four years.

"You can make four or five thousand dollars if you're one of the more prominent players on the team," he said.

Sam Bowie said that speaking engagements were "easy money."

"There are players that have been through that program that have made a living off of speaking engagements," Bowie said. "I've spoken at events where you can get $250 to $500. . . . I've received that type of money.

"If I was to speak at a place and a guy gives me an envelope with $500 in it, do you take that and give it back to him, saying that the NCAA says we can only accept $100?"

The NCAA manual says players may receive only "actual and necessary expenses" for speaking engagements and other public appearances. The UK athletic department has set a rate of 18 cents a mile for expenses, according to letters sent to groups who requested speakers. At that rate, a player driving to Fulton in far western Kentucky, one of the farthest points in the state from Lexington, would be reimbursed $108 for the 600-mile round trip.

At times, Bowie said, he would appear for nothing at a charity event. Other times, he was disappointed with what he was paid.

"I can recall Bret Bearup and myself maybe driving two, three hours away from Lexington, and the envelope would be $75," Bowie said.

But Bowie and Bearup had plenty of other opportunities to make money.

"Bret probably spoke more than anybody in the history of Kentucky," Bowie said.

Bearup just laughed when asked about Bowie's comment.

Others said that players would sometimes ask for certain annual appearances because of a group's reputation for paying well. None would identify the groups.

Several players from the last few years said payments for appearances usually ranged from $100 to $500.

McKinley said that "probably about $200" was the most he received on any occasion. Accepting the money did not concern him, he said, because he would never tell the NCAA about it and it would be "very difficult to prove."

Verderber said he was paid for several speeches each spring.

"Someone would call me and say they would pay me maybe $100 to speak," Verderber said. "But the money wasn't the reason I went. I went because I felt I had something to say to kids, mainly about education."

Walk-on player Bo Lanter (1979-82) also found speeches to be "a good source of income." Lanter said he made "several hundred dollars" a year by speaking and said he figured other players made more.

"That's just common sense," said Lanter, now a Lexington businessman. "I would think someone would pay more for Sam Bowie to speak that they would for Bo Lanter."

Forward James Lee (1974-78) also said he received excessive payments for public appearances.

Speaking payments have grown since his senior year, Lee said. "I think winning that championship made it easier for the rest of those players."

Randy Stacy, who left UK in November 1984 after more than four years as an assistant sports information director, was often responsible for matching appearance requests with players. He said that he informed people of the NCAA rules restricting payments but that he was still aware that payments were being made.

"I think we would be terribly naive to think that that wouldn't happen," he said. "But it's something I made sure that I didn't become involved in."

Several players said that they were likely to receive more money for an appearance when they made the arrangements through a booster or friend instead of through the sports information department.

"A lot of times, folks dealt directly if they knew the players, which was fine with me," Stacy said. "There was no way I could police that. I was glad to have it out of my hair."

Stacy said it was impossible to fill all the requests for speakers.

"There just wasn't enough people to do it," he said. "That's certainly not one of the areas of the job that I miss, because it was a hassle."

★ ★ ★

The sale of complimentary game tickets at inflated prices was an accepted and expected source of income for many UK basketball players during the last decade.

Nine former players told the *Herald-Leader* that they sold tickets, but not all would say how much they made or to whom they sold the tickets.

One who would was Shidler, who said he sold his tickets to Hall's attorney, Cecil Dunn of Lexington.

Shidler said that three years' worth of season tickets brought him $8,400 in cash and got him a discount on an apartment he lived in one summer.

He said that he could have made more but that as a freshman he was too naive to know that UK season tickets were so valuable. That year, Shidler's four tickets went to family and friends.

But Shidler soon learned that his teammates viewed income from the sale of tickets as "something to make life a little easier during the year until we could get a summer job."

The next summer, Shidler said, he gave two season tickets to the manager of his apartment building in exchange for reduced rent.

That left two other tickets, which Shidler said he sold to Dunn. Shidler said that he could not recall precisely how the deal was initiated.

But he said that it left him—a self-described "little peanut from Lawrenceville, Illinois"—"on top of the world," with a wad of $100 bills in his pocket.

Shidler said that Dunn offered $600 each for the two tickets and paid the full amount when he received them.

The arrangements changed in the next two years, Shidler said. He said that he asked for $800 each for four tickets as a junior and $1,000 each for four tickets as a senior.

Dunn, who often traveled with the team and was regarded as an insider during the Hall years, did not hesitate to raise the payments, Shidler said.

The last two years, 1978-79 and 1979-80, Dunn received the tickets directly from the basketball office and paid Shidler in increments —usually $500 at a time, Shidler said.

The payments were made in Dunn's downtown Lexington office, Shidler said.

"I'd call him and say I'm coming down, or can I come," Shidler said. "I think the first time he gave me $500 he said 'If you run out, you need some more, just call.' And so whenever I needed more, I'd just call him.

"He'd say, 'How much do you need?' I'd say, 'I don't know, $500 again would be OK,' and he'd just pull it out of his wallet.

"I was completely comfortable. It wasn't a problem," said Shidler, who did not know what Dunn did with the tickets.

"After we made the transaction, it was really no longer my business, and I really didn't care what he was doing with them," Shidler said. "He could have been wallpapering his house with them as far as I know."

Despite several attempts by the *Herald-Leader,* Dunn declined to answer questions for this article.

"After I read it I might be able to respond to it," Dunn said. "Now I just don't want to.

"I have for the last 20 years represented Joe (Hall) and also been his friend and both legally, ethically, and as a friend I wouldn't want to say anything that any way hurts him, even if it hurts me."

Until August 1, 1980, the NCAA permitted college players to sell their tickets at face value, which at UK was $60 for a lower-arena season ticket in 1979-80. After that date, players received tickets but were forbidden to sell them.

Starting with the 1983-84 season, players were no longer given actual tickets. They were allowed to put names on a pass list at the ticket window. Starting this season, only relatives, friends and fellow students designated by the players may be on the list. The passes may not be sold.

The *Herald-Leader* made an open-records request for the names on the pass lists, but UK denied the request, saying that disclosure could violate people's privacy. The newspaper is suing in Fayette Circuit Court to force disclosure of the lists.

UK players said they continued to sell their tickets in recent years despite the rule changes. As Master put it, "You're always going to get around something. . . . That's the way the world works." Master said, however, that he never sold his tickets.

McKinley, who graduated in May, said "the majority of the guys" on the team sold tickets, for as much as $100 each for a single game and between $1,000 and $1,500 for a season ticket.

Other players, including Master and Mike Ballenger, said the $1,000 to $1,500 range was right.

Asked to identify his teammates who regularly sold their tickets, McKinley said: "Well, I think you'd be pretty safe (saying) just anybody that . . . wasn't from Kentucky. I mean, you can just take your pick."

He said players without family nearby generally didn't have anything to do with their tickets except to sell them.

Bowie, however, said that he turned down offers for his tickets, even though his family lived in Pennsylvania. Bowie said that he rejected offers of up to $2,500 for a single season ticket.

"It's tempting," Bowie said. "I mean, here I am, out of town, my people don't have money. For me to say that at one point . . . I didn't consider it, I'd be lying. But I can honestly say that I never sold my tickets.

"As a matter of fact, a lot of times I gave my tickets to some kids from black neighborhoods, 6, 7 years old, that weren't fortunate enough to get in Rupp Arena. And a lot of times I never even used my tickets."

Bowie said that he and other UK players heard "constant talk" about what they could get for a season ticket. The going rate he heard was $1,500 to $2,000.

Kevin Grevey, a free agent who played for the Milwaukee Bucks last season, said he never sold his tickets, either, but that ticket selling by players was also "pretty common" when he was at UK a decade ago.

"It was pretty standard practice that guys sold their tickets," Grevey said. "I personally feel that when a kid goes to school and gets four tickets, those are his tickets and he should be able to do what he wants to with them."

The players who said they sold tickets described a variety of arrangements: Some sold tickets directly to boosters, and others relied on higher-profile teammates to make a deal for them.

Some examples:

• McKinley, who is from Independence in Northern Kentucky, said that family or friends usually filled his seats. But he said that when he had an extra ticket or two to a game, he would sell them.

• McKinley said that he relied on teammate Bret Bearup to find buyers, who paid up to $100 a ticket.

"He got the money for me," McKinley said. "He knows a lot of people around here."

• Bearup said that he did not mind helping a teammate sell his tickets.

"I helped Troy out because I knew people wanted tickets," Bearup said. "I didn't make any money from it, but I wanted to help because nobody ever did that for me."

Bearup would not name anyone to whom he sold tickets, but he said he usually got about $50 a ticket.

• Scott Courts said that in 1977 he learned the value of tickets from Rick Robey, a senior at the time.

Selling tickets "was as common as brushing your teeth," Courts said.

Courts said that Robey sold his season tickets for him and delivered "something like $2,250" to him in a room on the first floor of Holmes Hall, where the players then lived.

Another former player said that immediately after Robey delivered the money, Robey bragged about what he had done.

• Robey said that he never sold season tickets for Courts but that he did help Courts, Chuck Aleksinas and one other player sell their NCAA playoff tickets during the Wildcats' 1978 championship run.

Robey also said that he sometimes matched alumni interested in tickets with teammates who had extras. "I kind of played the mediator there, because I think I knew everybody in town," he said. "They would come to me."

"I've bought tickets before for particular games and stuff like that, but I was not in the ticket business," Robey said.

• Aleksinas, who now plays professional basketball in Spain, wouldn't comment on whether he sold his tickets during 1977-78, his only full season at UK, but he did talk about Robey.

"I can remember him always trying to get tickets off us," Aleksinas said. "I remember him as the business type, trying to make a dollar here, dollar there."

Four other players said they sold tickets:

• Mike Phillips (1974-78) said that he sold his tickets on a game-by-game basis when he was not using them for family or friends. "If I didn't have any use for the tickets, I didn't see any reason just to let them go to waste," he said.

Phillips said that he did not remember how much money he made from the tickets.

Phillips said that he sold them only to people with whom he felt comfortable because he did not want trouble.

A well-known scalper often tried to get his tickets, Phillips said, but "even if you are going to try to make a profit off your tickets, you're not going to go out and just sell them to anybody."

• Dwight Anderson, who led the Continental Basketball Association in scoring last year with an average of 27.5 points, said that he twice sold his UK season tickets.

Anderson would not say who bought the tickets or how much he was paid, but he said that the tickets were worth enough to make a special trip back to Lexington from Dayton, O., after he left UK.

"That was important," said Anderson, who finished his collegiate career at the University of Southern California. He said he had the UK tickets for his sophomore year, "and I wasn't using them."

"Somebody told me they were worth a lot of money," Anderson said, laughing as he recalled the incident but not willing to share the details.

In comparison, his USC tickets were worthless, Anderson said. USC basketball lacks a following like UK's, so the demand from boosters for tickets and the supply of money for players were far less than they were in Lexington, he said.

At times, Anderson said, he was left holding tickets on the way to a USC game, so he gave them to youngsters at the door of the arena in Los Angeles.

• Tim Stephens and another player, who asked not to be identified, also said they sold their tickets.

★   ★   ★

Former players said they also received free or discounted clothes.

Fred Cowan said that he received about 10 suits from Maynard Hogg. Hogg said that the suits were second-hand and that he gave them to Cowan "as a friend."

Verderber said that a close friend associated with the program once game him a gift of five new dress shirts.

Macy said that he enjoyed discounts at a Lexington clothing store that extended the same privilege to other players.

"Now whether that's illegal or not, I'm sure that the NCAA would say it is," Macy said. "That's like getting some money, too, if the discount is big enough.

"I would prefer doing something that way . . . because then you're at least still paying something for it."

Macy would not name the store.

★   ★   ★

Former players said they could get free meals almost anytime.

"You can get spoiled. You really can," Ballenger said. "Just because you sign autographs doesn't mean you deserve free meals all the time."

One of the most popular spots to get a free meal was Cliff Hagan's Ribeye on Winchester Road, the players said. Hagan is co-owner with Bill Wilcoxson, who operates it.

Bowie said he and other players could eat for free at Hagan's Ribeye "without question."

Courts said he knew about Hagan's Ribeye even before he came to Kentucky in 1977. He said that Wilcoxson called him and told him, among other things, that the Wildcats often ate in his restaurant and "usually it was taken care of."

Other players who said that they ate free meals at Hagan's Ribeye with a date or with other players were Dwight Anderson, Mike Ballenger, Jimmy Dan Conner (1972-75), Bo Lanter, Jim Master, Mike Phillips, Rick Robey, Jay Shidler and Melvin Turpin (1980-84).

Asked whether players and their dates sometimes had dined free of charge at Hagan's Ribeye, Wilcoxson said: "No. No. Not that I know of. . . . They were never afforded that opportunity."

Hagan also denied it.

"We're not running that place as a charitable institution, I guarantee you," Hagan said. "I'm not aware anybody ever got a free meal there, other than myself and Billy Wilcoxson."

In 1978, the NCAA made an inquiry to UK about the restaurant after a newspaper article quoted Anderson as saying that free meals were available there. The inquiry was dropped after Hall wrote a letter saying that players were not allowed to have free meals anywhere in town.

However, players told the *Herald-Leader* that Hagan's Ribeye was not the only place in Lexington where they got free meals either from the management or other diners.

"When I was at Kentucky I thought I had it made," Grevey said. "There weren't too many bars and restaurants I couldn't walk into and get a free dinner or a free drink."

At times, the players also ate for free by signing their names on a bill and having it charged to the UK Athletics Association, said Master and a UK senior who used to live in Wildcat Lodge with the players.

According to NCAA regulations, a school may pay for its athletes to eat out when they have practiced late or during a school vacation, if the school cafeteria is closed. However, the players said they sometimes signed for free meals when the cafeteria was open.

Master said that he and his teammates took advantage of the athletic association's arrangements with several restaurants, such as Clara's, a Chevy Chase restaurant that has since closed.

UK had arranged for players to sign up for their meals when it was proper for them to do so. But Master said that he and his teammates sometimes dined out when "we weren't supposed to."

"We were the ones that were in the wrong," Master said. The coaches "did their job and tried to keep us out of trouble, but, you know, it's hard to keep a 19- or 20-, 21-year-old kid out of trouble if he doesn't want to stay out of trouble."

A current UK senior named Tom Malasto, who because of his close friendship with Roger Harden lived in Wildcat Lodge as a freshman, said that even he signed players' names when he ate with Harden at Clara's.

"Like, I'd sign Master's and he'd sign Beal's," Malasto said. "They wouldn't even know."

Malasto said the coaches put an end to the practice during his sophomore year.

The *Herald-Leader* was unable to interview Harden for this article because of Sutton's instructions.

Bowie said that the signatures sparked an "extremely" humorous series of events.

"I can recall Joe B. holding a team meeting, wanting to find out who forged whose name," Bowie said. "I remember that real well 'cause that was one of the few incidents that I wasn't involved in. So I kind of love that."

Tom Heitz said it was hard to turn down an offer of a free meal.

What was he going to do, Heitz asked, "throw a rampage and say, no, you can't do that?"

Judge's Comments

For sports reporters, 1985 ranged from the high of Pete Rose's assault on Ty Cobb's record to the low of the death of a Clemson runner whose body contained traces of a prescription drug given to him by a coach. The stories presented distinctly different reporting challenges.

Most of the challenges are fun. Pete Rose punched his 4,192nd hit. Hagler and Hearns exchanged that many during 10 minutes in the ring. Tom Seaver returned to New York to pick up his 300th win. Villanova showed up, uninvited, at Lexington, and ended Georgetown's one-year reign. Chris Evert Lloyd and Martina Navratilova battled for the championship of the French Open in a match so classic that even the loser admired it. Spend A Buck earned 2.6 million of them in one race.

There were oddities, too. Such as Andy North winning his second U.S. Open, and practically nothing else. Refrigerator Perry went from an overweight defensive lineman to a national folk hero on offense.

All of those events have one thing in common: The participants held press conferences. To a reporter, covering them is like shooting free throws during a big game. If you've practiced enough, you are going to hit most of them.

Nobody held a press conference for Jeffrey Marx and Michael York. In fact, most of the information they dug out on violations in the Kentucky basketball program was accomplished by climbing stonewalls and ignoring threats.

That the loyal Kentucky fans didn't want to hear the news that many of their players were routinely paid illegally by boosters only added to the amount and difficulty of the reporting involved.

The reporters interviewed 33 former Kentucky basketball players. Many of them spoke for publication. The newspaper named names. And it was villified.

Marx and York deserved better. They did their job. If more sports reporters would do the same, perhaps the athletic establishment would stop cheating.

Marx and York produced a solid piece of reporting and wrote it unemotionally and clearly. By exposing the seamy side of the sport so that it could be cleaned up, they demonstrated that they are bigger fans of sports than the boosters who were paying money under the table.

Float Like a Butterfly

by John Keating of the Dallas Times Herald. This unusual camera angle catches platform diver Bryan Hansen at the height of his glory, 80 feet above the pool with viewers straining to watch during a diving meet in Dallas. Copyright © 1985, Dallas Times Herald/John Keating.

Always Look UP!

by Bernard Brault of La Presse newspaper. Boxer Johnny Herbert seemed to have more on his mind than his opponent as he received instruction between rounds of a 1985 boxing match in Montreal. The object of Herbert's attention was a young lady who signaled round numbers to the crowd. Copyright © 1985, La Presse, Bernard Brault.

Best Magazine Story

Memoirs of a Miner

HIGH SCHOOL FOOTBALL

By *MIKE TRIMBLE*

From Arkansas Times Magazine
Copyright © 1985, Arkansas Times Magazine

Most of us are doing pretty well, I guess. Salty Crowson is selling insurance and raising a short ton of kids over in Conway, and Jonesy is a college professor with a highly praised book under his belt. Satchelbutt Wilmoth married his high school sweetheart; ditto Bud Richards, who, last I heard, was running a very used car lot out on the highway and serving on the Bauxite School Board. I earn three squares a day just sitting in a chair, typing.

I don't hear much from the members of the 1960 Bauxite Miner football team—except for Salty, who handles my insurance and always calls around my birthday to remind me that I am one year closer to dying—but every year about this time I start thinking about them—Salty and Satchel and Bud and Rolleigh and Harold Selby and Dan Reed and the rest—and I wonder if they are still as embarrassed as I am at getting beat by Bryant.

I don't mean getting beat by Bryant last year, or even the year before; Bryant doesn't even play Bauxite in football anymore, having outgrown any semblance of athletic parity with the Miners since becoming the landing field for Little Rock's white flight about 10 years ago. I mean getting beat by Bryant in 1960, the year that Rolleigh and Dan Reed and Bud Richards and Jimmy Birmingham and Bill Ramsey and Jonesy and Johnny Holland and Paul Mansfield and I were seniors.

I am getting embarrassed right now, just thinking about it. My God! *Bryant!* Until 1960, Bryant had *never* beaten the Bauxite Miners. *Ever!* They had seldom even scored. Until 1960, the Bryant game was the annual laugher—always played at home because Bryant didn't have its own field; always played against a hapless bunch of skinny, inept players whose uniforms didn't even match. I remember lining up as an eighth-grader against a Bryant tight end who played in cowboy boots.

We had started the 1960 season as the undefeated District 5-A champions. In 1959, the mighty Black and Gray had roared through the schedule like a turpentined kitty. We had rocked 'em; we had socked 'em. We had Kicked Butt. Now, only a few months later, it was ashes, all ashes. *Sic transit gloria mundi!* The Bryant Hornets had beaten the Bauxite Miners, and before the season was over, so had just about everybody else. The center had not held, and I was the center.

Huckledy-buck.

★   ★   ★

Football was serious business in Bauxite when I grew up there. We had basketball mainly so the coaches could make sure that the football players didn't get too fat or have too much fun during the off-season. The student body went to the basketball games so they could meet up with their boyfriends or girlfriends and hold hands, and some parents went to make sure that's all they did, but it was football that everybody really cared about. Photographs of past Miner teams were enshrined by Ed Ricketts in his barber shop, in the glass display cases that held the Wildroot Cream Oil and the Lucky Tiger hair tonic.

They were formidable-looking, those old-timers in the pictures; they looked like men. R. M. Frey, the other barber, assured us that they *were* men—men to conjure on; men to be reckoned with. There, in one cracked and faded picture, holding one of those old-timey fat footballs and looking grim as a pallbearer, was George Cole. He had gone off to the University of Arkansas and had played football there, winning fame as a dropkicker. Now he was a Razorback assistant coach. And in another picture, a more recent one, was Moose Mize, who had terrorized enemy running backs and who, not even half-trying, the story went, because it wasn't football, had gone to the state track meet as Bauxite's only representative and had won the whole blessed thing *by himself!*

And in still another photo, Muscles Campbell, the ultimate Miner hero: unequaled all-around athlete and the most punishing straight-ahead runner the Arkansas Razorbacks ever had. Denied lasting stardom with the Chicago Bears only because of crippling knee injuries, Muscles was the epitome of what it meant to be a Miner. When he got married while still in college, the *Pick and Shovel* ran two photographs side-by-side: one of the newly married couple walking down the aisle; the other of Muscles hitting a home run for Bauxite's entry in the Central Amateur Baseball League. The caption was: "A Bat in his Hands; a Girl on his Arm." The *Pick and Shovel* was our newspaper. It was a monthly.

Those pictures were our icons. As little boys, when we played sandlot football on neighborhood teams (there were two: the Holly Street Hoodlums and the Norton Town Nightmares—I was a Nightmare), we not only assumed the identities of the well-known Razorback stars of the day—the Carpenter brothers, Lamar McHan, Dave Hanner, Billy Ray Smith (the elder), and Bud Brooks—but those in our local pantheon as well: Moose Mize, Muscles Campbell, his younger brother Pug, Knob Grimmett, Pedro Williams, and 'Tater Sweeten. (We were referring to Little 'Tater, of course, not Big 'Tater. Big 'Tater was not as big as Little 'Tater, but he was Little 'Tater's daddy, so he was Big 'Tater. Big 'Tater did not play football as far as I know. Little 'Tater won a football scholarship to the University of Houston. He got his picture in the *Pick and Shovel* for attending school at Bauxite for 12 years without ever being absent, or even tardy.)

Some of you may think I am making these names up, but I'm not, as anyone who grew up in Saline County can tell you. If there was one thing the town of Bauxite could do better than produce football heroes, it was think up nicknames for its male citizens, athletes or not. Everyone knew Buckethead Stiles, and Sourgut Green became so used to his moniker that he adopted it officially after dropping the slightly less-than-genteel "gut," even running successfully for Saline County judge with "Sour Green" imprinted on the ballot. We also had Chigger Chase (small but tough), Beaver Williams (overbite), Duroc Stuckey (red hair), Hollywood Duvall (moved in from California), and his cousin Paddlefoot (yes, very). Satchel Wilmoth's brother was called Shorty, and their daddy was called Bottle. There were Sonny Bono (before the no-talent singer), Jiggs Bono, Goober Hamilton (before the TV show), Chago Dial, Hooty Hodge, Slick Parsons, Hick'rynut Williams, and Doughnut McKelvy. Those are just off the top of my head; I could think for a while and name as many more, but you get the idea.

As we played our sandlot games on autumn afternoons, all us Hootys and Jiggses and Goobers and Chagos, we dreamed of wearing the Black and Gray, of one day being enshrined in the barbershop display case, next to the butch wax. What would Frey the barber say about us to that next generation of little boys as they gazed at the gallery of immortals? It was a question of some gravity, and even at the age of 9 or 10 we were preparing to assume the mantle of Miners by assuming in play the names and jargon of our heroes. The coach of the Bauxite Miners of that era was an ebullient man named Bob Banks, whose trademark was a nonsense word he'd use to pep his boys up in practice or in games. "Huckledy-buck!" Coach Banks would shout. "Huckledy-buck!" the little boys would scream as they rolled about on their backyard gridiron.

Huckledy-buck.

★   ★   ★

The years dragged rapidly by in that contradictory way that years pass in a country town. There was junior high football, in tattered, hand-me-down uniforms and equipment, and finally, in the ninth grade, I became a Miner.

But only barely. I spent my ninth-grade season trying to stay alive in practice. Physically a late bloomer, I was counting on puberty to transform me at any moment into a tall, well-muscled young athlete like the teammates who trounced me regularly in practice scrimmages. On game nights, I was on the bench and secretly glad to be there.

My neighbor on the bench was Wop Ware, but he was not as content with his lot as I. Wop was a ninth-grader, too, but was about 18 years old, having pursued learning at his own leisurely pace. Wop smoked, drank beer when he could get it, and had a girlfriend over at Benton who worked in a dime store. I was a pudgy bookworm who wore thick glasses. I do not know, even to this day, what made us soulmates, but that is what we were. Wop had gone out for football in order to impress his girl, but he hadn't considered the possibility that his physical limitation might keep him from the starting lineup. For one thing, he was so bowlegged that he could hardly run. "That boy couldn't stop a pig in a two-foot alley," Frey the barber once remarked as Wop left the shop after a trim. The smokes and the beer probably didn't help, either.

"This is embarrassing," Wop complained to me on the bench during the first game. "Betty's gettin' more exercise than I am just going to get a cold drink at the concession stand!"

Having nothing better to do, I addressed the problem, and by the third quarter, I had a solution. Having learned from Wop that Betty knew next to nothing about football, I suggested that he tell her to show up on Wednesday nights, when we played our B-team games, and simply let her believe that she was watching a varsity contest. The ruse apparently worked: Wop told me happily the next Thursday that Betty's only comment was that the crowd had certainly dwindled since the last game.

The rest of my freshman year was generally spent in shining the lettermen's football shoes, packing their gear for road trips and periodically checking for the appearance of body hair. On road trips, I would make sure I got a seat on the bus right behind Don Morrison, a huge but gentle farm boy who would spend the time on the road talking with an assistant coach about animal husbandry.

Until then, most of my information about sex had come from a couple of impromptu backyard lectures from Gerald Magby, and while Gerald's information ultimately proved to be pretty accurate, I thought it too fantastic at the time to give it any credence. The lore imparted by Don Morrison, on the other hand, had the ring of authenticity about it, dealing as it did with the real, honest-to-gosh world of bulls and cows, boars and sows. This wasn't theory; this was fact, and I stored away as much information as I could. It was to cause several very embarrassing moments a few years later.

The summer after my ninth-grade year was spent in heavy thought. Puberty had finally arrived, but it hadn't wrought the miracle I had expected. I looked a little better in gym shorts, but the muscular body I had ordered had apparently been out of stock, and I was sent instead an oddly shaped model that was mostly legs. I looked like a pair of pliers. Running summertime windsprints with my teammates, I would make the same marvelous up-and-down pumping motions with my arms and legs as they, only to see their backs get smaller as they left me in the dust. Clearly, if I was going to see any action as a sophomore, I would have to rely on my brains, not on my athletic ability.

My plan was to pick out some specialty and become proficient enough at it to guarantee some playing time. The specialty had to be easy—I knew my athletic limitations—and it had to be something nobody else wanted to do, because if they did, they could surely beat me out. I toyed with the idea of placekicking, but gave it up quickly; I could get no distance, and besides, there were others interested in the job. Same with holding for the placekicker; for some reason, that job seemed unofficially reserved for the quarterbacks, sort of like the Jewish seat on the Supreme Court. Finally, I hit upon it; I would become a snapper; that is, I would center the ball for punts and placekicks.

It was an inspired choice. Nobody was interested in making long snaps. First of all, a snapper looked undignified, all scroonched down with his head between his legs, looking at the world upside-down. Secondly, anyone assuming that position was extremely vulnerable to getting his can knocked off by a vicious noseguard or a blitzing linebacker. No doubt about it, the job was mine if I wanted it. Moreover, sheer repetition could assure a modicum of proficiency, and with no competition, I'd be in like Flynn. I wouldn't be a starter, but I would be getting into the game before the outcome was decided, maybe even getting my jersey a little dirty.

It worked. I never got very good at snapping—about one in four attempts would soar over the punter's head and into the end zone—but no one else had thought to practice at all, since they didn't want the job, and I was the best of a bad lot. Before the first game of my sophomore year, the coach announced that I would snap for punts. Huckledy-buck!

★   ★   ★

I guess it is time to introduce you to my coach. Bob Banks, the Miner coach of my childhood and the inventor of huckledy-buck, had quit to take a job at one of the aluminum plants. (He stayed in the game, though, as a referee. He officiated at many Miner games, and will appear at other places in this narrative, as sort of a Greek chorus.) My coach was a short, muscular man named Dan Bass, and true to the tradition of the town, he had a nickname. It was Tick.

There is a lot of dissatisfaction among my friends over football coaches, and it is a dissatisfaction I share. The macho image, the teaching of sport-as-warfare, the idea that coaching somehow provides the best training for school administrators—all of that disturbs me.

Coach Bass was different, but he wasn't different in ways that would be evident to most of my friends. His habits were traditionally masculine: he used a paddle liberally, and his favorite way of greeting one of his players was to hit him—hard—on the upper arm. Yes, he taught civics, and yes, he later became an administrator, and yes, he wanted very badly to win football games.

And he could lose his temper. His trademark was placekicking the team medicine kit after a particularly inept play on the part of his charges. The kit would fly open, and the team managers would scurry about gathering up the tape, scissors, Ace bandages, Firm-Grip, and analgesic balm before they rolled out onto the field of play. On the surface, he would not appear to fit your average liberal's idea of an enlightened educator.

There was an important distinction, however, though a subtle one, and not subject to easy analysis. It was, I think, a sense of fun, a realization that we were playing a game, and that although part of his job was to make sure we played it hard and well, the larger part was to preserve that fun, for his players and for himself.

There was also—he would poke me on the arm *really* hard for saying this—a gentleness that manifested itself when it was needed. Nothing gushy, just an awareness of when to turn the volume down.

I first became witness to that during my sophomore year. For some reason that defies analysis to this day, Coach Bass had filled an open date by scheduling a road game with the Warren Lumberjacks. The Lumberjacks were out of our classification to begin with, and that year they were riding high under Coach Micky O'Quinn. There probably weren't a handful of teams in the state outside what was then known as the Big Eight that could have stayed on the field with them.

It was a slaughter. I was getting in the game only when we punted, and it seemed that I was logging as much playing time as anyone on the team. They'd score in two plays; we'd run three plays and punt. They'd score in two more plays; we'd run three more plays and punt.

Finesse was not the strong point of the Lumberjacks; they simply beat you into the ground. For a while there, the contest resembled one of those games in an animated cartoon, with platoons of stretcher-bearers carting off the wounded in an unending procession.

At one point, when another woozy Miner was being helped off the field after emerging from a pileup looking through the earhole of his helmet, Coach Bass signaled for a replacement. The candidate for duty, whom I will refrain from identifying, looked down at Coach Bass, then over to where Howard Page was lying on a stretcher, his leg bent all funny.

"If it's all the same to you, Coach," said the reluctant gladiator, "I'd just as soon not."

This exchange took place near the end of the bench, where I was taking a blow between punts, and I was probably the only person other than the two principals who heard it. I was amazed at my teammate's action—I did not yet know wisdom when I saw it—and waited for the explosion. It didn't come. Coach just said, very gently, "OK, son; just go on over there and sit back down." He even gave the player a reassuring shot on the arm as he walked away.

Huckledy-buck.

★   ★   ★

The Lumberjacks blew us out in '58, but nobody else did, and behind the passing of Buddy Harp and the defense of Terry Allen, we won the district championship by beating the Magnet Cove Panthers in the last game of the season. My shuttle-diplomacy-style specialty had earned me a letter, if not sports immortality, and that summer, our team picture went up in a place of honor in Ed Ricketts' hair tonic case.

In 1959, nobody even touched us. Jimmy Davies, looking like a mole as he squinted around his contact lenses, bowled over defenders like ninepins, and Jimmy Birmingham just blew right past them behind the blocking of Ragon Don Kinney, Jiggs Bono, and Goober Hamilton. We hardly ever had to punt, but we were so far ahead so much of the time that I logged a lot of playing time as a second-teamer. The last game was against Magnet Cove, and it was a romp in a driving rainstorm. After the game, we took our sodden, mud-covered uniforms and threw them around the dressing room with glee. On the Monday after the game, Pete Hopper, the principal, solemnly called all the football players out of class and led us to the gym, where he pointed out the ravaged locker room. The floors were covered with a thick coating of dried mud. The walls were covered with a thick coating of dried mud. Even the ceiling, 15 feet high, was covered with a thick coating of dried mud.

"Boys," Mr. Hopper intoned, "I am real proud for you, winning the championship and all, and I'm not even going to make any big fuss about this mess. I just want to know one thing. How in the world did you do it?"

That next summer was a time for more figuring. I was tired of spending my athletic career looking at an upside-down punter. I had had enough of being a face on the team picture; I was ready to be singled out to young boys by Frey the barber; I was ready to hear the roar of the crowd.

I figured my chances were good. I had more experience at center and linebacker than any other of the returning players. I wasn't very good, but the experience alone should give me an edge. Besides, I was a senior, a two-year letterman. Bauxite was a United Steelworkers town, and seniority should count for something.

We reported to two-a-days ready to romp and stomp again. We were the undefeated Miners, and we aimed to stay that way. We should have known something was up by the cautious tenor of Coach Bass's opening chalk talk. The year before, he had laid it on the line: "Boys, I really don't see how anyone on our schedule can beat us." This year he said: "Boys, we can win again," but he didn't say how many.

Well, we won three, right off the bat, probably from sheer momentum and the intimidating effect that we had striding into opponents' gyms wearing our "Undefeated District 5-A Champion" jackets.

Then we journeyed to Lonoke County for a game with England, and the roof fell in. They were big and they were fast, and they weren't scared by our uniforms. In short, they were a pretty good football team. But the middle of the second quarter, it was 25-0, and their subs were starting to come into the game.

We had started bickering among ourselves.

"My man? My man? What act of Congress made him *my* man all of a sudden? He was *your* man till he knocked you on your butt three plays ago!"

"If you can't hold him out, Trimble, at least wave at him as he goes by."

Only Bud Richards kept his cool. He was off by himself, giggling. I inquired as to the reason for his high good humor in light of the fact that we were getting our clocks cleaned.

"I'm gettin' 'em," Bud chortled. "I'm gettin' 'em. I'm pulling their leg hair in the pileups!"

About that time Rolleigh stormed up in high dudgeon.

"Some sumbitch is pulling my leg hair in the pileups!" he roared.

Bud looked shocked. "They shouldn't oughtta do that," he said indignantly, and he trotted off to get in position for the next play.

We held them to 25-0, partly because they played a lot of subs and partly because Rolleigh played like a madman for the rest of the game. Bud and I decided on the bus trip home to continue the hair-pulling ploy for the rest of the season. "It sure got ol' Rolleigh fired up right enough," Bud reasoned.

Three more drubbings followed, at the hands of Cabot, Gurdon, and Sylvan Hills. The word was out now: the Miners could be had. One of the games was in a cold rainstorm, and for the first time, I felt some sympathy for those Magnet Cove players we had beaten in the rain the year before. When you're winning, playing in the rain is fun; when you're losing—no, when you're getting slaughtered—it is miserable. Your fingers are so cold that you can't bend them, and your knuckles get scraped, and they burn with an icy fire. There is no warmth on the field; there is no warmth on the bench. The only warmth is in the mud, and when you're lying there at the bottom of a pileup, you mutter under your breath to the others: "Get up slow! Get up slow!"

Huckledy-buck.

★　　　★　　　★

I discovered an interesting phenomenon about this time. Always before, when the Miners had won, I would go home and dream about the game all night, tossing and punching the pillow, replaying each block, each tackle, each long snap to the punter. With that first loss, I quit dreaming. I would fall into bed and sleep the sleep of the dead until morning. I have never slept so soundly.

Things were getting grim, both in practice and around town. Coach Bass complained that we were entirely too jocular for a team that played as badly as we did. He made Bud Richards remove the flame job and pinstriping from his helmet, and threatened extra windsprints.

Townsmen were beginning to grumble. Frey the barber somehow linked our misfortunes to the general moral decay of Western civilization.

"I just can't figure out what's the matter with you boys," he complained from under his green plastic eyeshade as he scraped the back of my neck with a straight razor. "It's—well, it's *somethin'*, but I can't figure out what it is. I'll tell you one thing, though." Now he was gesturing with the lather- and neck-hair-covered razor. "You wouldn't catch Moose Mize layin' flat on his back gettin' run over by no Gurdon *Go-devil.*"

He pronounced "Go-devil" as though it meant "pansy."

"I think you boys have had it too easy, is what I think. Them big ol' silver helmets! George Cole didn't wear no silver helmet. He didn't wear a helmet at all, silver or another kind. You got pads on your knees and pads on your shoulders. You even got fanny pads. You can't tell me Satchelbutt Wilmoth needs no fanny pads. I don't know what's the matter with you boys. You be needing any butch wax today?"

It was much the same elsewhere about town. Charlie Gibbs quit giving us free big orange soda-pops on Saturday mornings at his cafe in Swamp Poodle. "I don't back no losers, boys," he said.

Our only ally, it seemed, was Henry Henning, the custodian of the Community Hall. For those familiar with the writing of Larry McMurtry, Henry can be described as our Sam the Lion: wise, caring, never condescending, a counsellor with a pushbroom and a big ring of keys.

"What them old boys don't tell you," Henry mused as he lit a Lucky and leaned on his broom, "is that them teams with Moose Mize and 'Tater Sweeten on 'em didn't win all their games neither. Not even Muscles' team won 'em all. Some of them teams didn't win hardly any. Them old boys don't tell you that 'cause they don't really remember it theirselves. What they remember is 'Tater and Moose and Muscles and how good they was, and how much fun it was to watch 'em play, even when they got beat.

" 'Course," Henry added, giving his soothing logic that ironic Henry Henning twist that we had come to expect, "you boys ain't all that much fun to watch."

We took all this in silence, we bearers of the Miner flame, partly because there wasn't much we could say in rebuttal and partly because we knew help was on the way in the form of the Bryant Hornets. We might be bad—hell, we were bad—but at least we weren't

Bryant. The hapless Hornets carried the effluvia of defeat about them wherever they went; it was as much a part of them as their ragged blue uniforms. The worst insult any Bauxite football player could be subjected to still was "You looked like Bryant out there." (We had begun to hear that some.)

Well, the Hornets were coming to town, and woe unto them!

Huckledy-buck!

★   ★   ★

It started out quite well, really. We took the opening kickoff and moved the ball easily, mostly on a couple of long runs by Jimmy Birmingham and Bud Richards, some up-the-middle plowing by Johnny Holland, and some short passes from Salty Crowson to Chris Brazil and Harold Selby. Bud and I got in some good leg-hair pulling, too. Salty took it in for a score not five minutes into the game, and we lined up for the kickoff with smirks on our faces.

They did not stay there long. On the second play of the series, I blitzed between the center and guard and put a monstro hit on the Hornet quarterback for a sizable loss. I was laughing from the sheer pleasure of it all when I suddenly realized that the guy I had creamed was laughing, too.

He was laughing because he didn't have the ball. I looked up just in time to see a blue jersey recede toward the horizon at an unbelievable pace. (It was years before I saw anything move that fast again: it was in the movie "Star Trek," when the Enterprise went into warp drive.)

His name was Louis Besancon, and he was a west wind that played football. We had heard of him, of course: the *Benton Courier* had carried a story about him the spring before when he set some records at a track meet. But good grief, that was *track!* What did *track* have to do with anything? More specifically, what did track have to do with football?

Plenty, as it turned out. To make it mercifully short, Louis Besancon ate our chili. He scored on long runs, dump passes and long bombs, around end and up the middle. We did not score again. When the final horn sounded, and the visitors' stands erupted into a miniature V-J Day of screaming, dancing, hugging, and kissing, we slunk to our dressing room.

"This one's going to be pretty hard to explain," Rolleigh muttered.

Huckledy-buck.

★   ★   ★

I have never quite forgiven my parents for making me get a haircut on the Saturday after the Bryant game.

"Pitiful!" said Frey the barber. "Pitiful!" He stepped hard on the first syllable each time, and punctuated the accents with a none-too-gentle swish of his razor on the back of my already-crimson neck. "You boys were PIT (swish!) iful out there."

There was no refuge anywhere. Henry Henning stood on the

steps of the Community Hall and surveyed us with sad, reproachful eyes.

"Bryant." He sounded like the voice of doom. "Pitiful."

"If we're so all-fired pitiful," said Rolleigh, "seems like somebody would take pity on us."

But no one did, except Coach Bass. Maybe he figured we were hopeless, that no amount of cajoling and medicine-kit kicking would get the job done. Or maybe it was relief. Maybe he figured that if he hadn't been fired or lynched after the Bryant game he'd never be fired or lynched for anything. At any rate, he lightened up. He started joking around in practice again, and the zing returned to his howdy-doo pops to the arm. In one game—another blow-out—I was being beaten to death by a maniacal middle linebacker who lined up right in front of me and pumped his feet furiously until the ball was snapped.

"Why's he doing that, coach?" I asked during a time-out.

Coach gazed at me intently for a few seconds before answering. "He's trying to tire himself out so he'll get his second wind quicker."

Huckledy-buck.

★   ★   ★

Have I by any chance left the impression that the Bryant game was the low point of the year, the final and complete humiliation, the absolute depths of the slough of despond? If so, let me make haste to correct it. What I *meant* to say was that the Bryant game was our lowest moment as a team. I, myself, as an individual, still had pages to write in the annals of athletic shame.

It was at Lonoke, and we were taking our by-now familiar drubbing. By some unusual circumstance, the Jackrabbits were forced to punt—their third team must have been in—and Jimmy Birmingham, our speedster, fielded the ball near the sideline on about the 20.

He crossed the field toward the Bauxite stands, and as sometimes happens on such plays, a lane suddenly opened for him. All at once, I realized that Jimmy could go all the way if he got only one block, and I realized, too, that I was in the perfect position to make it. The only man with a shot at Birmingham was skulking along the sideline in front of our bench, watching the progress of the ball carrier. I had the perfect angle on him. I would spring Birmingham loose for a touchdown and at last—at last!—hear the approving roar of the crowd that had occupied my dreams since childhood. There was no way I could miss; the poor chump was so intent on Jimmy that he didn't even notice that I was about to knock his block off.

I didn't realize anything was wrong when I felt the satisfying "thunk" of the hit. I didn't realize anything was wrong when I was suddenly enveloped in darkness. I finally realized something was wrong when I reached to pull a few obligatory leg hairs and touched smooth, hairless skin.

That's when I realized I had coldcocked a cheerleader.

I was no stranger to embarrassing moments; no one on that

Miner team was. I had made a fairly regular thing of sailing the ball over the punter's head in my three years as a snapper, and I once had retreated from my linebacker's position to field a short punt only to have the ball strike me squarely on the top of my helmet. But this was different. With one ill-timed leap, I had opened up a heretofore undiscovered vista of football buffoonery. Worse, the thing was somehow connected to the dark and mysterious world of sex: I had boldly gone where no man had gone before, but I had done it in a clown suit, before an audience of angry and derisive critics. It seemed to be a terrifying Freudian dream, but it was real.

All of that flashed through my mind in an instant, to be replaced by a more practical and immediate dilemma: how in the hell was I going to get out of there?

Careful not to touch anything, I backed out from under the voluminous skirt to determine whom I had hit. It was Myrtle Baxley, the homecoming queen and Bud Richards' main squeeze. I turned around in terror. There was nowhere to go.

The roar of the crowd? Yes, there was some roaring, all right. Birmingham, who had been clobbered by the lone defender, was roaring. Myrtle's mamma was roaring. And above it all, I heard a shrill voice shout, "Congratulations, Trimble, you finally hit somebody!"

It is amazing the number of different thoughts one can entertain in times of panic. I thought of my father: he would be mortified by the bonehead play. I thought of my mother: she would be incensed that I had forgotten my manners and hadn't even helped Myrtle to her feet. I thought of Bud Richards: he would kill me if I had harmed his beloved Myrtle, and he wasn't going to be too happy about where I had ended up, either. I would have thought some more, but about that time, Coach Bass kicked the medicine kit.

Impartial observers said later that it was the best medicine-kit kick of coach's career. It tore the top clean off the hinges and sent Band-Aids fluttering like confetti. I didn't actually see it—my back was to the bench—but almost immediately after I heard the sound of the impact, I saw a fat roll of adhesive tape roll rapidly past me and toward the spot where my team was gathering for the huddle.

I know it does not make any sense now, but I somehow became convinced that I had to beat that roll of tape back to the huddle. If I did not, I might as well keep on running clear out into the wilds of Lonoke County to wander forever among the soybean fields. I began to run. I had never run so hard. There was fire in my lungs and a lump of ice in my soul. I caught the tape about five yards from the huddle and pulled up, panting, in front of my teammates, who were looking at me as though I were a crazy man. The tape rolled to a stop, and a referee picked it up and put it in his pocket. Then the referee looked at me and winked.

"Huckledy-buck," said Bob Banks.

Huckledy-buck.

★   ★   ★

Myrtle was not injured; thus I was saved from an untimely death at the hands of Bud Richards, though once more before the season was over, I was to wish that Bud had gone ahead and done the deed.

Have I by any chance left the impression that the Lonoke game was my own personal low point of the season, the night of my greatest humiliation? If so, let me hasten to correct it. What I *meant* to say was that the Lonoke game was the night of my greatest *public* humiliation. There was one more, a *private* humiliation—shame might be a better word—that I have not shared with anyone until this very day.

It was the last game of the season, at Magnet Cove. The Panthers had had their season finale spoiled for two straight years by the Bauxite Miners; now they were ready for revenge.

I do not recall whether Magnet Cove had a particularly good team that year. I do know that they had Randy Stewart; they couldn't have needed much else.

Many of you will remember Randy Stewart. He made all-Southwest Conference as a center for the Arkansas Razorbacks about 1965, and I understand he's now some kind of corporate face card for Exxon down around Midland, Tex. In 1960, Randy Stewart was a center and linebacker for the Magnet Cove Panthers, and he was of a type not often seen in the backwaters of Arkansas football: legs like tree trunks; a torso like a sack of wrecking balls, and a neck as big around as a sewer pipe. For that last game of the season, for my farewell to football, my final chance to salvage some respectability, Randy Stewart was—to use a term so loosely as to be ridiculous—"my man."

Huckledy-buck.

★   ★   ★

I have played in football games in which I feared we would lose. I have played in games in which I feared we would be disgraced. The 1960 Bauxite Miner-Magnet Cove Panther game was the only game in which I feared I would be killed. This was not an irrational fear that began the week of the game and built slowly, irreversibly as the day of the contest neared; this was a fear that manifested itself—unexpectedly but fully supported by the empirical evidence—about the second play of the game, when Randy Stewart tore the helmet from my head with a forearm shot, wrenched both of my arms from their sockets with a double flat-handed shiver to the shoulders, and tromped the length of my now supine form into our backfield to all but decapitate Salty Crowson, who had stopped in the middle of a roll-out to gape at the carnage, as people sometimes will be reflexively struck dead in their tracks when they come upon a particularly bloody car wreck.

"Punt!" I begged in the huddle.

Salty thought it over and shook his head in the negative.

"Why not?" I whined.

"It's second down. We can't punt on second down!"

"Why not?" I croaked again. "It ain't gonna get any better."

Salty shook his head again. I looked over at Rolleigh, the right guard and the strongest man on our team. "I sure could use some help."

Rolleigh gazed for a moment across the line, where Randy Stewart was standing under a cloud of steam that made him look like a volcano about to erupt.

"I'm a little tied up right now," Rolleigh said. "Why don't you try me again tomorrow at the barber shop?"

I looked around the huddle at my other teammates. All of them remained in their hands-on-knees huddle stance, staring silently and intently at their shoelaces.

"Thanks, men." I had meant it to sound sarcastic, but the tremor in my voice spoiled the effect.

We finally did punt, but, as had become a pattern in our games, the Panthers scored in about three plays, and we were again on what must laughingly be called the offensive. Three more running plays and a punt resulted in my getting a chipped tooth, a bloody nose, and a mouse the size of a golf ball under my left eye. By the end of the first half, it was all I could do to drag myself to the visitors' locker room. I lay on the floor, a wet towel on my head, as Coach Bass made his traditional rounds around the room, speaking encouragement to each player in a quiet voice and giving a critique of the first half of play. When he got to me, he said softly, "Protect yourself son," and then moved on.

On our first possession of the second half, Randy Stewart slammed me so hard on the helmet that the suspension webbing broke, leaving my head to rattle around like a baseball in a bucket. I was on my third helmet of the night, and the end wasn't yet in sight. That's when the primal instinct for survival took over; that's when I inflicted upon myself the final and complete humiliation.

That's when I tried to make a deal with Randy Stewart.

I have forgotten or repressed the actual words I used to put forth the proposition, but the gist of it, delivered through the earhole of his helmet as he lay atop me in a pileup, one arm around my neck and the other around the ball carrier, was that what the hell, this was the last game of the season and they were going to win big anyway, and I'd do everything possible to stay out of his way, even tip him off to the flow of the play before the snap if he wanted me to, if only he would lighten up and let me survive. He did not say anything when he let me up; he just smiled.

I was hopeful. A smile is a smile, right? The next play was to be a sweep around right end, and true to my end of what I hoped was our bargain, I indicated the direction of the play with a none-too-subtle rolling of the eyes.

As soon as I snapped the ball, I headed to the left, opposite the flow of the play. I looked over my shoulder and my heart stopped. Randy Stewart was not moving with the ball. Randy Stewart was not even looking at the ball, and it was clear that he was not even going to try to make the tackle. Randy Stewart was heading right for me, and I knew I was a dead man. The words that sprang to my lips just before the impact were a lie, an outrageous and despicable lie that came not from my brain but from some deeply buried survival gland wherein dwelt the hope that a man of principle might also be moved to pity.

"My sister has polio!" I screamed.

★   ★   ★

I was sitting up; I could tell that much. I could see the toes of my shoes in front of me, pointing up, but I couldn't ascertain at what point my body was making contact with the ground. I seemed to be floating. Hazy figures moved in and out of my field of vision. Someone seemed to be holding up some fingers, and asking me how many I saw. I thought for a moment that I was in jail: black bars ran up and down in front of my eyes. Then the floating sensation gradually subsided and the jailhouse bars became the black stripes on the shirt of a football game official. Again he asked me about fingers. I replied, apparently correctly. The official grinned at me and winked.

"Huckledy-buck," said Bob Banks.

Huckledy-buck.

★   ★   ★

The barber shop at Bauxite has been torn down for years, and while I mourn the passing of a landmark of my youth, sometimes I think it is for the best. If the barber shop were still there, where would the picture of the 1960 Bauxite Miners be? In the restroom? Or would it be in the hair tonic case, but pasted on backward, with its public side saying only "A Kodak Paper"? Or worst of all, would the picture be displayed normally, with one face inked out, one ignoble and undeserving gladiator consigned to nonperson-dom by the ballpoint of Frey the barber? I do not know.

There is another thing I do not know. As I recall the defeats and the long bus trips home that followed, the split lips and the pratfalls, the busted medicine kits and the knocking of cheerleaders on their megaphones, I do not know why I loved it so, or why I love it still.

Perhaps it was the insularity of it all. We were very small frogs, but we performed in a pond commensurate with our size. Our world was bounded by Pine Haven to the east, Swamp Poodle to the west, Crumby Town to the south, and the Baptist Church to the north; it was so familiar to us that we did not so much live in it as wear it, like an old, comfortable suit of clothes. Or perhaps a security blanket.

I have said that football was important to the town, and it was, but it was important as football, nothing else. Schoolchildren in Bauxite were seen as children, not as representatives of the town as a whole, or as surrogates for the thwarted ambitions of grownups, or as metaphors for the political or spiritual state of the country, Frey the barber's plaints notwithstanding. Nobody ever accused us of being anything but bad football players.

And so we were free to play, and it was play, and it was fun. Grantland Rice was wrong. It is not how you play the game that counts; it is that the game is played.

I have seen the big-time high schools play. Sometimes they do it on AstroTurf, and their coaches wear those fancy headsets just like the one Freddie Akers wears. Their players are big and fast and marvelously talented, some of them, and they have my respect and my good wishes, but I cannot give them my heart. My heart is with the slow and gawky country boys, as they take to dusty, dimlit fields on starry autumn nights.

Judge's Comments

Sitting in judgment of sports journalism used to be an easy task. You were handed a pasteboard box brimming with the tearsheets and photocopies and in a few hours of scanning could separate the Wheaties from the chaff. You were obligated to give each entry a fair hearing. But you knew without even opening the box which publications and individual writers would settle in the top 10. There simply weren't many writers—or editors—willing to stray from the beaten path. Much of what you had to endure was about as provocative as a report on wastewater management.

Those not-so-good-old days are over.

Today's entries are as imposing as "War and Peace."

The past year produced many remarkable achievements in sports and in sports reporting and writing. There was a wealth of excellent entries. Yet even among the excellent, only a few stand out as exceptional.

The best of these efforts is by Mike Trimble writing for *Arkansas Times.* The essense of "Memoirs of a Miner" is captured in the subhead: "Only triumphs are replayed in dreams; the vanquished find solace in heavy, unremembering sleep."

Trimble chronicles hard times with the Bauxite Miner football team. He does so with wit and insight, vignettes and analogies, and some awfully good writing. Listen:

On the second play of the series, I blitzed between the center and the guard and put a monstro hit on the Hornet quarterback for a sizeable loss. I was laughing from the sheer pleasure of it all when I suddenly realized that the guy I had creamed was laughing, too.

He was laughing because he didn't have the ball. I looked up just in time to see a blue jersey recede toward the horizon at an unbelievable pace. (It was years before I saw anything move that fast again: it was in the movie "Star Trek," when the Enterprise went into warp drive.)

It's an old story with an old message: Someone has to lose. But it's only a game. Even if it does shape the way we look at the world forever after.

It's also a new story because Trimble had the passion and the skill to make it fresh and enduring.

"Memoirs of a Miner" is a prize in itself.

Dick Young's America

GENERAL

By *ROSS WETZSTEON*

From Sport Magazine
Copyright © 1985, Sports Media Corporation

Idols grow old like everybody else. Dick Young was once the patron saint, the most respected sportswriter in America, the one who changed all the rules, the guy who brought street smarts into the sports pages. He's still the dean of American sportswriters, the most widely read and highly paid sports columnist in the country—and yet it's not easy to find a colleague who has a good word to say about him.

When you finish reading one of his columns in the *New York Post,* they say, you have to take out your handkerchief and wipe the spittle off your face. "Young Ideas," the title of his column, is "the greatest misnomer since Charley Winner." As a baseball and football writer "he used to hang out with the players, but now all he does is suck up to the millionaire owners." As a boxing writer "he would have no problem picking out Larry Holmes at a DAR convention." "His values are sick and corrupt," says a former *New York Times* sportswriter. And yet after saying all this—and adding that his "My America" tirades would embarrass Jerry Falwell, that his cranky obsessions are turning his column into a one-man vigilante gang— even his sternest critics are unanimous in conceding that "the son of a bitch was still the best day-to-day baseball writer who ever lived." "The younger writers all loathe him," says a veteran who's worked with him more than 40 years, "but the thing they still have to learn from us old-timers is that you can only hate Dick Young 90 percent of the time."

It's partly a matter of generational style. Sitting in the front row of the press box at the World Series, the Super Bowl, the championship fight, bobbing his head up and down like a belligerent bantam, rapidly clawing out notes in his lefthanded scrawl, Dick Young, even at 67, looks like he should be in a '30s B movie—the only thing missing is a snap-brim fedora with his press card jauntily stuck in the band. Dick Young belongs to the days when sportswriters banged out their stories on carriage-snapping typewriters, a cigarette dangling from their lips, a shot glass of bourbon at their side.

But it is his confrontational style that's made him so many enemies. You're drawn in by his lean, breezy, rat-tat-tat, three-dot prose, and then you realize what he's *saying* (a litany of Genghis Khan causes, from anti-unionism to Red-baiting to good ol' capital punishment), and even more clearly the tone in which he's saying it (not just caustic but downright churlish; not just opinionated but out-and-out ranting). Is it any wonder that colleagues who began their careers by imitating his street-smart stance, his wiseass skepticism, now regard him as a doddering fossil?

People who've been reading Dick Young for only 10 years or so remember little more than his vicious vendettas (almost single-handedly driving Tom Seaver out of New York), or his ethnic insensitivities (advising his Spanish-speaking readers to leave their spray cans at home when visiting the reopened Yankee Stadium), or his hit-and-run blind items ("I've heard a rumor why the Johnny Benches split up," he once wrote, "and I'll never believe it"—end of item), or his mad-dog savaging of "druggies" (he could understand an athlete wanting a little on the side, he commented on the Edwin Moses prostitute/drug bust, but using those controlled substances was unforgivable). Dick Young is not a writer Hallmark would hire.

And yet if you go back more than 10 years there's another side to Dick Young. In the evolution of sportswriting from adolescent mythologizing to tell-it-like-it-is honesty, Dick Young was arguably the single most important transitional figure. There's a better way to describe the arc of Dick Young's career than to say he was a street-smart kid who rose to patron saint who degenerated into crotchety old man. And that's to say that while his politics may be as reactionary as Louis XIV's, his professional role has been as radical as Robespierre's. What his detractors fail to understand is that there are many battles they don't have to fight because Dick Young has already fought them—and won.

★   ★   ★

"What good can you say about a writer," snips a columnist for a national newsweekly, "who thinks his greatest contribution to the English language is the word 'horsespit'?" Well, one thing you can say is that when Dick Young began covering the Brooklyn Dodgers in the mid-'40s, baseball writing was characterized by a different kind of horsespit. One New York daily would lead off its story, "The mighty bats and nimble gloves of the visitors from St. Louis yesterday vanquished. . . ." But Dick Young was writing, "This story belongs on page three with the other axe murders." When he'd begin his stories with fabled leads like "It was so cold out there today even the brass monkeys stayed home," he singlehandedly replaced the pompous poetry of the press box with the cynical poetry of the streets. "It may not seem that innovative today," says Vic Ziegel, executive sports editor of New York's *Daily News,* "but at the time we felt like people must have felt in the '20s when they first heard Louis Armstrong."

"How you going to deal with a guy whose enemies list makes Nixon look like Gandhi?" asks another young sportswriter. Well, one way you can deal with him is to remember that when Dick Young first began covering baseball, sportswriters were shameless shills for their teams, keeping the players at a heroic distance, settling for phonily alliterative nicknames like Joltin' Joe or the Splendid Splinter. So when Young brought his cut 'n' slash opinions into his coverage, writing "it was a typical 400-foot Gene Hermanski drive, 200 feet up and 200 feet down," readers were shocked. Mythic figures, bullspit; Dick Young drank in the same bars as these guys. If we take the warts-and-all closeups of today for granted, we're neglecting to give him credit.

Dick Young, they say, has broken so many stories because he's a mouthpiece of management. Come again? When Dick Young first began covering baseball, writers routinely showed up in the press box five minutes before the game and only visited the locker room if the press-box toilet was broken. "I had to stop by the clubhouse at 11:00 one morning," says a colleague from those days, "and Dick Young was already there, sitting on his haunches beside the trainer and a ball player, taking notes. That was the first time I ever saw a writer in the locker room at *any* time, so don't tell me he got handouts from the front office."

Then they say Dick Young is contemptuous of his colleagues, a competitive son of a bitch who'll knee you in the gut for a beat. But his critics don't know this story—it's never been printed until now. Joe Trimble, Dick Young's colleague at the *Daily News,* is sitting at his typewriter in the press box at Yankee Stadium, staring at a blank piece of paper. An hour ago Don Larsen pitched a perfect game in the World Series and now the press room downtown is freaking out—where's Joe Trimble's story? "I'm blank," Joe Trimble says to Dick Young in a coldsweat panic. "I can't write a word." Dick Young calmly rolls a piece of paper in his own typewriter, types out a sentence, takes out the paper and hands it to Joe Trimble. "The imperfect man pitched a perfect game." Forty-five minutes later, Joe Trimble's story is finished, it's the best story of his career, he wins *awards* for that story—and Dick Young never says a word.

Brash, vulgar, pushy—that's yet another count in the indictment. But hey, the man is a reporter, not a hired grin. Dick Young walks into the press conference where it will be announced that Doug Flutie has signed with the United States Football League. He sees a row of chairs occupied by TV people, celebrities, Donald Trump favorites and flunkies, sees the newspapermen standing three and four deep at the back. So he walks up the steps to the stage, sits down on a wall in front of the podium and takes out his notepad. Donald Trump's security goons politely ask him to move. Choosing his words with the care if not the vocabulary of Flaubert, he informs them that this is a press conference, that he's press and goddamned if he's going to *budge* They find him a chair near the podium. Christine Brinkley may be there to get her picture in the paper, but Dick Young is there to get his *story.*

★   ★   ★

"Gimme a beer," says Dick Young. "Whadda ya wanna know?"

Some of your younger colleagues think. . .

"Shit, those young guys. They don't work hard enough, they don't work the phones, they don't have any respect for themselves as professionals. I remember when the *New York Times* started giving days off in spring training! They're in Florida, for Christ's sake, and they want a day off! Me? I only write five columns a week these days. Piece of cake."

Mike Lupica of the New York *Daily News* says. . .

"Mike Lupica? He's a newspaper version of a spoiled-brat ball player," Dick Young snaps. "He writes bullshit based on his lack of experience."

Dick Young's not an off-the-record guy. Skipping all over the place, talking just like his Friday column, "Clubhouse Confidential," a sentence, three dots, on to something else, three dots, on to something else. Next question?

Murray Chass of the *New York Times?* "He'd sell his soul for access." Maury Allen of the *New York Post?* "Careless with facts and quotes." Jim Murray of the *Los Angeles Times?* "Just a gagster." Dick Young is the same with nearly all his colleagues. Not angry, not even sarcastic, just matter-of-fact rat-tat-tat. Next question?

Howard Cosell? "Howie the Shill? A fraud. An ass. A *pompous* ass. Those are the good things I can say about him. Now what about the other side?" Dick Young leans back in his chair and grins from sideburn to sideburn. He's feeling almost *benevolent.* Lucky you didn't catch him in a bad mood. "Cosell gets more and more obnoxious over the years, but people who say I go after him too much don't realize that I've never written a whole column about him. He's not worth it. Just a little shot here and there."

(For his part, Howard Cosell declines to comment, but he once told an interviewer, "He's a sick, troubled person. He's a hate merchant, crazed, who's been writing trash and abuses the First Amendment.")

You were saying how you used to steal papers when you. . .

"Not steal, *borrow,*" says Dick Young sharply. "We used to borrow papers from the candy store, check out the box scores, then put them back." A law and order kid. "I had a wonderful childhood. Sure, my parents were divorced when I was 3, but it pisses me off when I hear about some guy who sobs his way to the electric chair because he came from 'a broken home.' *I* came from a broken home, and I always felt I was one of the luckiest guys alive."

Dick Young's mother was an American Jew of German descent, his father a Russian Jew. From age 6 to 12, he was boarded out with an Italian Catholic family. Talking about growing up in Washington Heights (a lower-middle-class neighborhood in upper Manhattan), about getting an 87.5 average in high school ("and a better education than lots of colleges give you these days"), about playing stickball in the streets ("I was one of the best around"), about going to the old Madison Square Garden or the Polo Grounds ("I was always a Giants fan"), he'll sometimes go three sentences in a row without bursting into an angry denunciation of the hoods and druggies who've desecrated his idyllic past. The Depression '30s? Idyllic? There's no nostalgia quite as proud as that of a man who survived hard times.

After graduating from high school, Dick Young went to California to stay with his father, a cameraman in Hollywood. Didn't work out. Los Angeles Junior College; kicked out when he couldn't afford the non-resident fee. Joined the Civilian Conservation Corp.; shipped to upstate New York, helped build a state park, still proud of that. Heard the *Daily News* was hiring, $15 a week. Hitchhiked to New York, turned out they wanted college graduates. Said he'd go to college at night. Took classes at New York University, worked his way up at the *News.* Finally, after five years, covered his first game, at the Polo Grounds, then given his first beat, the '46 Dodgers, and before long another big promotion, this time to patron saint.

"I didn't even want to be a sportswriter," he says. "I wanted to be a hotshot newspaperman like Walter Winchell. I wanted to be a stop-the-presses guy, competing with the other paper for the scoop and for the girl. I didn't go for that fancy writing—still don't. Some guys think they can fool sports fans with, quote, good writing, unquote, but the fan knows when he's being bullshitted by a cute line. If you've got the story you report it, if you don't you write it. A newspaper isn't like a book, for Christ's sake. When you're through with it you throw it out and buy a new one."

★   ★   ★

Dick Young writes over 4,000 words a week—which adds up to nearly 10 million words in his career, 100 books or so give or take a "War and Peace." For nearly four decades Dick Young *was* the *Daily News,* the most popular feature in the country's largest-selling newspaper—a survey once showed that he was singlehandedly responsible for over 50,000 sales a day. But then, in 1981, rumors began to circulate that the *Daily News* might fold, and suddenly there's Dick Young, the man who chastised Tom Seaver ("Be a man and honor your contract") breaking his contract and jumping to the *New York Post.* Hypocrisy was the kindest word they used. Loyalty, horsespit.

"People think they see an *analogy,* right?" Dick Young uses the word scornfully, like an epithet. Suddenly his anger seems less genial. "Just for openers," he says, "there's a helluva difference between a guy who works 45 years for an organization and a guy who works five years. And as for the money, the difference wasn't that great. I only got a raise from $115,000 to $125,000 (he makes $155,000 now). My dream situation was to work for 50 years at the *News* and then have a good-bye party when I reached 69. But there I was, 63½ years old, they're talking about closing down the world's greatest newspaper and how many places will give a job to a guy 63½ years old?"

A lot of people feel Dick Young has lost his pop in the *Post,* that the Goetz-for-President tabloid has encouraged his pugnacity at the expense of his populism, turning him into a knee-jerk Neanderthal. Drugs, for instance.

"Nothing is as bad as drugs," Dick Young says furiously. "*Nothing.* I get so angry when I see our country threatened by drugs. Ballclubs used to punish a guy for the slightest moral deficiency, but nowadays they welcome him back with open arms. I'll get out of this business before I'll beg a druggie to talk to me."

Where does this rage come from, a bad experience? "Me? I only take one *aspirin,* for Christ's sake." The Dick Young segue—even in his fury he retains his humor. "I even gave up *Camels*—that was the closest thing to heroin in my time."

Race? That's a bit more complicated. Dick Young was one of Jackie Robinson's earliest champions, but according to one of his colleagues on the Dodgers beat he once confided, "I can never forget he's black" (to which Robinson responded, "I never *want* him to"), and was always closer to the nonmilitant Roy Campanella.

"I was all for Jackie," says Dick Young, "but he thought everything that happened to him was because of his color. Racism was sometimes a crutch for Jackie. I can understand it, but that doesn't make it right. And don't give me any crap, racism is a two-edged sword. Blacks are as racist as anyone these days—maybe more so."

This isn't the kind of speech that's going to win Dick Young any Brotherhood of Man awards. But while this kind of insensitivity appalls his white colleagues, his "I won't bullshit you" stance has won him the grudging respect of many black athletes. Take Ali, for example.

"I was down on Ali at first," Dick Young admits. "I felt he was exploited by the Muslims. He was a commercial racist, he didn't hate white people, he just pretended he did in order to sell tickets. Anyway, one day Bundini Brown came over to me and said, 'You guys should talk,' and I said, 'I'd be glad to.' We had long discussions after that—politics, religion, everything. I still disagree with him, but we respect each other now. In his dressing room after his last fight, down in the Bahamas, we even kissed each other on the lips."

OK, that answers the question: Does Dick Young ever change his mind about *anything?* Still, one wonders if Ali really belongs in Dick Young's America. "My America," he calls it, President Young addressing his constituency, a land of afternoon ball games, hardworking newspapermen, respect for Mom—and electric chairs.

"I know it bugs people. That's why I do it. I use 'My America' almost facetiously now, just to needle people. But look, I was brought up in the greatest country in the world. To me, patriotism isn't a matter of flag-waving but of the work ethic and respect for authority—those are the values I was brought up on."

In Dick Young's America, drugs are evil, unions are ruining sports and black athletes use racism as a "crutch." But it's revealing that he'd even *suggest* he's only kidding. Dick Young's politics are in the grand old tradition of American populism, of the little guy, of the boys in the bar, of the blue-collar, of the hardhat—of *democratic* bigotry.

"To me, there's no such thing as a liberal or a conservative. It's only this case, this case, this case—whose side deserves to be attacked at a particular time." In Dick Young's defense, it has to be pointed out that he's led the fight for access to locker rooms for women sportswriters. "They're just doing their jobs," he says, "they deserve to be treated like professionals. Why do the so-called liberals always lay claim to what's right?"

★   ★   ★

Wiseass, sarcastic, swaggering—with a gutter wit, a toe-to-toe combativeness and most of all a tabloid cynicism that's been elevated to the status of a political philosophy—never forget, Dick Young comes from the '30s of The Front Page, not Norman Rockwell; he grew up in the Depression of Our Gang, not Eleanor Roosevelt. At times he seems less interested in changing your mind than in getting your goat.

"Today's writers don't have enough guts," he says. "They let themselves be pushed around. The players give them all that crap and they accept it"—it's hard to tell who ticks him off the most, the players or the press. "They even have ropes around the batting cage in spring training! Jesus Christ, how'm I supposed to do my job?" Three dots later and he's off on druggies again, then three dots and he's after the goddamned unions, then three dots and he's dumping on a lazy colleague or a spoiled-brat player or even his own paper. " 'Today is Friday, the Post learned exclusively'—what the hell's happened to our profession?"

When you read this stuff in his column you're reminded of the obstinate dogmatism of the self-educated, but when you *hear* it it almost has a certain . . . charm. Even in his most vitriolic tirades there is a spark of wit, a flash of style. Dick Young may be the most opinionated, abusive, foul-mouthed bastard in an opinionated, abusive, foul-mouthed business, but still. . .

At the press conference after the first Ali-Frazier fight, Ali went into one of his harangues, berating the judges' decision and announcing that he was going to organize a nationwide vote to let the *people* decide who won the fight. Everyone's furiously scribbling notes when Dick Young's voice suddenly pipes up. "You'll lose," he tells

Ali. "Most of the brothers are in the slam and are ineligible to vote." The reporters are aghast. Ali is speechless. But then suddenly he leans back and roars with laughter, the reporters join in and the harangue is history.

So what if he sometimes dresses like a cross between a senile hippy and a linoleum salesman—plaid pants, Day-Glo jackets, even, for a time in the '70s, a medallion on his chest with a Miami Beach sport shirt open to his waist. What really keeps him young is the sharp one sentence comeback, the snappy putdown. Dick Young, an embittered old man? No way. He's still a brash, cocksure, pugnacious, candy-store kid who happens to be 67 years old.

In the meantime, the beat goes on—"In the sweatshop conditions of his Florida spring training camp," Dick Young will write on a typical day, "where he works two-to-three hours a day and spends the rest of the time around the pool or on the golf course, Kent Tekulve has warned the plantation owners of baseball that the players are running out of patience. They aren't going to put up with their terrible lives much longer. 'We don't want a strike, but if our backs are to the wall we'll do it' . . . a wall that most people wouldn't mind being backed up against. . . . The players want to strike? Let 'em."

"A repugnant person," says a writer who used to be on Dick Young's staff at the *Daily News*. "He'd always try to graft his sensibility onto your work. At the Montreal Olympics, for instance, he'd even change my leads, adding phrases like 'the dreaded Russians and their Red sisters. . . .' He somehow managed to be both corny and vile at the same time."

Dick Young's going to retire a year from January—at 69—50 years on the beat, the last of the great tabloid newspapermen. "Me and my wife, we own a piece of sand in Arizona. I like to cook, raise flowers. I think I'll even try a novel." A novel? "Sure, I'll keep writing my crap as long as someone is willing to pay for it. The same stuff, only I'll fictionalize it." Dick Young breaks into a malicious smile. "All those bastards, they'll have a helluva time trying to figure out who the hell I'm talking about? Hah, I'd love to see their faces!"

Hometown Bids Maris Farewell

BASEBALL

By *BILL PENNINGTON*

From the Bergen Record
Copyright © 1985, Bergen Record Corporation

Rudy Maris leaned hard on the church pew and took off his glasses to rub one eye. "I'll never understand what they did to Roger," he said of his second son. "Everybody here knew he didn't deserve all the trouble they gave him back in New York. We really knew him. We didn't need anyone telling us what he was like.

"Now I see that all those writers are doing stories about how he really was a nice guy. Well, poor old Roger is lying in a box over there; it's not doing him much good now."

Here in Fargo, S.D., Rudy Maris' message was on the lips of everyone in town. Since 1961, when Roger Maris hit 61 home runs, overtaking a legend and stirring an ugly prejudice in the baseball community, people in Fargo have been trying to explain their hero to outsiders and explain to themselves a misconception they cannot fathom.

Yesterday, for the final time, the townspeople embraced their local hero, trying until the very end to convince the world outside their snowy farm community that a decent, honest man had somehow been misunderstood and distorted.

"When others have confused their position with injuries, a just man will always find his place," Roger Maris Jr., 27, read from the Bible during the funeral service yesterday. "His place is reserved. His honesty will be rewarded."

And when Roger Maris' eldest son stepped down from the altar, the more than 1,000 in St. Mary's Cathedral were moved to applaud. Since the funeral was televised live locally, it's likely that in homes throughout eastern North Dakota, heads nodded in approval.

In Fargo, where the high temperature yesterday was 2 degrees, there was a touching, extraordinary display of warmth for Maris, who died of cancer Saturday at 51. He was born in Hibbing, Minn., but was reared in Fargo. He always considered Fargo his hometown. In their outpouring yesterday, it seemed as if the townspeople hoped to finally insulate him from the unhappiness that followed his dream season of 1961.

"He didn't want acclaim or fame," the Rev. Al Bitz told the congregation, which included several teammates of Maris' from the 1960-66 Yankees and the St. Louis Cardinals, to whom Maris was traded by New York after the 1966 season. "That's probably why he had his troubles with the press. He just wanted to do his job and do it to the best of his ability. Then, he didn't want to be bothered with what he thought was unnecessary. He just wanted to go home to his family and friends."

"If Roger was with me and Whitey and a couple other friends he'd be fine," Mickey Mantle said as he stood in front of the red brick church after the service. "He just wasn't good in the public eye. But what a great guy."

Mantle wept through parts of the service. "You always knew he was your friend," he said. "He was the kind of guy who would tell you so, just to make you feel better. Not enough people got to know him that way, that's all."

In Fargo, they did. The 1980 census reported a population of 61,000 here. It also reported that the average family had five children. In this close community of families, people often work together to keep their farms going, trying to fend off the large combines. And yes, everybody knows everybody else.

Rudy Maris was a supervisor for the railroad. Roger's high school coach, Sid Sander, says he thought Maris' strength with a baseball bat came from hammering ties on the tracks as a youngster working with his father.

"He was a great athlete at every sport," Sander said. "One day in a football game at Devil's Lake, he ran back four kickoffs for touchdowns. The other coach told me he didn't want his team to score any more because he didn't want another kickoff run back for a touchdown."

Maris led the Fargo American Legion baseball team to a state championship in 1952. That was his vehicle to a professional baseball contract.

"But he always came back to Fargo every year no matter what," said Jim McLaughlin, who was a coach for the Legion team. "He'd work with our youngsters, and he'd play cards with the same guys he did before he went to New York and became famous. He didn't join a country club and move to a new part of town. That wasn't Roger."

"He's more than a guy with a bat and pinstripes to us," said Boyd Christenson, who operates Prairie Public Broadcasting. "He was our friend."

Ed Colpeck, a childhood buddy of Maris', said during a prayer service Wednesday night: "Forget New York City. They couldn't have known Roger. Let's remember him hanging out at the bowling alley with all the rest of us. Remember the admiration this town's kids would have in their eyes when Roger came back here. Remember all the benefit functions he would attend."

It was this dedication to Fargo that touched many in the town. "We're all very proud that Roger chose to come home to be buried," McLaughlin said during Wednesday's service, his voice cracking. "We all know how much that means to us."

"It was his request to come back," Maris' widow, Pat, said Wednesday, flanked by her four sons and two daughters. "This is home. Here are his roots."

"It's a place with a lot of good times," Maris' older brother, Rudy Jr., said. "You know, before. . . ."

Before. Before he went to New York and won two Most Valuable Player awards. But he could win no popularity contests. The story goes that Maris was taciturn with reporters, which bred contempt and unflattering articles.

Of course, more than the press burdened Maris. New York fans took sides, too. He was chasing Babe Ruth, an American icon. And he was dueling Mantle. Mantle and Whitey Ford were the two most popular Yankees that season.

"I think the only time he enjoyed that year was the time on the field," said Pat Maris. "But after the games he would sit for two or three hours answering questions. A new wave of reporters would come to his locker every 15 minutes. This happened every day."

"It's true the guy's hair really fell out," said John Blanchard, a catcher and outfielder for the Yankees who had the locker next to Maris' in 1961. "I got spooked. I said: What do you have, ringworm?' He said it was just nerves."

"But the worst part," Pat Maris said, "is that when it was over, when he accomplished so much, he still didn't get any credit for it."

Which has led some to believe that Maris considered the '61 season a nightmare. There is even a quotation often attributed to Maris in which he claims to regret breaking Ruth's record because of the problems it caused.

"I've read that so many times because it gets picked up over and over. It's ridiculous," said Rudy Jr. "He cherished the record. He prayed to God to break the record. He was a religious, quiet man, and he set a goal. He was the kind of guy that didn't brag about it after. That wasn't necessary. He would beat you, and you knew he beat you."

"Ah, but I think the lack of recognition and all the stuff they were saying about him bothered Roger for quite a few years," Maris' father said. "My other son (Rudy Jr.) says to forget about it, but I can't. Roger had a lot of bad breaks."

Maris was buried in Holy Cross Cemetery in North Fargo, under a barren, flat spot near an access road.

Television cameras followed the ceremony over his grave. Dozens of Fargo residents had driven out to the snowy plain, and they watched the scene—TV crews, photographers, reporters.

After the Maris family had left, after the TV cameras had been stored in their vans, many people came forward to lay hands on the casket. A few said, "Goodbye, Roger." Then they walked back through the knee-deep snow to their cars.

On the way back to town, they passed a sign that surely must have raised their spirits: "Fargo, Visit the Home of Roger Maris."

Proud Moment

by Odell Mitchell Jr. of the St. Louis Post-Dispatch. Sometimes the little things in life mean the most. All it took was a return during a tennis class for handicapped children to create this proud, priceless smile on the face of St. Louisan Delores Foston. Copyright © 1985, Odell Mitchell Jr., St. Louis Post-Dispatch.

Splash, Crash!

by Paul A. Souders of the Montgomery County Journal. With a mighty splash and resounding thud, two kayaks collide while the paddlers try to negotiate the rapids near Great Falls, Md., on the Potomac River. Copyright © 1985, Montgomery Journal photo by Paul A. Souders.

Age Hasn't Cooled The Fire Inside Ali

BOXING

By *IRA BERKOW*

From The New York Times
Copyright © 1985, The New York Times Company
Reprinted by Permission

The sprawling, three-story house was quiet, except for the tinny too-wa, too-wee of birds in a small aviary next to the office room on the first floor. It was early on a recent morning and the cool, shadowed office was dimly lit by two antique candelabras which had a few of their small bulbs burned out. An antique lamp was also lit and with its slightly crooked shade peered over the large black mahogany desk scattered with letters and an Islamic prayer book. Nearby were several open boxes stuffed with mail.

Behind the desk, three large windows opened onto a back yard, half in sunlight, with cypress trees and pruned bushes and a swimming pool. Along another wall in the office, a pair of black men's shoes stood by themselves in the middle of a brown-suede couch. In another corner, a television set, with another on top of it, rested on the Oriental rug that covered most of the floor of the room. On the wall facing the desk was a marble fireplace without a fire.

Suddenly, a torch appeared in the doorway. The fire, burning at the end of a rolled-up newspaper, was followed by a large man in black-stockinged feet who trotted into the room. "Hoo, hoo," he said, as the flame burned closer to his hand, and he tossed the torch into the fireplace. Quickly, the logs in the fireplace crackled with the flame, and Muhammad Ali, the torchbearer, watched them burn. Then he sat down in an armchair in front of his desk and in a moment closed his eyes.

He said something, indistinct, in a gravelly mumble, and the visitor, in a chair facing him, asked Ali if he would repeat it.

"Tired," he said, with a little more effort, his eyes still closed. It was 8 o'clock in the morning and Ali had been up since 5:30 saying his daily prayers.

He stretched his legs. He wore a light blue shirt, unbuttoned at the cuffs, which was not tucked into his dark blue slacks. At 43, Ali's face is rounder and his body is thicker than when he first won the world heavyweight championship by knocking out Sonny Liston in Miami in February 1964. The 6-foot-3 Ali weighed 215 then and is now about 240 pounds.

In the ensuing years, he would weigh as much as 230 in the ring as he lost and regained the title two more times—an unprecedented feat in the heavyweight division. Ali, who was stopped in a one-sided bout by Larry Holmes while attempting to win the title yet a fourth time, retired five years ago, but he is hardly forgotten.

A few days before, he had been at ringside at the Hagler-Hearns middleweight title fight in Las Vegas, Nev. Numerous ex-champions were introduced before the bout. Ali was saved for last.

He was asked now how he felt about that moment. He said nothing, and it appeared he was sleeping. Then: "A-li, A-li, A-li," he said, opening his eyes and mimicking the chant that arose among the 16,000 fans when the ring announcer introduced him.

"I had to go like this," he said softly, raising his right index finger to his lips, "to calm the people down.

"A lot of fighters, when they quit no one ever hears of them again. But I've gotten bigger since I quit boxin'. Look at this," he said, nodding to a box in the corner, "people from all over the world writin' me. Thirty-one boxes full of fan mail in four years."

One was from Bangladesh, sent to "Loos Anjeles," and calling Ali "my unknown Uncle." Another from West Germany asked "Mr. Ali" for his autograph. A third was from Drakefield Road in London and sent to the New York Presbyterian Hospital, where Ali had gone late last summer for a checkup. He has been diagnosed as having Parkinson's Syndrome, a nerve disorder.

Ali asked the visitor to open the letter and read it aloud.

"I am very sorry to know of your temporary problem," wrote the Briton, "and wish you most sincerely a rapid recovery. Many of my friends who are fans of yours are thinking the same, that you will in a very short time be back to your old poetic self and come and see us in dear old London. . . ."

Do you still write poetry? the visitor asked Ali.

"No," he said, "no more. That was in a different time. Eighteen times callin' the round. 'That's no jive, Cooper will fall in five.' 'Moore in four.' "

The visitor recalled a personal favorite, when Ali predicted how his first fight with Liston would go, it turned out that Liston didn't answer the bell for the seventh round. Did Ali remember the poem?

"Mmmmm," he said. I wasn't sure what he meant by that.

But he began, his voice still very low:

"Ali comes out to meet Liston,

"And then Liston starts to retreat.

"If he goes back any farther, he'll wind up in a ringside seat."

He paused thoughtfully, then continued.

"And Liston keeps backin' but there's not enough room,

"It's a matter of time—There! Ali lowers the boom.

"Ali lands with a right—what a beautiful swing!

"The punch knocks Liston right out of the ring. . . ."

Just then the phone rang. "My phone's ringin,' " he said. "Hold on." He reached over to his desk. "Yeah, naw, naw," he said sleepily into the phone. "I wouldn't try that for no $5,000, you crazy?" He nodded. "Check ya later." And hung up. "Where was I?"

He was reminded that he had just knocked Liston out of the ring.

"Who woulda thought," he continued, "when they came to the fight,

"That they'd witness the launchin' of a hu-man satellite.

"Yes, yes, the crowd did not dream when they laid down their money,

"That they would see a total eclipse of the Sonny."

Ali's voice was fading again. "I wrote that 22 years ago," he said, his words getting lost in a throat. "That was a long time." He is taking voice lessons from Gary Catona, who had come into the room during the recital of the old limerick. Catona is a voice and singing teacher who three weeks ago had come to Los Angeles from Austin, Tex., to try to help Ali speak more clearly.

Ali began to speak more slowly and less distinctly over the last several years. There was much speculation about him suffering a variety of illnesses. During his hospital visit in New York last September, doctors determined that he had Parkinson's Syndrome.

Catona believes that the only problem with Ali's voice is that his vocal muscles are weak, that they lack resonance.

Ali was asked what was wrong with his voice.

"I dunno," he said, "somethin'."

"Muhammad never really had strong vocal muscles," said Catona. "He used to scream out his words. His normal speech was never a normal speech."

★　　　★　　　★

Ali and his voice teacher schedule a one-hour lesson every day, but Ali travels a lot and they don't always connect. "But he's good when we do it," said Catona. "It's like building body muscles, you've got to work at it. He sings the sounds of the scales. 'Ah! Ah! Ah!' " Catona sang, his voice rising at each 'Ah!'

Catona and Ali had already had the session at the piano in the living room, and beyond this Ali was asked what he's been doing with himself lately.

"People are interested in you," he was told. "You're one of the most popular figures. . . ."

"Popular niggers?" he interrupted.

"Figure," the visitor repeated.

Ali looked at him playfully out of the corner of his eye.

"What am I doin' now, oh, I'm so busy," he said, growing serious now. "I'm busy every day. I've got all this mail to answer—they're startin' fan clubs for me all over the world, in Asia, in Europe, in Ireland, in China, in Paris. But my mission is to establish Islamic evangelists, and to tour the world spreadin' Islam."

He converted from Christianity to the Islamic faith 21 years ago, changing his name, as the world knows, from Cassius Clay to Muhammad Ali.

On the shelf above the fireplace stood a Sports Illustrated cover from May 5, 1969, laminated on a wooden plaque. The cover showed the young boxer wearing a crown, with the caption, "Ali-Clay—The Once—and Future?—King."

What's the difference between Cassius Clay and Muhammad Ali? he was asked.

"As much difference as night and day," he said. "Cassius Clay was popular in America and Europe. Muhammad Ali has a billion more fans all over the world. Cassius Clay had no knowledge of his self. He thought Clay was his name, but found out it was a slave name. Clay means 'dirt, with no ingredients.' Cassius—I don't know what that means. But Ali means 'The most high,' and Muhammad means 'worthy of praise and praiseworthy.'

"Cassius Clay had Caucasian images of God on his wall. Muhammad Ali was taught to believe that there should be no image of God. No color. That's a big difference."

He rose and got a large briefcase from under his desk. He withdrew several religious pamphlets with pictures of Jesus Christ. All but one was white. Then he took out a Bible and opened it to Exodus 20:4, and asked the visitor to read it. "Thou shalt not make unto thee any graven image, or any likeness of any thing that is in heaven above. . . ."

"Ooohh," said Ali. "Powerful, isn't it. But what are all these. Man, you thought boxin' was powerful. Boxin's little. These pictures teach supremacy. The Bible says there should be no pictures of God, no images, he should be no color. But you see that God is white. Tarzan, King of the Jungle, was a white man. Angel's food cake is white, devil's-food cake is black. Man, ain't that powerful?

"Cassius Clay would not have the nerve to talk like this—he'd be afraid of what people might say or think. Ali is fearless, he's hopin', prayin' that you print this. Cassius Clay would not have the courage to refuse to be drafted for the Vietnam War. But Muhammad Ali gave up his title, and maybe he would have to go to jail for five years."

He rose again and this time brought back a plastic box, flipped up the latches, and opened the lid. It was a box of magic paraphernalia.

He took two red foam rubber balls and made them become four right before the visitor's eyes, then turned them into a box of matches, then made them disappear altogether. His eyes widened in mock shock. He still has the fastest hands of any heavyweight in history. It was a very good trick.

How did he do it?

"It's against the law for magicians to tell their tricks," he said.

"It's a tricky world," he said.

He next transformed three small unstretchable ropes of varying sizes into the same size.

He made a handkerchief disappear, but, on the second showing, he was too obvious about stuffing it into a fake thumb.

"You should only show that trick once," he said, a little embarrassed.

He redeemed his virtuousity by putting four quarters into the visitor's hand, snapping his fingers, and ordering the quarters to become two dimes and two pennies. The quarters obeyed. He snapped his fingers again and the quarters returned; the pennies and dimes vanished.

"It's magic for kids," he said. "It's my hobby. See how easy they can be deceived? But these aren't childish things. They make you think, don't they?"

It was mentioned that perhaps Ali's best magic trick was transforming the small house he lived in as a boy in Louisville into this 22-room house with expensive antique furniture. He made more than $60 million in ring earnings and endorsements. "But the government took 70 percent," he said. He says he is financially secure. He doesn't do commericals, for example, because, he said, "I don't need the money."

★   ★   ★

He lives here in Wilshire with his two children by Veronica Ali, 8-year-old Hana and 6-year-old Laila. They employ a live-in housekeeper. His six other children live with his two former wives.

"My wife likes antiques," he said, walking into the living room. He pointed to a tall clock against the wall. "It's 150 years old," he said.

Gary Catona now took his leave, and arranged for a session the following morning. Ali led his visitor for a tour of the house. "I'm not braggin'," he said, "just showin'. I don't like to talk about what I have, because there's so many people hungry, homeless, no food, starvin', sleepin' on the streets."

In the dining room is a long dark table with 12 tall, carved chairs. On the second floor are the bedrooms. In the kids' rooms, toys and stuffed animals tumbled across the floor. There's an Oriental sitting room, and guest room.

The phone rang. "City morgue," he answered. He spoke briefly and hung up.

They ascended the carpeted staircase to the third floor. On a wall are a pair of red boxing gloves encased in glass. One glove is signed, "To the champion of champions—Sylvester Stallone." On an adjoining wall is a robe with multi-colored sequins that bears the inscription, "The People's Choice." In the corner of the case was a photograph of a man with his arm around Ali. It is Elvis Presley, who gave Ali the robe.

In the adjoining room is a large pool table with a zebra skin lying over it. Trophies and plaques and photographs line the wall and cover the floor.

He was asked about recent efforts to ban boxing.

"Too many blacks are doin' well in it, so white people want to ban it," he said. "But how do I live here without boxin'? How would I ever be able to pay for all this? Look at Hearns and Hagler. Two poor black boys, but now they help their mother and father and sisters and brothers. It's from boxin'.

"There's more deaths in football than boxin'. Nobody wants to ban football. You see car races. 'Whoom, whoom.' Cars hit the wall, burn up. Motor boats hit a bump. Bam! Don't ban that, do they?"

Going back down the stairs, the visitor is met by a nearly life-size painting of Ali in the ring wearing white boxing trunks. He is on his toes and his arms are raised in triumph. The signature in the corner of it reads, "LeRoy Neiman, '71."

Did Ali miss fighting? "When the fight's over," he said, "you don't talk about it anymore."

The visitor asked about his health. "I don't feel sick," Ali said. "But I'm always tired."

How did he feel now? "Tired," he said, "tired."

A doctor friend, Martin Ecker of Presbyterian Hospital, has said that if Ali takes his prescribed medication four times a day—the medication is L-Dopa, which is effect peps up the nervous system (the disease does not affect the brain)—then Ali's condition would be improved substantially. The medication does not cure the disease, but it increases alertness.

Ali is inconsistent in taking the medication. He believes it doesn't matter if he takes the medication, because he is in the hands of Allah, and that his fate is sealed. Days go by when he doesn't take the medicine. But when friends urge him to, or when he is going to make a public appearance, then he is more inclined to take his dosage.

Did he feel that after 25 years of amateur and professional fights, of countless hours of sparring, that he had taken too many punches?

He stopped on the second-floor landing. He rubbed his face with his hands. "Uh, uh," he said, softly. "Look how smooth. I very rarely got hit."

As the visitor turned from Ali and opened the door to go, he heard an odd cricket sound behind his ear.

The champ smiled kindly but coyly. There was either a cricket in the house or something that sounded like a cricket in his hand.

Walking to his car in this quiet, elegant neighborhood, and then driving out past the security guard at the gate, the visitor realized he would not plumb the mystery of the cricket sound in Muhammad Ali's house. It's a tricky world, he recalled, and he would leave it at that.

After the Fall

MOUNTAIN CLIMBING

By *STEVEN WILL*

From Women's Sports and Fitness
Copyright © 1985, Steven Will

Sometime in early May 1980, Kate Bull scratched the following entry in her diary. The letters are broken and uneven, barely legible —the legacy of a broken wrist.

"Where do I begin? How do I start to sort it all out? I believe I loved Peter MacKeith more, and liked him more, and respected him more than any sweetheart I have ever known. I never thought in future terms like I did with Peter MacKeith. The weekend of April 25 changed all that. . . ."

On that day, Kate and Peter left Fairbanks with their friends, Jon Holmgren and Tobi Norton, for a three-day climbing trip to Old Snowy, a 9,200-foot mountain in the heart of Alaska's Delta Range. Kate had met Peter earlier on an expedition to Mt. Shand and, though the climb itself had been unsuccessful, their relationship had grown and flowered.

Kate was a 20-year-old college student from Massachusetts. An avid and experienced climber, she had come to Alaska in 1978 in search of adventure and had quickly fallen in love with the chilling pleasure of scaling frozen waterfalls. Peter loved her youthful vigor and enthusiasm for life, and the way she inundated him with questions about every mountain expedition he had ever taken.

And there were a lot. Peter was 10 years older than Kate and his record read like a Who's Who of famous mountain ranges. He had climbed in the Andes, Greenland, the Hindu Kush and Alaska, as well as in his native Scotland. Listening to him talk, Kate was fascinated by his quiet self-assurance and perpetual smile that made her feel calm and safe when she was with him.

In the weeks following the Mt. Shand trip, Kate had discovered a rare well of sensitivity within Peter. She opened her heart to him, sharing pain and sorrow over the recent death of her father. Peter, in turn, told of the climbing death of his friend Andrew, of how he had tried to revive him for over an hour, but failed. Ever since then, he had been climbing much more cautiously. "I don't ever want to die in the mountains," he told her.

But death seemed as remote as Mt. Shand, as they skied across Castner Glacier toward the mountain. Old Snowy was not considered a particularly difficult ascent, and because the face they were planning to climb was steep and coated with ice, they didn't have to worry about avalanches. It was springtime in Alaska, a season of clear skies, long days and plentiful snow—the perfect time for Kate and Peter to bag their first summit together.

★   ★   ★

As nightfall approached, the two adventurers separated from Jon and Tobi and headed up the glacier on their own. They were eager to get an early start the next morning so they could reach the top of the mountain before it got dark.

They pitched a tent at the foot of the O'Brian Icefall and were off again by sunrise, leaving behind all their equipment except what they absolutely needed to make the climb. By 9 a.m. they had climbed the icefall, skied across Old Snowy Basin and could see the face of the mountain soaring thousands of feet above them, shimmering in the sun.

Kate was flushed with excitement. She had never climbed such a sheer face of alpine ice before and wondered what mysteries it held in store. Would it be too hard and unforgiving? Would she become its master or merely a survivor?

The route they took up the mountain started in a steep couloir, or gully, covered with several feet of soft snow. The climbing was slow and tedious. They had to punch out each step, tamp the snow, add weight, and then punch again. Soon they both were panting and bathed in sweat, thinking about nothing else except making the next step. And the next. And the next.

After a while, Peter grew tired and Kate took over the lead. She soon pushed them all the way to the boundary between snow and ice, between couloir and face. But when Kate stepped off the snow, her confidence began slipping. This was different. The cold, blue ice of the mountain wasn't like the waterfall ice she was accustomed to. It was as hard as rock and the freshly sharpened points of her crampons barely nicked it.

She asked Peter to take over the lead again and he marched ahead, switchbacking up the face, his ankles bent downhill to keep the crampon points in contact with the ice. Kate imitated his example, but her ankles tired rapidly and her hold seemed tenuous.

She asked Peter what would happen if one of them fell.

"You hope you can stop yourself," he responded. "Do you think you could?"

She hesitated, imagining herself trying to sink the pick of her axe into the ice while skimming down the face. It didn't seem possible, but she answered yes.

They debated the merits of placing protection. Running the rope through ice screws would increase their margin of safety, but the prospect of torquing screws into such solid ice was daunting. It would take time, time they didn't have if they wanted to reach the top. They climbed on.

Three hundred feet from the summit, Kate became extremely nervous and said so. The expanse below looked deadly.

"If you fall, just yell," Peter reassured her. "I'll be able to hold you."

Kate looked up at Peter, connected to her by 30 feet of rope. Sunlight danced off the ice of Old Snowy's face, reflecting in Peter's sunglasses. He was smiling. The image stuck in her mind, touching her with wonder and awe.

"We're going to do it, Kate!" Peter shouted.

"We sure are," she agreed.

Immediately above them, though, the ice steepened. Kate took one look and moved toward the relative security of a snowy ridge. "Good idea," Peter called out and headed in the same direction.

Those were his last words.

★   ★   ★

It happened in less than an instant. Kate heard a scraping and looked around to see Peter's body shooting down the face of the mountain. She had just enough time to turn toward the mountain wall and think about slamming her tools into the ice. Then the rope pulled taut and yanked her off.

They fell 100 feet, picking up speed as they bumped and crashed against the iron-hard ice. Kate was sliding on her belly. She careened off a bump and caught a glimpse of Peter. What would happen, she thought, if he stopped and she kept falling? Would she crash into him and crunch her crampons onto his skull?

They fell 300 feet, hurtling down the mountain at terminal velocity. Kate focused on trying to keep her crampons from snagging on the ice and tearing at her legs.

They fell 700 feet. Kate made a final, desperate attempt to slow down, forcing the pick of her hammer into the ice. The hammer chattered noisily and then was gone. And so was Kate.

They fell 900 feet, 1,000 feet. Crampons and ice tools were torn from their limbs. They bounded and rolled, the rope snarling around them. Limbs cracked, snapped, shattered. Still they fell.

★   ★   ★

When Kate regained consciousness, she was lying on her back in the snow, with her head pointed downhill. She opened her eyes and could hear Peter several yards away, gasping for breath.

Her left leg was in bad shape. When she tried to lift it out of the snow, her foot just dangled there, as if it were hinged at mid-calf. But even though she could see the damage, she didn't feel any pain.

She didn't have time. She needed to free herself from the tangle of rope and try to help Peter. Each time she moved, however, she and

Peter slipped farther down the icy slope, leaving a thick smear of blood behind them. When she finally broke loose and crawled over to Peter, he had stopped breathing.

She turned him over. His face was covered with blood, and there was a huge gash in his forehead. It was a gruesome sight. Kate turned away and emptied her bowels into her pants.

She felt as if she were edging into the Twilight Zone. Everyday reality no longer seemed to apply. "This is serious, Kate," she said aloud. "This is not a game, a practice, a test. This is it."

She tried to give Peter mouth-to-mouth resuscitation, but there was too much blood. Then she tried to get his heart beating, but her right wrist failed under the pressure. She worked clumsily for 15 minutes, maybe 20. No breath. No pulse. No Peter.

Yet, somehow, she felt his presence in an ethereal way. After he stopped breathing, she had the sensation that he was still there, separated from his body and watching over what she was doing.

She didn't analyze the phenomenon; she didn't analyze anything. She just kept moving, with a new sense of urgency, as if something beyond her control were directing her actions. She didn't have time to think, to grieve. She had to find Jon and Tobi, to get someone up there. She had to hurry.

★   ★   ★

Leaving Peter's body in a tangle of rope and blood-soaked snow, Kate rode another thousand feet down the couloir on her back pack, trying hard not to bounce her shattered leg against the icy slope. When she reached the large, solitary black rock where she and Peter had stashed their skis and poles, she cleaned the mess out of her pants and tried to assess the extent of her injuries. The damage to her left leg was obvious, but it looked as if her right wrist and ankle were broken, too. Obviously, skiing out would be impossible.

It was early evening. Dark clouds obscured the sky and snow threatened. Jon and Tobi should have been there by now, camping near the route for an early ascent. Where were they? Had they decided to turn around and go home?

Her mind clicked off the possibilities. It was late Saturday. She and Peter were scheduled to ski out on Sunday, but no one would really expect them back in town before Monday. If they didn't show up by Monday night, someone might come looking on Tuesday. But that was three days away, maybe four, if you counted the time it would take a rescue party to ski in from the road.

Kate felt cold and thirsty. She longed for the quart of Tang she'd left with Peter at the top of the couloir. Somehow she had to get back to their tent, where her sleeping bag and cook stove were. Back several miles across the basin and down the icefall—not an easy trip.

First, she fashioned a splint for her leg from the metal stays inside her pack. Then she tried to rig a sled, placing the pack on top of her skis. It didn't work. She tried kneeling on her skis. That didn't work. She tried sitting on her pack and pushing with ski poles. That didn't work, either. She tried three more variations. It began to snow.

Kate slept that night in a small hollow five or six inches deep on the lee side of the black rock. Sleep was intermittent. As soon as she closed her eyes, thoughts of Peter floated into her mind. "Peter's dead. Peter's dead," she said to herself, trying to extract some meaning from the hard-edged words. But, for some reason, she felt completely detached from his loss, except for that strange feeling, fainter now than before, that he was watching her from a distance, making sure she was all right.

Utter silence engulfed her. Though she no longer trusted her senses, her body was shivering and she knew that if she fell asleep for a long time, she might die from hypothermia. But death didn't seem like such a forbidding prospect. Peter had already tried it out, after all, and if she died in her sleep, at least she would be with him. She drifted off.

When she awoke, the air was warm, almost balmy, and the snow had stopped falling. Kate got up and built one more sled, positive this time that she would succeed. But it fell apart too, so she started crawling. Planting one ski pole into the snow, then the other, she shuffled her knees forward, over and over again in endless repetition. The minutes crept by slowly, easily outpacing the meters. By the end of 10 hours, she had traveled only two miles.

All she could think about was getting something to drink. She fantasized about water, milk and tall glasses of apple juice and imagined herself arriving at the tent and melting shovelfuls of snow on her cooking stove. But the tent seemed so distant now; it might as well have been pitched on the moon.

Night began to fall, and Kate dreaded the thought of trying to find a place to sleep on the bleak and snowy floor of the basin. She came to the edge of a crevasse that stopped her in her tracks. It was only three or four feet across and, if her leg and ankle weren't broken, she could have leaped over it easily. But, as it was, all she could do was sit there and wait.

For quite some time, she had been hearing voices but thought it must be a hallucination or the wind playing tricks on her. Then, suddenly, she heard a far-off shout and saw two shadowy figures moving toward her across the snow. Her heart starting racing. It was Jon and Tobi.

"Where's Peter?" asked Jon softly, as he skied up to the edge of the crevasse.

"He's dead," answered Kate, in a matter-of-fact tone that surprised her.

Saying the words aloud to someone else made the experience seem real for the first time. It was true: she was alive and Peter was dead. She had survived.

She looked up at her rescuers' stricken faces and started to sob.

★   ★   ★

When Kate arrived in Fairbanks, she was greeted with an outpouring of sentiment unlike anything she had ever experienced before. Her hospital room was alive with friends and relatives giving her hugs and words of encouragement. Her mother flew in from Massachusetts to lend her support. And in all the excitement, Kate had little time to reflect on what had happened to her.

The news media, of course, portrayed her as a heroine, but Kate felt uncomfortable in that role. What she did, she insisted, wasn't courage or heroism, but an act of survival, pure and simple. "Once you're there," she said, "you've gotta do what you've gotta do to survive. You're going to fight."

Peter's funeral came and went. Kate was released from the hospital in a wheelchair and moved into the basement of her landlord's home. She started keeping a diary to occupy her mind and played the banjo night and day, even composing a bluegrass tune called "Old Snowy."

Whenever she tried to drift off to sleep, though, she would think about the accident and relive the nightmare over and over again in her mind. She became obsessed with an impotent, all-consuming wish to alter the course of past events. Anything might have done it, she thought. A later start that morning, an extra word spoken during the lunch stop, taking the time to put in the ice screws; anything, and Peter might still be alive.

She missed Peter, ached for him, longed for his support and comfort. She couldn't figure out why she was the one who had to survive. "So many times," she wrote in her diary, "I just wish I had died with him. Death was so easy for me to accept then, out there, and then I would be with him. Or at least not without him."

And the question tormented her; was he really dead when she left him? She had checked his wrist, his neck, and found no pulse, but how sharp were her senses? Did she miss something?

When Peter's body was recovered, it took two strong climbers several hours with extra ropes and pulleys to lower him to the glacier. Even if he had been alive, there wasn't much she could have done to get him down the mountain. But still the question lingered.

Kate talked to her doctor, who assured her that, from the sound of it, Peter probably had died from a blow to the head or internal injuries. She also tried several times to find out the results of the autopsy, but never got an answer. Eventually, she just stopped asking.

★   ★   ★

She had experienced no initial grief when Peter died, and even afterwards, her sorrow had not been intense. She began to wonder if she had lost her ability to feel. "I should have felt it more deeply," she told a friend. "It's like my whole being doesn't feel the effects of things. I think it makes me more capable of being strong. But is it that I'm strong, or numb?"

By late May, Kate's depression began to lift, and she found herself instead on a roller coaster of uncontrolled emotions. "Emotional undulations are driving me nuts," she wrote on May 21. "At the Sandvick House I was laughing so hard my stomach hurt. Two hours later tears and sadness overwhelmed me in a torrential onrush of emotion. Why can't I just get over it without having to go through this?"

As May turned to June, Kate's emotional swings subsided and she shifted her attention to physical rehabilitation. The casts came off her wrist, then her ankle, then her left leg. She swam laps almost everyday and walked long distances until her leg muscles felt strong again.

Her body was going to be different. The sheared edges of her left tibia and fibula were pulverized, and as they mended, a massive lump of bone deformed her leg. But the bone was solid; her only structural problem was in her ankles. She had lost flex, and it became apparent that, as long as she was active, she would have pain. Hiking would be slow and bothersome, and running was out of the question.

The leaves changed color and fell, followed by snow. Kate wrote about Peter, talked about the accident and shed tears. She realized others had grown uncomfortable with the subject and began to restrain herself. At times she would break under the weight of unexpressed emotion, tears and sorrow raging through her. But even those outbursts became infrequent and, finally, rare.

★   ★   ★

As Kate's body got stronger, she contemplated climbing again. Two forces kept drawing her back to the mountains: one physical, the other spiritual.

"It's a physical high to be that strong," she said, trying to explain her motivation. "It makes me feel capable. I can do this, man. I'm tough and here's the proof—I did that climb.

"And there's also the connection with spirit that I get in the mountains. I remember feeling it poignantly that spring. I was doing a lot of thinking, trying to figure out if I had any spiritual feelings left at all. In the mountains I feel—well, I don't know what the hell it is and intellectualizing ruins it. But there's energy I'm linking into up there. It's beautiful. It's magical."

Kate's determination to rediscover that feeling carried her, 10 months after the accident, to the frozen falls on Dragonfly Creek. She had some doubts, naturally. She didn't know if she could handle it physically and was worried that she might become overwhelmed by a flood of bad memories and freeze midway through the climb.

Dragonfly was the first waterfall she had ever mastered—her home away from home. With a climbing partner, she limped through a grove of tall spruce trees and down a steep incline to the protected rock bowl where the frozen waterfall draped the rock in glimmering blue.

Thunk. She drove a pick into the waterfall, sensing the interplay between muscle, steel and ice. She swung her other tool, kicked in her front points and left the ground. Everything was as it should be: all memories positive.

But as she ascended, she felt the stealthy approach of fear. Her movements became clumsy, her placements uncertain. Fear moved closer, lacing its fingers through her mind. Her legs started trembling, and she called to her partner to let her down.

Later that day, while her partner was off on his own, Kate wandered back to the ice and started practicing again only six inches above the ground. She drove her tools, set her front points and moved carefully across the base of the waterfall. Suddenly, her tools popped and she dropped backwards onto the snow.

It could scarcely be considered a fall, but it triggered something in Kate and she began to cry. Was this it? Had she lost her touch? Would she ever climb again?

On the way home, however, she began to see things differently. She felt a little sad that she hadn't done better, but she realized this wasn't going to be her last attempt. It had felt good to cry. If nothing else, it had showed her that she was capable of feeling, that she wasn't just a stone wall.

The following week Kate returned to Dragonfly for another try. She had to force herself to strap on her crampons and take her first few steps, but once she was on the ice, her initial anxiety began to melt away. The ice was soft yet firm, a far cry from Old Snowy's rock-hard visage. She moved cautiously at first, testing each foothold several times. As she climbed up the waterfall, she developed an easy rhythm, swinging her hammers confidently and working the ice with all her former style. Fear disappeared—or at least was put on hold—and in its place came a feeling of strength, joy and fluid grace.

When Kate lifted her body over the top, she was breathing hard, but she felt elated. Below her, she could see the rapids of the Nenana River frozen in silence, walled in by the foothills of the Alaska Range. It was a beautiful view, perhaps the most stunning she had ever seen, and looking at it made her want to cry and sing and laugh all at once.

★   ★   ★

It's tempting to leave Kate atop Dragonfly, during her moment of triumph. But loose ends exist in real life that, if they can't be tied off, should at least be gathered and sorted.

Kate became a graduate student in geology at the University of Alaska. She buried herself in her studies and music, and occasionally made forays into the vertical world. Last year, she put a new route on 13,832-foot Mount Hayes and was the first woman to lead an ascent up Alaska's Bridalveil Falls.

And as time passed, the memory of that afternoon on Old Snowy became less vivid. She grew detached enough to see that her ordeal on the mountain had given her a real understanding of life—and death.

"There's so much involved in living and dying, and the effect someone's death has on other people," she said. "We live and die, and do what we have to in order to survive."

Then, one afternoon last year, Peter's mother and sister stopped by to visit Kate on a trip to Alaska. Inevitably, the conversation turned to the coroner's report. They revealed that the real cause of Peter's death had been exposure and that he may still have been alive when Kate left.

Her mind reeled. All the old questions came back. Had she left him too soon? And why did she live and Peter die?

But, eventually, Kate stopped trying to find a solution. She knew it was absurd to blame herself for Peter's death. All she could do was learn to live with ambiguity and go on with her life. No matter how hard she tried, there were some questions she would never be able to answer.

'Best' Team Won, Even If It Wasn't Most Talented

BASEBALL

By *THOMAS BOSWELL*

From the Washington Post
Copyright © 1985, the Washington Post

Thanks, we needed that.

After drug trials, a stupid strike following on the tedium of 1984, baseball was ready for the Kansas City Royals.

We needed the most preposterous postseason in history to end in the crowning of the wonderful, ridiculous, awful, spunky, lucky Royals as winners of the I-70 World Series.

Are they the worst team ever to win the World Series? Well, let's hope so. These guys deserve to be remembered. If they aren't the worst, let's say they were, anyway.

This is a club that merits more than, "Well, sure, they were pretty mediocre, but somebody sometime probably had even less talent and more luck." No, no, no. That won't do.

Was this the greatest never-say-die comeback performance in the history of baseball? Well, by all means, let's pretend it was. It's a fact that no Series winner ever before survived six sudden-death, win-or-go-home games.

Stop that whispering out there, you spoiled sports. We're trying to forget the '81 Dodgers. They survived five must-win games before the Series ever began, *then* lost the first two to New York.

Let's not let the facts get in the way of a fairy-tale ending. Just for today, let's ignore about 10 teams that accomplished comebacks so outlandish that it's almost impossible to compare degrees of difficulty. (In recent times, give me the '78 Yankees any day.)

Let's make sure we give K.C. its due. No baseball team ever did more with less, or had to dig out of deeper holes to accomplish it, than these Royals.

Let's hear it for a loaf of Brett, a slice of Biancalana and a pound of Balboni. Darryl Motley and Dane Iorg, we don't even know you, but when it comes to heroes, you're our kind of guys.

Whoever thought that the nation's sixth-graders would be able to pass a spelling bee on Saberhagen, Gubicza, Quisenberry, Leibrandt and Concepcion?

Let's be honest. Can we talk here?

Could the Royals have won the World Series if The Tarp That Ate St. Louis hadn't broken an itsy-bitsy teeny-weeny bone on Vince Coleman's knee?

Of course not. Don't be silly. Tito Landrum (.360) produced only three runs in the whole Series. Coleman can create that many in one havoc-riddled game.

Could the Royals have won without the fine work of Joaquin Andujar? No way. K.C. should vote the Cardinals' astronaut a full share.

Could the Royals have won without Don Denkinger? Maybe so. But maybe not, too. The Cardinals looked like they never recovered from the American League ump's bad call in Game 6 which let the leadoff Royal reach base in the ninth inning of a 1-0 game.

Given a break, K.C. hardly kicked down the door. Let the record show that while the Royals took a title on Sunday, the Cardinals gave it away Saturday.

Kansas City started the last inning of Game 6 with a grounder to first, a popup near the dugout and a terrible sacrifice bunt back to the mound. Before the Royals could figure out what happened, they had the bases loaded with one out.

Kansas City won 91 games and had to squeeze blood from stones to do that. They had the sixth-best record in baseball and that's about right.

The reason we like the Royals, the reason their triumph will warm baseball fans so much more through the winter than a Cardinal victory is the nature of the people who won. Who really cares about talent? Who cares that the Blue Jays, Cardinals, Yankees, Mets and maybe even the Dodgers could beat the Royals over a long fair season.

Sometimes it's better when the best team *doesn't* win.

The Royals' owner does not have himself drawn around his ball park on a chariot of beer kegs, nor does he have an odious commercial jingle blaring over the public address system between pitches. Royals stadium is not a tacky testimonial to the glories of peddling beer. It's a beautiful park full of water fountains.

The Royals manager does not denigrate teams before he plays them, then deny his cheap-shot quotes until they're played back to him on a tape recorder. He does not abuse Pulitzer Prize-winning journalists for asking a polite professional question. He does not push blame toward his players and away from himself. After he wins the pennant, he doesn't use four-letter words to rub his foes' noses in their loss.

The K.C. manager does not accuse umpires of deliberate prejudice when there is no evidence of it. He does not throw tantrums on the field when he loses. He doesn't lay on the charm for the national TV cameras, then bad-mouth the team that just beat him once he gets back to his office.

When Dick Howser of the Royals makes a hard decision and gets second-guessed nationwide, he stands like a little soldier in one spot for an hour and, politely, humorously, tells anyone who asks just why he did what he did and why he'd do it again.

The Royals are easy to like. Make that easy to love. George Brett, Frank White and Hal McRae—the soul of the team since 1973—are hard-nosed, honest and smart. They play hurt. And they've swallowed postseason losses in '76, '77,' 78, '80, '81 and '84 without losing their confidence, drive or leadership.

Dan Quisenberry not only is the best relief pitcher of his time, but a gentleman who minimizes his importance, mourns whenever he lets down his mates (whom he considers "real" players) and is a very funny fellow.

Some Royals have won tougher contests than a baseball game. Willie Wilson went to jail behind a drug rap and came back a stronger man. Lonnie Smith has beaten a bad cocaine habit.

You'd need a miner's helmet to find Royals General Manager John Schuerholz, he's so busy hiding from the credit for the team he's built. Nonetheless, he knows why his club is so special.

When the Royals trailed early in this Series, Schuerholz said, "I think the interaction of your players among themselves is more important now than it ever was. You can't say what makes good chemistry within a group of people. But you better pay attention to getting it, and then to keeping it."

For at least the last 10 years, the Royals have concentrated as much on building a team with character as they have on amassing talent or signing free agents. Many times, like the '77-to-'83 Baltimore Orioles whom they resemble, they have narrowly failed and been told they would never be world champions until they had more swagger, more muscle and less good humor.

Too soon the Royals will have to begin replacing some of the 35-and-over crowd that has given this club its tone: John Wathan, Greg Pryor, White, Iorg, McRae, Jorge Orta. Then, like the now inert Orioles, they may find how mysteriously difficult it is to build a team that is significantly better than any objective analysis would indicate.

Whether the Kansas City Royals are the "best" team in baseball at the moment is a question of definition.

That they represent what is best in baseball is beyond doubt.

And that's more important.

Pure Kareem

PRO BASKETBALL

By *SAM McMANIS*

From the Los Angeles Times
Copyright © 1985, Los Angeles Times

To capture the moment forever in his mind, Kareem Abdul-Jabbar raised both arms in exultation and took a long, sweeping look around the Boston Garden. He looked up at all those championship banners, down at the creaky parquet floor and over at the opposite bench, where the Boston Celtics were slumped in defeat.

If Abdul-Jabbar hadn't removed his goggles at that point, they might have gotten misty.

On Sunday afternoon in Game 6 of the NBA championship series, Abdul-Jabbar accomplished more than simply winning the fourth championship of his 16-year career. He helped the Lakers end 25 years of frustration at the hands of the Celtics, and that made it special.

Years from now, when Abdul-Jabbar recalls this series, he probably won't remember the score (111-100) or how many points he scored (29). And the fact that he won the Most Valuable Player award for his sustained brilliance throughout the series probably will be secondary.

No, it was the historical significance of the Lakers' 0-8 streak against the Celtics in final series that made it memorable. Not usually given to outward displays of emotion, even when the situation calls for it, Abdul-Jabbar was overcome with feelings of joy Sunday.

This championship, he said, was more satisfying than any of his previous three NBA titles—1971 with Milwaukee and 1980 and 1982 with the Lakers—or the three NCAA titles he won at UCLA.

Why?

"Because it was the Celtics," he said. "Boston has never lost the championship in the Garden. They never lost one to the Lakers. And they never lost one to a team with Kareem Abdul-Jabbar on it."

About the only thing Abdul-Jabbar could compare this to was

the 1955 World Series, when the Brooklyn Dodgers beat the New York Yankees for the first time after years of frustration.

"I guess I feel like Johnny Podres in 1955," said Abdul-Jabbar, referring to the Dodgers' pitcher who won the seventh game of that series. "This has got to be real satisfying because of the history of it. This is something I'll never forget, ever. It reminds me so much of that '55 Series."

In 1955, 8-year-old Lew Alcindor sat in the family living room in Manhattan and watched his beloved Dodgers. On Sunday, he rewound his memory and played it all back as if it had just happened.

"I walked in the living room and Yogi (Berra) was up and Gil McDougald was on second base," Abdul-Jabbar said. "Yogi hits it down the line and (Dodger outfielder) Sandy Amoros catches it. I jumped up and ran and yelled out my window."

Abdul-Jabbar, now 38, had a similar display of emotion after he had fouled out with 14 seconds to play in Sunday's game. Knowing that the Lakers were assured of winning the title, Abdul-Jabbar raised his right index finger in the air and screamed. In an instant, he was swarmed by teammates.

If Abdul-Jabbar wasn't 7-2 and 235 pounds, his teammates probably would have carried him off the court and into the locker room when it was finally over. After all, it was Abdul-Jabbar who mostly carried the Lakers in the championship series.

After the Lakers' 34-point embarrassment here in Game 1, in which Abdul-Jabbar scored only 12 points, he simply took over. He scored 30 points and had 17 rebounds in the Lakers' 109-102 win in Game 2, 26 points in the Lakers' two-point loss in Game 4 and a magnificent 36 points in Game 5 Friday. All he did Sunday in Game 6 was make 12 of 21 shots for a team-high 29 points.

"MVP?" Laker Coach Pat Riley asked. "There's got to be a better word."

There are certain aspects of Abdul-Jabbar's play in the series that are utterly indescribable. For a two-week span, Abdul-Jabbar was 24 instead of 38. People used terms such as "spry" and "rejuvenated," but even those didn't seem to fit.

In addition to sinking dozens of sky hooks, his specialty shot, Abdul-Jabbar was doing things he rarely did even when he was a young Buck in Milwaukee.

He dove on the floor once for a loose ball. He once grabbed a long rebound, dribbled the ball the length of the court and swished a sky hook. He took the wing on fast breaks. And, in perhaps his boldest move of the series that no one outside the locker room saw, Abdul-Jabbar walked to each players' stall before Game 2 and gave pep talks.

"He picked us up," Laker forward James Worthy said. "You think I can't let a 38-year-old outdo me? All us young guys get pumped up by that. This is the way I look at it: If he can be that committed, I can too."

Clearly, Abdul-Jabbar was especially inspired in this series. He admitted as much after Sunday's game, saying that he wanted to be assured of at least one more championship before retiring after next season.

If Abdul-Jabbar hadn't changed his mind in December and agreed to a one-year contract extension, this would have been the closing curtain of his career. But now, he's coming back for another season at the top of his profession.

Holding the Most Valuable Player trophy in his massive hands, Abdul-Jabbar couldn't stop smiling as he answered questions at a formal press conference.

Asked if he turned back the clock in this series, Abdul-Jabbar said: "I feel like I'm not any age."

Asked if perhaps he even surprised himself with his excellence, he smiled and said: "I've lived with me all my life. I know what I can do."

Others, however, weren't so sure Abdul-Jabbar still could play this well. At 38, nearly all professional basketball players are well into retirement, either coaching or selling insurance. But Abdul-Jabbar plays on, endures and even thrives on occasion.

Certainly, Abdul-Jabbar rose to the occasion against the Celtics. Actually, Kareem didn't rise until after he and the Lakers had hit bottom in Game 1. But, as Riley said afterward, that 34-point loss may have been a blessing.

"Personally, Game 1 was embarrassing," Abdul-Jabbar said. "It was terrible. I knew I could do better. I wanted to prove it to *myself* that I could do better."

When the Lakers held a meeting the morning after Game 1, Abdul-Jabbar stood up in front of the entire team and took responsibility for the loss. It was at that point, Riley said, that he noticed drastic changes in Abdul-Jabbar's game and attitude.

"It brought us together," Riley said. "Ever since Game 1, he had that look about him, a certain air about him. I've known Kareem well for 10 years, and I've never seen him like this. In practice, he was focused on one thing. No frivolity. He directed his total attention at what we were trying to do. He was more responsive to me than ever. And when the other players see that Cap (he's the team captain) is paying attention, they will, too."

Said teammate Kurt Rambis: "Kareem wanted it really bad. You could see it in his eyes. He's always been a leader by his actions, and he signaled to us that he wanted it. He put us on his back and carried us."

It is quite a burden Abdul-Jabbar carries with him. He truly is the most valuable player. The Lakers' raucous post-game celebration served as a vehicle for Abdul-Jabbar to release all the tension and pressure that had built up.

Although usually shying away from such things, Abdul-Jabbar joined in Sunday, pouring champagne over players' heads.

Also, he was extremely accommodating to photographers who wanted him to pose with the championship trophy, and he talked to the press for more than an hour.

But when a short, bald man in his 60s walked in the locker room, Abdul-Jabbar dropped everything.

"Dad," Kareem screamed. "Dad. I feel wonderful, dad. Where's mom?"

Ferdinand Alcindor, eyes red and voiced choked, shook his head.

"Your mother's outside and she's very proud of you."

Abdul-Jabbar is a proud man, which is why he will retire after next season. He will be 39 and he said he just feels it's time.

"There is a time for everything," Abdul-Jabbar said. "I feel that time is running out on me. Time is on my back and I don't want it to run over me."

Time, at least for a two-week span, was on Kareem Abdul-Jabbar's side.

The Hard Times Of a Hard Hitter

PRO FOOTBALL

By *RON BORGES*

From the Boston Globe
Copyright © 1985, Boston Globe

Hugh Green is talking for the record. He is explaining himself to the world. His eyes stare straight ahead as he speaks. A smile never quite manages to peek through the dark cloud he has wrapped around himself. He is cordial and forthright, but clearly he is speaking only because his business requires him to.

He is answering questions, but he is not entering into any conversations.

Then he decides to shift his approach. For just a moment, he stops merely answering questions. Now he is making a statement.

"I am a linebacker," he says, his voice rising with emotion for the first time in 20 minutes.

It is immediately clear that Hugh Green is not describing what he does.

He is describing who he is.

★   ★   ★

He became a man when he was 6, although like most men born so young, he didn't volunteer for the assignment.

The world made Hugh Green a man, forcing him to leave childhood behind before he had a chance to take it for a ride. Adulthood rushed in on him, making it clear that this world of his could be a hurting place whether you deserved the pain or not.

He had never known his father, but his mother was always by his side down in Natchez, Miss., ready with a cool drink and a warm smile. But then Hugh Green ran home one day and someone told a 6-year-old boy that his mother had died.

When you are 6 and there is no father to protect you and no

warning that from today on you will walk alone, your insides begin to hurt.

It changes you, although perhaps you don't know how or why. You just know it changes you.

"I'm not happy my mom died," he says now. "But if she were alive today, I don't think I'd be where I am. My mom's death changed my whole life. I grew up without a mother, father, brothers or sisters. That's a challenge for anyone. I grew up within myself.

"I had to accept responsibility at an early age. I solve my own problems. I set my own pace. I don't depend on anyone else for answers."

"I am a linebacker."

★   ★   ★

The man-child was 13. He had been living with his aunt and uncle, Lucy and Eltee Berry, since his mother's death. They took him in, raised him, cared for him, loved him in their way. But he was not their son and they were not his parents, and so one day the man-child decided life there was too hard and he walked away. He would depend on no one.

The first night, he slept in an old bus, but by morning he was confused and a little scared, so he climbed into a tree to think about his life, and a local policeman spied him.

"How old are you?" the cop said.

"Thirty-five," the man-child replied.

Green ended up standing before a kindly judge who suggested he try football instead of the highway. He did, but his first team went 0-4. Hugh Green never forgot what that feeling of loss was like. For the rest of his life, he decided, he would dedicate himself to winning.

"My uncle, well, he made me come up the hard way," Green says of those years. "If I asked him for a nickel or a quarter, he made me borrow it and pay him back. It took me a long time to understand why he was as tough as he was. I understand now."

"I am a linebacker."

★   ★   ★

It didn't take long for Hugh Green to become a star at Natchez North High, but because he was small for a defensive lineman, he went relatively unnoticed by everyone but the people who couldn't block him.

The same could not be said for the kid across the river, however, one Raymond (Rooster) Jones. Jones was a running back who could move. He was the fastest thing to hit Pascagoula, Miss., since the highway opened; so the college recruiters came from everywhere to watch.

One of them was an assistant coach from Pittsburgh who noticed on a film of Jones running that he was always being caught by a little guy from North Natchez High.

The coach investigated, and before long, not only was Rooster Jones going to Pitt, but so was Hugh Green.

Green showed up as a freshman in 1977 hell-bent on winning. For the first practice, his new teammates came out in shorts. So did an unknown commodity named Green.

By the afternoon practice, Hugh Green was a starting member of the Pitt Panther defense, although when the season opened against Notre Dame, an upperclassman named Mike Lenosky was in for the first play.

On the second, Hugh Green replaced him. Green never missed another play.

By the end of his sophomore year, he was named to Pitt's all-time all-star team.

By the end of his junior year, he was the only underclassman ever selected as a finalist for the Lombardi Trophy.

By the end of his senior year, he finished second in the Heisman Trophy voting, won the Lombardi, saw his No. 99 retired, was part of an 11-1 team and won four national player-of-the-year awards.

He was also still a man alone, a man focused on winning.

"Nobody in college football could block him," recalls Jackie Sherrill, now the head coach at Texas A&M but then Green's coach at Pitt. "Once, he was rushing the punter against Boston College. The guy ducked under Hugh and started running when Hugh jumped to block the kick, but in midair, Hugh wrapped his legs around the guy and dragged him down. There was no question who was the best football player in the nation that year. Hugh Green is the best linebacker in the history of college football.

"It got to the point where we wouldn't let him practice much for fear he'd hurt one of our guys. One day he asked me why I wasn't calling his number. I said, 'Who do you want?'

"He said, 'The big boy.' "

The big boy was All-America tackle Mark May, who stood 6-foot-6 and weighed somewhere between 280 and a ton. Hugh Green, at the time, weighed 219 pounds and stood 6-2 on his toes.

"He grabbed May like he was a dishrag," Sherrill says. "And Mark May was a great football player."

He was great, but he wasn't Green.

"If I don't crush somebody on a play, I'm disappointed," Green once said while explaining his philosophy of life as he knows it. "Let's be truthful. Fans like the sport because of the violence . . . which is also why I like it."

"I am a linebacker."

★   ★   ★

For more than five years, Green toiled in Tampa Bay, doing all he could to convert a loser into a winner.

He made tackles from stateline to stateline. He rushed the quarterback. He intercepted passes. He was arguably the best linebacker in America, Lawrence Taylor or no Lawrence Taylor.

But he couldn't make the Buccaneers a winner, even after back-to-back All-Pro seasons in 1983 and 1984. He was still the same Hugh

Green, but his team was a loser, and for the first time since he was 13, he wanted out.

"It wasn't the absence of winning that got to me," Green says now. "It was the absence of giving 110 percent. It was like a losing cause. It kept me emotionally down in so many ways. I had always felt I was the kind who gave full effort. I didn't know if I could still do that.

"You get to the point where you say you're having a great year, but you look in the win column and see nothing there. You look at yourself and say, 'Am I doing all I can to help the team?' Losing hurts."

Finally, on October 2, he walked out, just as he had 13 years earlier when he climbed a tree in Natchez. Soon he was back, but the Bucs got the message.

Within days, Green was gone, traded to the Miami Dolphins. The price was first- and second-round 1986 draft choices plus $300,000 in bonus money, which he agreed to leave behind. He hadn't depended on anyone for his answers. He had walked out until he got to a place where he could be a winner.

"Hugh felt his unhappiness might hurt the young players here," says his close friend, Tampa linebacker Cecil Johnson. "He was a player people looked up to, and when he started to talk negative, he knew it was affecting people.

"There were a lot of hearts hurt when Hugh left, I don't mind saying. But you have to hand it to (Tampa Coach) Leeman Bennett. He did right by Hugh."

Now Hugh intends to do right by the Dolphins.

"I'm getting more comfortable now," Green says. "It takes time to learn the defenses and the personnel. Until you do, you end up not being the athlete they knew you as, but you can't let the change frustrate you. You have to work harder.

"We played Tampa the second game I was here, and people wondered how I could go right out and do that to my old teammates. Miami had always been our archrivals, but I had to reverse roles. It wasn't difficult. I'm a football player. I'm paid to do a job. Logos shouldn't affect a person.

"But I was lost a lot that day. I didn't know what we were doing. It was the worst game I ever played. I always try to at least play a game that's a 7 or an 8. A 7, and I want to shoot myself. Anything less, and I'd just jump off a bridge.

"But now I'm getting back to where I should be. I'm starting to know what I'm doing again. I'm returning to my old self."

"I am a linebacker."

★   ★   ★

Already they are noticing in Miami that Hugh Green practices the way most NFL players play. He hits you on Tuesday and on Wednesday and on Thursday just as he would on Sunday.

He hits friend and foe alike.

He hits.

Always.

"When we played Tampa last year in an exhibition game, he blindsided me," recalls Dolphins quarterback Dan Marino, Green's former teammate at Pitt and present host at his Miami home. "I'm telling you, I've still got the bruise. And he *likes* me, so just think what he does to people he doesn't like."

The same thing, that's what he does, because that is what he learned 20 years ago when he was 6 and his whole world collapsed. He learned you play for today.

"I've always competed, and things have turned out the best for me," Green says. "You always go full speed and the odds are life will work out to your benefit.

"I go full out in practice. Some guys don't like it, but that's me. You never know when things will end. That time may seem far ahead of you, but then, like that, it's over.

"If you're a man, you go out and work your whole life so your kids will be proud of what you accomplished. You have to show those kids how hard you've worked because they have to know you don't get nothing easy in life. That's the way life is.

"If I hadn't always been like this, if I hadn't gone full out, I wouldn't be where I am. I wouldn't be the person I am."

He wouldn't be "a linebacker."

Mom, Apple Pie And Wrestling

WRESTLING

By *MICHAEL DAVIS* and *MIKE KLINGAMAN*

From the Baltimore Sun Magazine
Copyright © 1985, the Baltimore Sun

The Civic Center has been awash in villainy for almost two hours. At 9:45 p.m. on a Saturday, America is on the ropes again, and from his $9 seat, Yard Dog decides he just can't take it any more.

This is what he sees:

During a tag-team match, a feral-looking Nikita Koloff is pounding the bejeebers out of Dusty Rhodes, a.k.a. the American Dream. Koloff is using a chain. Outside the ring, Ivan Koloff glares, Rasputin-like, at the crowd, growling something which sounds like Cookie Monster speaking English backward. The crowd does not like this. It would like the Koloffs nuked.

"Shut up, you bleeping commie! USA! USA! USA!"

Cue, Yard Dog, who, in an unpremeditated wave of patriotism, hurls himself ringside like an MX missile and sprays the contents of his soda cup on the suspect Russians.

Yard Dog, a scruffy bike type, is immediately hustled off by four security men. His army fatigues disappear behind a moving patch of blue. But he is remembered by someone in the crowd.

"You got em, Yard Dog, you uneducated moron, you! USA! USA! USA!"

The crescendo of tired Olympic cheers builds from this blue-collar anvil chorus. It's Oriole Section 34, cubed.

"These folks are Working Class Only; ain't nobody here with a whole lot of money," says Ralph Herndon, a 310-pound house detective who, in blue coveralls, looks like a black Haystacks Calhoun. He came from Washington for the show, and is sitting amid an odd melange of skullcaps and USA hats, of Meade High School lettermen's jackets and Iron Maiden T-shirts. The kids say professional wrestling is camp, sort of like "The Rocky Horror Picture Show" with C-minus choreography.

Nearer the ring, a man and woman are sharing french fries. The fries and their hair are identical colors: half-black, half-brown. Behind them, a middle-aged, greased-back Elvis cheers his T-shirt's namesake: The Boogie Woogie Man.

The Boogie Woogie Man, a.k.a. Jimmy Valiant, has long blond hair and the name Chewbacca on the seat of his pants. He and his tag-team partner, Bob Backlund, are Good. Their opponents are Evil. They are Billy Graham, who is bald, and the Barbarian. What seem to be pulsating corpuscles atop Graham's skull make his pate look like a half-finished lobotomy, or $2.29 ground round. "You could have nightmares about the way the top of his head looks," says Oriole announcer Tom Marr, who is ringside.

The Barbarian, less repugnant, is wearing a choke collar, with studs, and has the equivalent of a large black tarantula painted over one eye.

The Good are not amused. The Boogie Woogie Man calls them slimy dogs, and groins both within a five-second span. Good triumphs, in 10:13, less time than it probably took to apply the Barbarian's makeup.

Grace Johnson, 59, is ecstatic. She lives in Westminster and arrived by bus. Mrs. Johnson likes wrestling for "the excitement, the men." From her second-row seat, she has had both. Once, Backlund gave her a sweaty hug, staining her blouse with his blood. Her granddaughter, Kathy Watson, swooned over the blouse and traded for it. Mrs. Johnson got the flowered knit sweater she always wanted; three years later, Miss Watson still hasn't washed the blouse.

Last year, Mrs. Johnson—a great-grandmother—was hit with a chair thrown by the Samoans. She received only a sprained knee, but now her 3-year-old grandson Maurice, nicknamed Bam-Bam, balks at attending the matches, "because Nana got hurt."

Others are taunting the wrestlers, hoping for their own badge of courage. Fred Creutzer of Parkville—Dr. X to the crowd—wears a white mask with a black X and barks insults at the ring, like some yippy chihuahua who gets underfoot. Too often, he succeeds. George (the Animal) Steele, who has a green tongue, once chased him up the aisle. "I've been spit at, called names and grabbed," says Mr. Creutzer, who works in a Mars supermarket freezer.

Dr. X has an American flag in his pocket. It is there to pay tribute, not to tease. "This is for Sgt. Slaughter," he says softly. "He shook my hand at the Capital Centre; he's U.S. of A. all the way."

As Slaughter's match approaches, the flags multiply, and Mickey O'Shea becomes more visible. In his Sunny's Surplus uniform, Mr. O'Shea is a scaled-down clone of Sgt. Slaughter. He has the same mustache, same hair (short and bald on top), same look (a pouting frown with jutting jaw). Mr. O'Shea, who is from Randallstown, looks so much like Slaughter that the Iron Sheik took a swipe at him last year.

★   ★   ★

The Saturday night security detail earns its pay at the Civic Center. They're often abused by the customers ("Chicken-head biters and geeks," is how one guard described the crowd) and often abusive. Wrestling shows are their anathema. Says one guard: "If wrestling were the only thing on TV, I'd turn on the radio."

With courage fueled by alcohol in excess, one sorry patron recently transgressed the tenuous yet perceptible breach between spectator and performer. "Didn't take an instant before Rowdy Roddy Piper saw the guy coming toward the ring," says Larry Beatty, a world-weary shock trauma technician who works many a Civic Center card. "Before the guy even touched the rope, Piper broke his nose. A second later the police were dragging the sucker away."

Wrestling's most unfortunate moments occur when spectators blur the distinctions between fantasy and reality; when they begin to take all the raging bull from ringside too seriously.

The wrestlers certainly don't. Backstage the performers have been known to kibitz, chain-smoke and share stories of their children and the lonely road, not unlike long-haul drivers at a 66 truck stop. They are serious only about two things: performing well and avoiding injury. (A wrestler recently dodged a misfired dart aimed toward the Civic Center ring by a fan. "It landed right at my feet," said usher Bob Greco. "I still have the dart at home.")

"The truth is, wrestlers are intelligent, approachable, rational, real people . . . and great athletes," says 30-year-old promoter Gary Juster, a backstage heavyweight in the National Wrestling Alliance. "We don't have a high percentage of Rhodes scholars, but we don't have a high percentage of illiterates, either.

"When problems arise in arenas, it always strikes me the reason is the wrestlers are professionals while the fans are not," he says.

Often a fan incident can change the course of the evening's script. "A villain who senses things are getting out of control will take a fall quickly and end the match," says Gerald Morton, an English and drama professor at Auburn University-Montgomery, who was co-author on the recently published tome *Wrestling to Rasslin'* (Popular Press, Bowling Green State University). "They won't mess around. These guys have been shot at and stabbed before by fans, so they must always take precautions to protect themselves from some fans. But they must do it in such a way as to not turn off the rest of the audience."

No one is more aware of the crowd's visceral ebb and flow than Slaughter, the 36-year-old, 6-foot-6, 305-pound ersatz marine.

Government records reveal Slaughter, a.k.a. Robert Remus, never served time in the U.S. Marine Corps, though he claims to have been a drill instructor from 1966 to 1973. Slaughter dodges all questions about his armed service record—for good reason.

"We've been 'interested' in Slaughter for a couple of years, since he began using our paraphernalia, but the guy has been very elusive," says Capt. Jay Farrar, of the Public Affairs Office of the U.S. Marine Headquarters in Washington. Captain Farrar's office has received 50 complaints in the past year from true-blue marines, citing Slaughter's abuse of the uniform. "What they really didn't like—and we know of two such cases—is when his opponents staged attacks on people wearing dress blue uniforms, whom we strongly believe were not Marines. Then Slaughter came in and rescued the guys."

However, the USMC could do little (until last fall, when Congress passed a law prohibiting the use of the Marine Corps emblem and insignia by civilians). "That gave us recourse to fight back," says Farrar, whose office fired off a letter demanding that Slaughter stop because his actions "reflect discredit on those who have served." Neither Slaughter nor his former Connecticut agent, Mark Sotichek, ever replied.

"Our next step is to try and get the U.S. attorney's office involved," says Farrar. "From a public relations standpoint, it may not be worth the effort. You've got to look at this broad-minded. Sgt. Slaughter isn't a bad buy. He's trying to uphold good things. But he's abusing something that Marines hold near and dear to us, just for showmanship."

Slaughter's response? "We have no comment on that," said Maria Passerelli, his secretary-booking agent in Westport, Conn.

Slaughter was born August 27, 1948, and grew up in Eden Prairie, Minn., a southwest suburb of Minneapolis. From all reports he was an unremarkable (save for his stature), well-mannered student at Eden Prairie High.

Slaughter is recalled fondly by John Ryski, his football line coach, as being "a quiet, shy kid who didn't particularly like contact sports at first. He was never muscular, but from his sophomore year on he was awfully big and awfully strong." Legend has it "Big Bob" broke off an arm of a seven-man practice sled one day. "Aw, it was rusted," Ryski remembers him saying.

After high school Slaughter worked for his father's roofing business and then became a barber. He broke into wrestling in 1974 after attending a camp in Minnesota run by ex-wrestler Verne Gagne. That was back in a time when the military was in disfavor. Now, Slaughter is cresting majestically on the country's current nationalistic wave. Slaughter appealed to Republican leaders—to no avail—to allow him to recite the Pledge of Allegiance at an Inaugural Ball last January. "If Mr. T can be Santa Claus at the White House, then Sgt. Slaughter ought to be allowed to recite the Pledge," he reasoned.

Thanks to geopolitics and the nation's jingoistic frenzy, the Slaughter character, a Bad Guy turned Good Guy, has become, in effect, an American Phenomenon. (Except the story in *USA Today* soon.) "It's nice to walk down the aisle now and have people shaking my hand instead of spitting on me," he says. "That abuse gets old."

Since its earliest days, the plotlines of wrestling's passion play have been directed by political and cultural swings.

"After World War II, the sneaky Japanese and the Nazi Germans were standard villains," says Morton. "Now, new national foes like the Iranians and the Russians have given birth to new confrontations."

You can't attend a wrestling card these days and not expect to find bogus Russian villains, like Ivan and Nikita Koloff or Nikolai Volkoff, scheduled in a feature match. The dreaded 305-pound Volkoff, who regularly is pelted with produce, begins each match by singing "Hymn of the Soviet Union," the Soviet national anthem, in a voice that Ray Didinger of the *Philadelphia Daily News* wrote "would clear Red Square on May Day."

Thus, the satisfactions of pro wrestling in these nationalistic times are lip-smacking good to commonfolk: They not only see us win the battle of the Superpowers at ringside, they witness a character like Sgt. Slaughter twist Uncle Ivan's arm until he says "uncle."

As Morton told the *Los Angeles Times:* "Wrestling is such a broad spectacle or drama, it plays itself out like a soap opera does. It can change quickly to react to current events. It is not confined by intellectual concerns and it can do what its audience wants it to do.

"Wrestling will put in the ring the representation of our greatest nightmares and then try to destroy them. That's why people go, because they're willing to buy that. Evil is simple enough for them that it can be represented. It's cathartic."

Slaughter crossed the metaphysical brink between Evil and Good on a night in 1983 when he overpowered the Iron Sheik in Allentown, Pa., a pig-iron city where the scars of unemployment are all too visible. It was the perfect setting for the fiery eruption that would propel Slaughter clear out of Hades. Or Allentown, at least.

The moment of transmutation was both preposterous and ingenious. Promoters had claimed that the Iron Sheik, a scuzzy fiend who formerly fought as the Sheik, presumably in his pre-Geritol days, was descended from a line of wild-eyed Iranians. He was said to be a distant cousin of the "kooks who had held Our Boys hostage in Eye-ran!"

Before the match, the Iron Sheik waved the flag bearing the likeness of Ayatollah Ruhollah Khomeini. Slaughter countered by unfurling Old Glory and unlocking the gates of wrath. "I stood up for America that night," says Slaughter, "just like everybody in the hall wanted to."

Ever since, it's been the Sgt.'s stripes forever pounding in the hearts of his legion fans. He gets fan mail by the gunnysack delivered to the Connecticut headquarters of Cobra Inc. USA, Slaughter's corporate barracks. Fathers line up to have their sons photographed with him. "Mothers have asked him to baptize their babies, and others swear he has healing powers," says Passerelli, who books

Slaughter's travel, answers the mail and fields the ever-growing commercial offers being thrust his way.

Examples? This year, Hasbro Industries discussed creating Sgt. Slaughter action figures as part of the G.I. Joe merchandise line. Slaughter, a budding recording artist, already has cut a 45 on the Camouflage label and intends to follow with an album. ("He wants to do a couple of ballads and a few recital numbers," says Passerelli, who would not disclose whether Slaughter's warblings recall John Wayne or Wayne Newton.)

Slaughter says he worked everyday of 1984, except New Year's Eve and Christmas Eve, and will allow no letup in '85. "The only states I haven't wrestled in are Alabama and Utah," he says with regret. "But I'll be appearing in Salt Lake City soon. . . . and I've invited the whole Osmond family to come out!"

Spend an hour with Sgt. Slaughter and you walk away wondering where his act begins and ends, since he seems to slip in and out of his public persona easily. "It's like a politician, or anyone else who comes in contact with the public," says promoter Juster. "You hear the adulation all the time, and after awhile you begin to believe it all."

Slaughter says he is a patriot and "a throwback to the old-time athlete. I don't smoke, I don't do drugs and I drink only occasionally." He says he often speaks to school groups and has worked with the disadvantaged. He has helped raise money for the restoration of the Statue of Liberty.

He appears to have a heart proportionate to his massive frame. He says he is a favorite son of Vietnam veterans, and that the sunglasses he always has on his person were among the personal effects of a serviceman who was killed in Southeast Asia. They were given to Slaughter by the man's school-age son in Atlanta.

Clearly, he has a soft spot for young people. This night, he would pose for snapshots with two young boys, minutes before entering the ring. "He is a good kids' person," says Larry Beatty, the medic. "I've seen him stop and give autographs to children at almost the moment he steps out of the ring. If I had just spent 20 minutes in the ring with a 400-pound guy who was acting like he wanted to make eight ounces of orange juice out of me, I'm not sure I would be ready to talk to anybody for a while."

For his labors, both in and out of the ring, Slaughter likely will make an estimated $250,000 to $500,000 this year, vaulting him into wrestling's select company of perhaps a dozen millionaires-in-the-making. He took an Andre the Giant-sized step toward financial independence recently by breaking away contractually from second-generation promoter Vince McMahon, whose World Wrestling Federation is by far the country's most powerful.

The wrestling industry, which generates an estimated $250 million annually, thrives in what sociologists might call a closed society. Its leaders operate in virtual obscurity, their movements all but undetected. As with the mob, secrets just don't leak easily. "If only our CIA were as controlled and enclosed," sighs author Morton, "our country would be in better shape.

"And when you understand the jockeying that goes on between the three top promoters (Juster's NWA, McMahon's WWF and the Midwest's American Wrestling Alliance) you can begin to see how vicious this business can be," he says.

Wrestling, the nation's No. 3 spectator sport behind auto racing and horse racing, has been a consistent draw for decades. But the sport is in the midst of a giddy television resurgence, thanks to cable TV in general and MTV in particular. Three of the top 10 programs on cable during October were wrestling shows on either the USA Network or Superstation WTBS, according to *Advertising Age*. MTV and McMahon have formed a marriage of convenience, co-promoting wildly successful rock 'n' roll challenge matches at Madison Square Garden and elsewhere.

In February, MTV promoted and televised "the war to settle the score," a comic book come to life, before a Garden sellout of 22,000. Like Popeye defending Olive Oyl, WWF champion Hulk Hogan—upholding the dignity of that flower of maidenly virtue, Cyndi Lauper —fought to a draw against the evening's Bluto, Rowdy Roddy Piper. What promoted these wrestling vidiots to duel was Piper's effrontery of breaking one of Lauper's gold records over the head of Capt. Lou Albano. The latter, a former wrestler-turned-manager, played Lauper's overweight and overwrought father in the Lauper video, "Girls Just Want To Have Fun."

The WWF claims that "35 percent of all young people in America, 18 to 34, are proud to call themselves wrestling fans." MTV, which wants to be the nation's purveyor of sex, song and sock, believes if you have wrestling in your soul, it's likely you have rock—or is it rocks?—in your head.

There is a distinction between the wrestling spectator and the wrestling viewer. An *Advertising Age* survey in July revealed 45 percent of the cable TV viewers were 18 to 34. Fourteen percent attended college, 13 percent earn more than $40,000 a year and 11 percent are professionals. Watching wrestling on cable has almost become a Yuppie holy obligation.

Wrestling whips college basketball by a 3-to-1 margin in the ratings on USA Network, and the audience appears to be growing. The nation's No. 1 cable show is USA's *Wrestling TNT*, a bizarre wrestling news-and-talk show taped in Owings Mills. It is what TV would be like if the bomb fell and mutants took over the stations.

The TNT set is so tacky it could trap horseflies. It has the standard desk, couch and urban backdrop of the *Tonight* show, but the Manhattan skyline hanging behind host Vince McMahon appears to have been fashioned by somebody's Cub Scout den mother.

TNT's pattern is so vulgar and brainless it inspired critic James P. Breig of the *Long Island Catholic* to write: "Picture Johnny Car-

son on steroids and with a lobotomy and you have some idea of what
TNT is like." But the Friday night show is seen in 1.4 million homes
weekly and is considered a white-hot TV property.

Why? Because it has a unique sense of chaos. Last fall, they televised the nation's first triple-ring ceremony. Wrestlers Butcher Paul
Vachon and Diane Page exchanged vows on the mat, then they exchanged blows with some of the invited guests, including the Wild
Samoans. It degenerated into a brawl, climaxing with the lovely
bride being pelted with a coconut cream pie. She got her just desserts.

Slaughter, whom some merchandisers see as an alabaster Mr. T,
is himself a made-for-TV caricature. When time allows he continues
to make local TV car-dealership commercials, as he does for Larry's
Chevrolet, for small truckloads of money. There has been talk of
including the Sgt. Slaughter character in a Saturday morning action
cartoon show.

"Sgt. Slaughter knows the time is right to make it now while he
can," says author Morton. "In wrestling, anything can happen. He
could get injured and have his career ended overnight. And you always have to worry about the fans. They are fickle, and could turn
on him at any time."

This night, at a stop in Baltimore, in a match for "the NWA
champeenship of the world," the fans are turned on to him.

★   ★   ★

The Sarge enters first, marching in to "The Marine Hymn" and
gladhanding like a politician. Mickey O'Shea gets his wildest wish:
The two Sgt. Slaughters face and salute one another.

There are pockets of hate. Someone yells, "Hey, Gomer!" A plac-
ard reads, Slaughter the Sergeant. These people are craning to see
Ric Flair, a.k.a. Nature Boy, the champion who rides in on an elec-
tronic carpet of rock music, in a long white robe with pink-sequined
butterflies. The hair is platinum. He is Barry Manilow-brow.

Unperturbed by the dazzle, the Sgt. begins to disrobe: first the
hat, then the shirt, which he hurls at the darkened crowd. It is caught
by a man in the eighth row. What will he do with the keepsake?
"Wash it first," says Jerry Allen.

The match begins, and it is the Sgt. who has the upper hand. His
hand is in Flair's hair, messing about as if searching for fleas. Nature
Boy feigns insult, and a moment later he is parallel with the floor,
caught in a headlock and kicking his feet like a 6-year-old who has to
go to the bathroom. Bad.

But Flair gets up, as he must, and whacks the challenger's throat
with karate chops—once, twice, three times. Then he throws the Sgt.
out of the ring, where he lays at the feet of ageless Lena Warner, of
Glen Burnie. "Get in there, you jackass you!" screams Mrs. Warner,
who makes a menacing gesture toward him. Three ushers move in
on Warner. The Sgt. recovers.

But what is this, blood? Is the Sgt. bleeding? The ooze cues the
chant.

"USA! USA! USA!"

Now Nature Boy has the Sgt. in a headlock, and his face is purple, and a Marine in a Camp Hansen T-shirt is screaming, and Mickey O'Shea's sunglasses are steaming. First the hockey team in Sarajevo, and now this?

But the Sgt. breaks free and delivers the Slaughter Cannon, which is like a triple windup by Eddie Feigner, and suddenly Nature Boy is outside the ring. And defeated.

Sgt. Slaughter raises the championship belt. Whistles blow. Fists, both white and black, go skyward, but only momentarily, because now the Sgt. has been disqualified for throwing Nature Boy out of the ring. The generic crowd reacts accordingly.

"Bull----! Bull----!"

Briefly, they tangle again in the ring, and the Sgt. parades out with a satisfied look and the belt he'll have to give back. "Flair's got more money, he paid somebody off," growls the Marine from Camp Hansen. "You saw who carried the belt out, didn't you? The Sgt.'s gonna get a Texas Death Match and whip him."

The crowd of nearly 6,000 isn't particularly happy, but America didn't lose. It only got screwed. There's a difference, in pro wrestling as in life.

Soccer Somersault

by Mike Adaksaveg of the Journal Inquirer. University of Connecticut's Matt Addington gets the worst end of a collision with Harvard sweeper Ian Hardington during Ivy League college soccer action. Copyright © 1985, Journal Publishing Co. Inc.

What's Up Mr. McEnroe?

by Bernard Brault of La Presse newspaper. Tennis star John McEnroe wasn't wearing a disguise. He simply was performing his patented racket toss during action in an international professional tournament in Montreal. Copyright © 1985, La Presse, Bernard Brault.

The Clemson Nightmare

GENERAL

By *CURT HOLBREICH*

From the Pittsburgh Press
Copyright © 1985, the Pittsburgh Press

Stijn Jaspers, star of the Clemson University cross country team, had not been seen for two days. He missed his morning run. He missed classes. Phone calls to his dormitory room went unanswered.

It was a warm Friday afternoon last October 19, and on impulse Robert deBrouwer and Ellen DeSmet had chosen this day to marry. They wanted Jaspers, their friend and teammate, to wish them well. On their way to the county courthouse, they knocked on his door. No response. They called a resident adviser to get a key to the room. The curtains were drawn; the room was dark.

"I saw an arm hanging off the bed," deBrouwer said. "I was so upset I couldn't say anything. Ellen went into the room. She couldn't recognize him at first. He was all purple.

"She came out crying, 'He's dead! He's dead! Don't go in there!' "

★ ★ ★

On August 8, Jaspers, 23, ran the 5,000 meters in the Olympics for his native Holland. Two and a half months later, he was dead.

Dr. James Pruitt, a Seneca, S.C., pathologist who conducted the autopsy, concluded Jaspers died of congestive heart failure, the result of a heart defect at birth that left him with an almost non-existent left coronary artery.

Found in his room, however, was an envelope containing three capsules of phenylbutazone, a strong anti-inflammatory drug that is potentially dangerous to people with heart disease. Phenylbutazone increases salt retention in the body, which can increase fluid retention, adding stress to the heart. Jaspers did not have a prescription for the drug. Traces of it were found in his blood.

No direct connection between the phenylbutazone and his death was established.

Yet Jaspers' death unraveled a series of events that left the Clemson University athletic program reeling again—its basketball and football teams have been hit with five years of National Collegiate Athletic Association probation since 1977—and called national attention to the use of performance-enhancing drugs among college athletes. His death:

• Resulted in the conviction of two Clemson University track coaches for distributing drugs to athletes—the first conviction of its kind for college coaches;

• Prompted the discovery of what police believe was a drug distribution network accused of illegally providing almost 100,000 doses of performance-enhancing prescription drugs, including phenylbutazone and anabolic steroids, which were dispensed to athletes at Vanderbilt University in Nashville, Tenn.; Colgate University in Hamilton, N.Y., and Clemson in South Carolina;

• Led to the indictment of three Nashville area men, accused of conspiring and distributing performance-enhancing drugs, and;

• Helped spawn an investigation by the U.S. Food and Drug Administration into the black-market dispensing of anabolic steroids.

And, finally, as a result of Jaspers' death, Clemson will be a different place when the fall semester begins Wednesday.

It will have a new interim president, a new athletic director, a new chairman of the board of trustees, a new track coach and a new chief of campus security. The latest change came last Monday when H.C. (Bill) McLellan, the former athletic director, announced his retirement effective September 19 after 30 years of university service.

★　　★　　★

Ellyn Hutson met Stijn Jaspers in September 1983. She was trying to cross the campus on horseback, but the horse was not cooperating. Jaspers gave the horse a little tug. It cooperated.

Hutson, a senior majoring in animal science, and Jaspers lived on the same floor in the Clemson House. They had a common friend in Hans Koeleman.

"One day they both came down, and Hans said Stijn wanted to change his major to animal science and would I talk to him. I showed him everything. I took him to a livestock show just to see what was going on. It turned out he didn't care about animal science.

"I had promised myself this was my senior year. I swore I wouldn't go out with any guys. I didn't want to deal with it. I was going to graduate and I was going to leave. I don't know how he knew about that, but he kind of came in the back door. He kind of tricked me."

★　　★　　★

The week before his death Jaspers showed his girlfriend, Ellyn Hutson, several orange-and-white capsules. He said they were phenylbutazone.

Hutson, a graduate student in microbiology, had been dating Jaspers for a year and said she had seen no evidence to indicate he used prescription medications. She said Jaspers told her his coach gave him the pills because his left knee was sore.

She knew about the drug, commonly known as butazolidin or bute, and she vividly remembers what she told him. "They gave you that?" she said. "Don't take that. I give it to my horse."

Often prescribed by physicians to patients with severe rheumatoid arthritis, especially of the spine, phenylbutazone and related anti-inflammatory drugs have become popular among athletes wanting to reduce the pain and swelling brought about by stress injuries caused by heavy training.

She said she warned Jaspers several more times that night to avoid the drug, but the soreness behind his knee had hindered his training, and endangered his preparation for the NCAA cross country championships a month away. Phenylbutazone would help relieve the inflammation.

The most common side effect associated with the drug is stomach distress. The drug also can impair the body's ability to produce blood cells. ". . . those who may be subject to edema or congestive heart failure should not receive the drug," according to Victor A. Drill's Pharmacology in Medicine, a standard physician's reference book.

Jaspers, who was at Clemson on a track scholarship, was not a frequent user of phenylbutazone, his teammates and friends agreed. "Maybe two or three times a year," said Hans Koeleman, another Dutch runner and Jaspers' roommate during his last two years at Clemson. As for steroids? "Never," Koeleman said. "We'd try anything—special diets, vitamins, whatever—if we thought it would help. But steroids, that was a line we would not cross."

Nothing in Jaspers' medical history told of his heart problem, a condition that routine testing likely would not detect. By all outward appearances and previous examinations, he was a healthy, fit, Olympic-caliber athlete.

Finally, Hutson deferred to Jaspers' judgment.

"He knew more about running than I did," Hutson said last month in her first interview since Jaspers' death. "He was the one who knew best and I accepted it." She paused, then added her deepest regret, "I wish I had insisted."

★   ★   ★

Two days before Jaspers died, deBrouwer, a sophomore from Holland, said he had warned him about phenylbutazone. DeBrouwer had taken the drug while he had mononucleosis and it had made him sicker. "These are bad," deBrouwer said he told Jaspers. "Yes, I know," Jaspers said, "but I want to run fast."

The next day at practice, deBrouwer saw Jaspers for the last time. "He was training like a mad man," deBrouwer said. "When you take that stuff you're not supposed to train, but he was training like a mad man three days in a row. That day he had two hard workouts. He came in the (track) office and he looked so bad, really bad. His eyes were deep in his sockets like a zombie."

That night, he died.

Jaspers probably took two phenylbutazone capsules during the

48 hours before his death, said Pruitt, who did the autopsy. The level found in his blood was 8.0 milligrams per liter, well below the lethal dose of about 100 mgs. per liter. Pruitt concluded the dose was probably too small to have contributed to his death. That conclusion was supported in interviews with four physicians, all of whom are either experts in cardiology or pathology.

One of the experts consulted, Cyril Wecht, the Pittsburgh pathologist, offered a divergent opinion. His concern was that, although Jaspers did not have a lethal level of the phenylbutazone in his blood, the drug might have reduced Jaspers' inflammation and permitted him to train more strenuously than was advisable.

He said it could be argued that might have hastened Jaspers' heart failure.

"From a medical-legal standpoint, from what might have been on this particular day, he would not have died if he had not taken the bute," Wecht said. "Why? Because the bute did what it was supposed to do—cut down on the inflammation. The final reaction is that he ran at a pace his heart was not able to sustain."

In the end, however, no indictments were returned on any charges implicating Sam Colson and Stan Narewski, the two convicted Clemson coaches, in Jaspers' death.

★   ★   ★

Jos Hermans discovered Jaspers in Holland. He coached him, befriended him, then watched him go away to school in the United States.

"He was open to new things, new opinions, what was going on in the world," Hermans said. "His main reason for going to the United States was to find new borders, be surrounded with new opportunities."

Clemson, one new opportunity, was the perfect place to train because of the weather and the facilities. Jaspers, 6-1, 141 pounds, improved rapidly, running a 5,000-meter career best of 13:24.64, the fastest time by an American collegian last year. But he also often grew homesick for Holland. He didn't decide that he wanted to return to school for his junior year until September.

"I hoped he would go back for two weeks or a month and come back home to stay," Hermans said.

Instead he devoted himself to winning the NCAA cross country championships, partly as redemption for falling in the 5,000 in the Olympics.

"I still think he is alive," Hermans said. "It was like I still thought he was going to come back (to Holland) this year.

"The hurting," he said, "it doesn't stop."

★   ★   ★

On October 24, five days after the body was found, Hutson informed university police that Jaspers had taken butazolidin a few days before his death, according to Clemson University police files.

Six days later on October 30, Colson and Narewski were interviewed by university police. According to copies of the incident report, Colson "... stated that in the past he has given Clemson University athletes butazolidin. Coach Colson stated that he has a bad back and he gets the prescription from his doctor ... Coach Colson stated that he does not just give butazolidin out, only when an athlete has an injury and he feels butazolidin might help in the recovery."

Later that day Narewski told James Brummitt, then acting university public safety director, and N.W. (Mac) McCrary, a university investigator, that he was the one who gave Jaspers "five or six" of the butazolidin capsules that he had obtained from Colson. Narewski said "he had been at Clemson for approximately two years and from his experience while at Clemson he thought it to be a common practice to give athletes such drugs for injuries."

Nothing in the file indicates that the investigators questioned track team members about the dispensing of prescription drugs by the coaches until November 15 when Koeleman, Jaspers' roommate, gave a written statement. He provided little information.

On November 16, Brummitt and McCrary reported their findings to William Traxler, solicitor (district attorney) for the 13th Circuit of South Carolina who was responsible for prosecuting the case.

"As for why it took a month for the local police to come to the solicitor, I'm not sure," said Ben Stepp, who worked under Traxler. "Some people are trying to say it was a cover-up. But they (the university police) were really not sure what to do. They were concerned about blowing something up, ruining a lot of peoples' careers."

Until then, the only contact Traxler said he had received about the case were two telephone calls from McLellan, the athletic director, during which he was informed that the coaches had admitted to being the source of the phenylbutazone. McLellan did not return several phone messages left with his office. But Traxler said no hint of a larger problem was discussed.

"I know the gist of what they told me was they had two coaches that had given four or five phenylbutazone capsules to Jaspers," Traxler said. "I do not remember if they mentioned that (the possibility of a larger problem) to me or not. It was in their report. I can only tell you that my impression of what we had to do was limited solely to those four or five capsules."

Brummitt, who has returned to his previous job as chief of the university's investigative division, said the meeting with Traxler was routine.

"When we went to him we gave him a copy of everything we had, and we went over the report," he said. "Now we didn't sit down and pick out each word.

"Also you've got to look at what we didn't know, if he died from pills, died from heart attack. We didn't know if we had a manslaughter charge. It was nothing you could just go out and do in one or two days."

Traxler said he was proceeding under a timetable that would

permit him to present the case to a Pickens County grand jury on December 3.

★ ★ ★

Two events happened on Friday, November 30, that changed Traxler's timetable.

Paul Jaspers, Stijn's younger brother, had been sent from Holland by his family to find out further information about his brother's death, including his medical records. He went to visit Pruitt, who in his original autopsy report of November 7, wrote, "The finding of traces of phenylbutazone in the patient's blood is not believed to be a factor in his death." But Pruitt said he had begun to reconsider his finding.

"I didn't realize phenylbutazone was so dangerous," Pruitt said. "It's a dangerous drug. Until I got into this and really started looking at all the literature, I didn't realize there was such a controversy over phenylbutazone."

So as Paul Jaspers watched, Pruitt took a copy of the report and added with a pen the following phrase to his typewritten report, "but the possibility that the drug contributed to the subject's demise cannot be ruled out." He initialed the amended copy and handed it to Paul Jaspers.

"I talked with Mr. Traxler about amending the report," Pruitt said. "I hadn't done it yet, but I told him that we probably would be issuing an amended report. So when Jaspers' brother came in and asked the same question . . . I did change it because he's going back. The guy is going back to Holland and so I did change the report for him. I changed it because I was going to do it anyway."

Wecht, asked about the procedure, did not question Pruitt's judgment in making the revision, but he did consider his method unprofessional.

"That's terrible, really from a medical-legal standpoint," Wecht said. "There's nothing wrong with going back and writing an addendum. You date it and state what happened. But to write something in hand . . ."

Pruitt defended his work.

"If you make a mistake," he said, "you have to be willing to admit it and change your findings. That is what I did."

That same day, deBrouwer, along with Paul Jaspers, went to the police and told Brummitt he had received phenylbutazone from Colson. Colson has denied giving the drug to deBrouwer in statements made to South Carolina Law Enforcement Division (SLED) agents.

The campus police took deBrouwer to Traxler.

"When deBrouwer walked in," Traxler said, "you look at a worst case scenario. I said, 'I got one possibly dead because of phenylbutazone and I got another that got sicker because of phenylbutazone. What in the world is going on over there?' "

Traxler called off his grand jury presentation and decided to enlist the support of SLED to aid campus police in the individual interrogation of the men's and women's track and field teams.

Only then was university President Bill Atchley informed of the problem in a December 3 meeting with Melvin Barnette, vice president for business and finance, and Walter Cox, then vice president for student affairs and now acting president. Four days later, the interviews began.

Investigators found at least 20 track team members had gotten prescription drugs from the coaches. They found that anabolic steroids were distributed. Most of the steroids, Colson said in statements to SLED agents, were distributed to members of the football team's offensive line. Neither coach had a prescription for the drugs.

★   ★   ★

Stephanie Weikert, a 1982 All-America runner at Clemson, cherishes a snapshot of Jaspers. He wears sunglasses. His head is shaved, product of a lost bet.

Jaspers had bet Sam Colson, his coach, that he would break four minutes in the mile. He ran a 4:01. Out came the shears.

At first, his friends left him a clump of blond hair in the shape of a tiger paw, symbolic of the university's mascot. Then they shaved that, too.

"When I'm alone, and I sit down and look at this old photo album," Weikert said, "that's when it hits me, and I think of the old times and all the fun.

"He's just poised there with his bald head and John Lennon sunglasses."

★   ★   ★

The search for the Clemson coaches' source of the drugs led to an alleged pipeline of prescription drugs originating in Nashville. Participants are charged with illegally distributing almost 100,000 doses of performance-enhancing drugs between June 1982 and January 1985. About 5,000 of those doses are said to have been sent to Clemson.

Indicted and awaiting trial in Nashville, Tenn., are M. Woody Wilson, a pharmacist who formerly operated a pharmacy two blocks from the Vanderbilt campus; Thomas Patterson, a former employee of the store, and E.J. (Doc) Kreis, the former Vanderbilt strength coach who played football at Clemson from 1973-75 and who is a close friend of Colson. All three men have pleaded not guilty. Among the indicted co-conspirators are 31 past and present Vanderbilt football players.

Colson, 34, the former Clemson strength coach and women's cross country coach, is among those named as having received drugs. In the South Carolina case, he pleaded guilty on March 11 to eight counts involving the illegal possession and distribution of prescription drugs. He was fined $2,000 and given a three-year probation.

Narewski, 36, the head track and field coach, pleaded guilty to two counts. He was fined $750 and placed on a one-year probation.

Jack Harkness, 25, former assistant strength coach, has not returned from his native Canada to face charges on two counts. His case is not covered by treaty of extradition between the United States and Canada. Each count carries a maximum penalty of 18 months in jail and a $500 fine.

All three coaches have resigned.

"The case is closed," said J.P. (Pete) Strom, chief of the SLED, the state's investigative police force, and no further criminal investigation is planned.

★   ★   ★

Questions remain about the conduct of university and law enforcement officials during their investigation. Most of those concerns center on the four-week delay between the time Colson and Narewski confessed to university police last October 30 that they were the source of the phenylbutazone and Atchley being notified of that admission.

At least two administration officials, McLellan and Barnette, were made aware of the coaches' statements. Neither informed Atchley. It was only after deBrouwer told university police on November 30 that he had received phenylbutazone from Colson that Atchley was told on December 3.

"I was upset I didn't know about it and the reason why I didn't know it," Atchley said. He resigned effective last July 1 when he failed to receive a vote of confidence from the board of trustees. "No one told me that the source (of the phenylbutazone) was essentially our own people. If they would have, action would have taken place.

"They knew good and well, I'm pretty sure, from actions I was pushing in the past, I wasn't going to tolerate that. When you're dealing with drugs and people's lives and things like that, it was a very serious thing, and I wasn't going to tolerate that."

Barnette denies that the delay in informing Atchley was intentional.

"That is absolutely wrong and, if he believes that, he is wrong and he ought to know better," Barnette said. "There was absolutely no intent to withhold from him, and he didn't seem upset when we went to him and told him. It's after a lot of other things have happened that he is saying this."

The university board of trustees has refused to release a report prepared by a Greenville, S.C., private investigator hired by the board to examine the conduct of university officials in the matter.

"It is not in the best interest of the public to release the report," said Louis Batson, recently elected president of the Clemson board of trustees. "There are things that would not benefit the public to know. I don't think it would be harmful to the university, but there are some individuals that may be hurt by it. Several who testified were promised none of their testimony would be made public."

Both Batson and Strom said the report indicates no criminal wrong-doing by university officials in the investigation of Jaspers' death.

"We have a deep grief about our lost son," said Jaspers' father, Gerald, who has refused to be interviewed since his son's death. "There is a lot of mystery—a feeling I would say of things we don't understand."

★　　★　　★

Just past midnight on the night of October 17, the door to Jaspers' dorm room was open a crack. Hutson had done Jaspers' wash that night. She slipped in and left his basket of cleaned clothes by the entranceway. Jaspers, quiet but awake, was lying in the top bunk. He was exhausted from a hard day of cross-country training. He had put cotton in his ears to block out all noise.

The room was dark. Hutson never switched on the light. She never saw his face.

As she quietly closed the door, Hutson heard Jaspers' voice for the last time. "Ellyn," he said. She didn't want to disturb him. The door clicked closed.

Two days later, he was found dead. Among his possessions was a plane ticket home for December 16. That day he had planned to leave Clemson for good.

★　　★　　★

The road to Clemson is clearly marked by a path of giant orange tiger paws. The paws, symbolic of the university mascot, begin on the pavement of U.S. Highway 76 10 miles outside of town and lead into the bowl of Death Valley, the nickname for Memorial Stadium, the 78,915-seat football field.

Clemson, which was founded in July 1893, is an athletic power-house, funded in part by the IPTAY (I Pay Thirty A Year) organization. IPTAY, which was founded in 1934, raised $5 million in 1984, more than any athletic fund-raising organization in the nation. It was the sixth consecutive year IPTAY achieved that distinction.

"That town doesn't mind a winning team and the town doesn't care at what cost they do win," said Cornel Messam, a middle distance runner who graduated in 1984. "Anyone in town will tell you, they'll take another probation for a national championship."

Maybe no one has seen the divisiveness caused by the Jaspers investigation any clearer than Stepp, an assistant solicitor. He is a 1974 graduate of Clemson, where his father taught agricultural economics. His office wall is covered with Clemson memorabilia, including a poster-sized Sports Illustrated cover hailing Clemson's 1981 national college football championship. He saw the prosecution of Colson and Narewski split his old classmates.

"A lot of people got angry, 'You're picking on my Clemson,' " he said. "They (the coaches) violated the law, and we're entrusted to investigate under the law. But it was like you screwed Clemson out of a national title. It's crazy but that's how some people looked at it.

"My father taught there, I grew up there, I love it to death, but the right things need to be ferreted out. You just can't pretend something like this didn't happen."

Mays, Mantle Should Still Be Out

BASEBALL

By *STAN HOCHMAN*

From the Philadelphia Daily News
Copyright © 1985, Philadelphia Daily News

The casino pays Willie Mays $100,000 a year for 100 days of work. Mays plays golf with some gamblers, poses for pictures, signs some autographs, answers some questions about the toughest pitcher he ever faced and why he always ran out from under his hat.

The bars are full of guys who would like to play golf with Willie Mays, pose for a picture with him, ask him about the toughest pitcher he ever faced and why he always ran out from under his hat.

Maybe they saw him play when he caught the ball that Vic Wertz hit in the Polo Grounds. Maybe they grew up in New York when Mays played stickball with the kids in Harlem and was always chattering, "Say Hey," and it reminds them of their vanished youth.

Maybe they want a piece of a superstar even if it's just his signature on a bar napkin.

So how does the casino decide who plays golf with Willie Mays? That's easy. Their accountants tell them who bets with the black chips, who shows up on Saturday afternoon and doesn't budge from the tables until Sunday morning, except maybe to go to the john.

That's who gets to play golf with Willie Mays.

And suppose the guy who is used to betting with $1,000 chips also bets baseball. And suppose the guy is tired of losing.

And suppose the guy says to Willie Mays he has a 12-year-old son who adores Dwight Gooden and could Willie please as a very special favor introduce him to the young pitcher so he can get an autograph for his son.

And suppose the guy has lost $140 to Mays on the golf course that day, missing a four-foot putt on 18, and Mays figures what's the harm and he arranges a meeting with Gooden and the guy.

And suppose the guy does something easy like take Gooden out the night before he's supposed to pitch and gets him loaded and maybe even takes some pictures of Gooden that Hustler magazine would love to have.

Or suppose he does something hard, like introduce Gooden to some substance that makes the kid forget how tired he is or how tense he might be about facing the Cubbies the next day. Bowie Kuhn was a pompous, stuffed shirt of a commissioner, but he knew that things like that happen. He had seen Pete Rozelle go to the mat with Joe Namath on "associating" with undesirables, forcing Namath to sell his interest in a restaurant-bar.

The whole world knows it's legal to own a restaurant-bar. The whole world knows that it's legal to gamble in a casino in New Jersey.

But the Hilton hotel people spent $320 million to build a joint at the shore and now they might not get a casino license because the Gambling Commission doesn't like the people their attorney represented.

The New Jersey Gambling Commission running a cleaner operation than major league baseball? Say it ain't so, Peter Ueberroth.

Kuhn took the tough stand, barring two former heroes from baseball once they took jobs with gambling casinos. Sure, sure he knew that all Mays and Mickey Mantle did was play golf and shake hands and pose for pictures.

But he knew that they were doing all that with guys who bet big money at the tables, and guys who bet big money at the tables sometimes look for an edge when they bet baseball.

Mays has been away from the Mets for so long, maybe he doesn't even know Dwight Gooden. It has been so long since Mantle played catch with Yogi's kid, maybe he wouldn't know Dale Berra from Don Mattingly.

Owners do own race tracks, players do own race horses. Everybody and his brother plays the lottery. Betting on baseball is illegal in 49 states. Conspiring to fix a game is illegal in all 50.

Kuhn saw baseball's popularity survive its share of drunks and skunks in its ranks, but he wasn't sure the sport could handle a scandal involving fixed games. Or even the scent of a scandal. He didn't want to find out.

Kuhn liked Mays and Mantle, admired what they had accomplished as players, but he was concerned about the integrity of the game. So he did the unpopular thing and said they couldn't work in baseball if they shilled for a casino.

They could still play in old-timers' games, though. Mays showed up at the Crackerjack charade in Washington, just before game time, after weeks of haggling.

Those games are choreographed carefully, and when the promoters weren't sure Mays was coming, they didn't have him in the starting lineup. Willie pouted, turned, and left the ball yard. So much for good-will ambassadorship.

Ueberroth knows the game needs heroes and thrives on nostalgia, but he's opened a can of snakes here. He has made an exception to the rules for superstars Mays and Mantle.

What about Sparky Lyle, who also works for a casino? Suppose the Phillies wanted to hire Lyle to teach their relievers to throw the screwball. Was he heroic enough for Ueberroth?

And what about Denny McLain? Here's a 30-game winner, Cy Young winner. So, he's going to do time for extortion, loan-sharking and bookmaking. When he gets paroled, is there a place for a repentant sinner in baseball?

"How can you allow convicted drug users to play the game and then say Mickey and Willie are a bad influence on the game?" demanded George Steinbrenner, who has a couple of former drug abusers on his 40-man Yankee roster and wants Mantle to throw out the first ball.

Kuhn didn't say that Mays and Mantle were a bad influence on the game. He implied that high rollers are a bad influence on the game because they sometimes want a sure thing to bet on.

Steinbrenner's rhetoric is muddy as usual. Does he want baseball to ban drug users, not even giving them a second chance? Or is he saying that society is so loose, so damaged, that baseball has to soften its rules to match the world outside the ball yards?

Mantle's father and uncle died young. Mantle thought he was going to die young, too.

"If I had known I was going to live this long," he says, "I'd have taken better care of myself."

He'd have taken better care of himself and his finances. And if he'd done that, then maybe he wouldn't have to work for a carnival, shaking hands and signing autographs and playing golf with wealthy strangers.

Mays probably feels he got shortchanged at the pay window along the way. You can't blame him when arbitrators who don't know a fungo from fettucini now decide whether a guy should get $1,000,000 or $680,000 for a summer of playing ball.

The Mets kept him on the payroll as a "coach," but he didn't stick around for the games.

Now, he gets $100,000 for 100 days' work, and that includes visiting schools or hospitals. If a country club or a race track or an insurance company offered him $120,000 for 100 days' work, playing golf, shaking hands, he'd be gone from Atlantic City faster than you can say Leo Durocher.

How about a baseball team offering that kind of money? Mantle snickers at the thought, because he knows how baseball works. Mays talks vaguely about representing the game in foreign countries because he has never understood how it works.

The guys who get to play golf with Mantle and Mays will drop $400,000 at the casino tables before the year is up. That will pay for greens fees, flashbulbs and all the Jack Daniels they can drink.

It will pay for Mantle and Mays. And that is the name of that game. Baseball is better off not being a part of it.

The Gold That Tarnished

TRACK AND FIELD

By *DICK SCHAAP*

From Parade Magazine
Copyright © 1985, Parade Publications, Inc.

Carl Lewis was, by any reasonable measure, the biggest winner of the 1984 Olympic Games. He was also the biggest loser.

He achieved precisely what he set out to achieve. He won four gold medals—in the long jump, the 100-meter dash, the 200-meter dash and the 400-meter relay—matching Jesse Owens' 1936 accomplishment, which made Owens, for the rest of his life, an almost mythical figure. Yet Lewis emerged from the Games with his image clearly diminished.

Of all the neat tricks Lewis performed in Los Angeles, that reverse flip may have been the neatest, the closest to a true miracle. The only other major American athlete whose image suffered in Los Angeles was Mary Decker Slaney, and she fell far short of reaching her goals.

Lewis not only won his four events, he won every heat and every qualifying round of his four events. Consistently, in 13 appearances, he sprinted and soared to the brink of athletic perfection. The experts in his field recognized the magnitude of his brilliance: *Track & Field News,* the bible of the sport, named him the outstanding male athlete of 1984. The people of the largest nation in the world recognized his brilliance, too: 400,000 Chinese put Lewis atop a poll to select the world's finest athlete.

But in the United States, when Sports Illustrated chose its Sportsman and Sportswoman of the Year, the honors went to Edwin Moses and Mary Lou Retton, who won one Olympic gold medal each. The runners-up were the football player, Doug Flutie, and the tennis player, Martina Navratilova. Lewis did not even get a mention.

The New York Times, in its year-end review of sports, similarly snubbed Lewis. *The Times* cited 11 athletes on the front page of its sports section, and omitted Lewis. *The Times* ran photographs of 24 athletes and ignored Lewis.

If Lewis was, to a shocking degree, without honor in his own country, he was also without profit. Before the Games, his personal manager, Joe Douglas, compared Carl's commercial potential to Michael Jackson's and Lewis himself hinted that four gold medals might add up to millions in endorsements. But after the Games, the only product Lewis newly endorsed was a Japanese health drink. BIG BUCKS FADE AWAY FROM LEWIS read a headline in *The Sporting News.*

Carl found himself in a bizarre position: He had to make a comeback—*from* greatness.

His world had turned upside down. Before the Games, he had been placed on a pedestal, presented the James E. Sullivan Award, the most prestigious award for sportsmanship and skill an American amateur athlete could receive. He was besieged to pose for the covers of *Newsweek* and *Time* and *Gentlemen's Quarterly* and almost every other magazine short of the *Hog Digest.* He was hailed as a model young athlete, articulate, intelligent and exciting. But after the Games, he was pronounced aloof, arrogant and avaricious—a perfect target for sarcasm and satire. In a Halloween skit on TV's *Late Night With David Letterman*, a young trick-or-treater masqueraded in a tracksuit adorned with four gold medals. "And just who are you supposed to be?" Letterman asked.

"Give me 20 bucks and I'll tell you," said the youngster.

Rarely had an athlete so gifted and so successful been so maligned publicly. Privately, a whispering campaign that rose almost to a roar hinted that Lewis, with all his other flaws, was also a homosexual and, therefore, clearly unfit to appear on a box of Wheaties. One day not long ago, over an omelet and fresh strawberries, his own version of the breakfast of champions, Lewis confronted the whispers. He said the rumors themselves did not hurt him. "I'll tell you what hurts," he said. "That people are that malicious."

(Ironically, one source of the rumors was one of Lewis' more celebrated rivals, a man whose own sexual activities also came under public scrutiny.)

"Some people feel they have to beat their chests all the time to proclaim their masculinity," Lewis said. "That's not my style. The way my parents (both track coaches) brought me up, my best friend was Carol, my sister (one of the best female long-jumpers in the U.S.). And I was her best friend. Of course we influenced each other. She has some masculine traits, and I have some traits that people think are not too masculine. That's the way I am. If I feel happy, I'm going to laugh, and if my feelings are hurt, I'll cry. I don't hide my emotions."

Why should Carl Lewis, supreme athlete, have to defend his masculinity? Why should people snipe at him? What had tarnished his golden performance? Was it the fault of the media, which built him up, then, frustrated by his inaccessibility, tried to tear him down? Was it the fault of a public which demanded that its heroes all spring from a neat predictable mold? Was it the fault of other athletes who envied Lewis' ability and acclaim? Was it the fault of Lewis himself, consumed by his own importance? The answers are yes, yes, yes and yes, that everyone contributed to the decline and fall of Carl Lewis' image. But in the end, the fault lay basically with him, not that he was evil, but that he was different, that he refused to do things the conventional way, the acceptable way; that he refused to conform, to do what was expected not only of him, but of any hero.

Lewis is different from most athletes. Most don't collect delicate crystal. Most don't study acting with Warren Robertson, a Texan-turned-New Yorker who also tutored Jessica Lange. Most don't have the voice, or the nerve, to sing "The Star-Spangled Banner" at track meets or to cut a record called "Going for the Gold." Most don't have cousins who are barbers who create Grace Jones hairstyles for them. Most don't slip into gleaming skintight outfits that make Prince's costumes look sedate. Lewis does all these things, and he may even eat quiche. But that is hardly justification for the abuse he has taken.

On the track, in competition, Lewis made two blunders. First, he antagonized the press and the public—both thirsting for a record—when he took only one jump during the Olympic long-jump final, when he soared quite far enough to clinch first place but not far enough to endanger Bob Beamon's magical Olympic and world record of 29 feet, 2½ inches set in 1968. Then he elected to pass up his remaining jumps, to save himself from the chill and the physical strain.

Track and field experts knew that Lewis' decision, strategically, was a wise one, that risking injury and jeopardizing his third and fourth gold medals to seek a record that might be beyond his reach was foolish. But public relations experts knew that Lewis' decision was a disaster. He had talked too much about Beamon's record not to give it his best shot, or at least appear to give it his best shot. Instead, by resting while his rivals strained, he showed disdain for them and, worse, for the public, for the people who had paid $60 a ticket to see a great athlete perform greatly.

His refusal to push himself in the long jump, to risk himself, made his victory seem too easy. This was Lewis' second blunder. He made all his victories seem too easy. He not only didn't taste defeat, he didn't even get a whiff of it. His extraordinary excellence, paradoxically, made his extraordinary efforts seem commonplace.

Off the track, in confrontations with the media, Lewis blundered, too, with considerable help from Joe Douglas, his well-meaning but pugnacious personal manager. Lewis, for instance, always has been notoriously casual about keeping appointments, a habit unlikely to endear him to sportswriters and broadcasters on deadline. And Douglas always has been notoriously litigious, as quick to file a lawsuit as Lewis is quick out of the starting blocks. Douglas threatened to sue me and Random House for using a picture of Lewis in a mailing publicizing our book on the 1984 Olympics; in contrast, other athletes, and their agents, pleaded to have their pictures used.

Lewis and Douglas could so easily have manipulated the media to their advantage—flattery and kindness have corrupted more newsmen than bribes. Instead, their efforts to dictate to the press were so clumsy that the men and women of the media bristled. Then, when some reporters—in print and on the air—reacted as testily as spurned suitors, Lewis and Douglas succumbed to paranoia, certain they were victims of a vast media conspiracy.

During the Games, Lewis' refusal to live in the Olympic Village —to many competitors, the most meaningful and enduring of Olympic experiences—was an insult to his fellow athletes. His refusal to talk to reporters from the start of his first competition until the end of his 13th was an insult to the media.

It wasn't so much *what* Lewis and Douglas did—other athletes also skipped out of the Village and shied away from interviews with few consequences—as the *way* they did it. Both gave the impression that they felt Carl Lewis was bigger than the Olympic Games.

Can Lewis recover from such blunders? Can he revive an image as impressive as his credentials? Can he turn what is still a considerable income—approaching $1 million a year, thanks mostly to Nike and track and field promoters—into a gold mine? Can he become "popular"?

I think he can, but for a price.

Lewis will have to open up, not by appearing on talk shows and answering predictable questions, but by revealing himself, exposing his personality—even though he says he fears that people can't be themselves anymore. Carl Lewis, despite the mistakes he has made and the misjudgments both his friends and his critics have made, is good company: thoughtful, sensitive, considerate. He is able to handle both adulation and its absence, which is no mean trick.

One night, I watched him sit in an acting class, next to an attractive young woman who had not the slightest idea who he was, who knew only that he was young and handsome and trim and ebullient. She admired him only for those traits.

A few hours later, I watched him sit in an East Side Manhattan saloon and accept the attention of people who focused upon him purely because he was Carl Lewis, the Olympic champion, who had not the slightest idea what he was like behind the four gold medals.

He handled both situations with equal grace, more delighted, perhaps, by the young woman's attentiveness and lack of recognition, yet still at ease—not antagonistic—in the false spotlight of hero worship. His reactions seemed awfully mature for a man who is, after all, only 24.

Carl Lewis can regain admirers, I suspect, by displaying a sense of humor about himself, about his accomplishments, about his position. His wit is not inconsiderable; he should turn it upon himself. Self-deprecating humor has been a saving grace for other athletes, equally talented and confident, such as Muhammad Ali, Joe Namath and the British decathlon champion, Daley Thompson. Each has a sense of his own absurdity. Each can wink at his own greatness. Lewis hasn't winked often enough.

Lewis still faces a challenge that can truly test him—and elevate him: Bob Beamon's world record in the long jump.

"I've talked about it too much," Lewis says. "I've told the world I'm going to do it. I've told myself I'm going to do it. Now I've got to do it."

He will aim at the record during the Mobil Grand Prix series in Europe this summer. A noted computer specialist, Dr. Gideon Ariel, has determined, by blending tests and theories, that of all the world records in track and field, Beamon's is the one that comes closest to man's potential.

Dr. Ariel is not certain that the human body can withstand the exertion of jumping beyond 29 feet, 2½ inches. He has theorized that if Carl Lewis were to jump 30 feet, the target he has set for himself, bones might crack, tendons might tear.

"I hope he's wrong," Lewis says.

Perhaps, if he were to make an effort so supreme that he shattered his superb body in the process, the American public might embrace him once again.

Carl Lewis really isn't a bad guy. He shouldn't have to go that far.

Wildcats Pitch A Perfect Game

COLLEGE BASKETBALL

By *JOE HAMELIN*

Less likely things have probably happened, sometime, somewhere. The parting of the Red Sea is a very strong candidate. There was an earthquake in Indianapolis a couple of years ago. Marilyn Monroe married a writer once.

But an unlikely thing happened here Monday that will rank with the most unlikely of things that have ever happened anywhere, now and forever. Villanova beat Georgetown for college basketball's national championship.

The score was 66-64, and here is how it was managed: Villanova made 22 of its 28 shots, a percentage of 78.6, one never approached in the 46 previous national championships; and 22 of its 27 free throws.

It was as flawless a performance as any team ever gave in a game of such magnitude, and as unlikely a one. For Villanova, a team of bright and articulate individuals who think it is no crime to cry in public or embrace one another, there was extra drama in it. Alex Severance, its coach of 25 seasons through 1961, winner of 413 games, had died in his Lexington hotel earlier in the day. He was 80.

The Wildcats' unlikely victory, which followed unlikely tournament victories over Dayton, Michigan, Maryland, North Carolina and Memphis State, was this unlikely:

• Villanova had won 24, lost 10 on the season. Georgetown was 35-2.

• Georgetown had won 46 of 48 games, the last 17 in a row, one of those by six points, one by seven, one by nine, the rest by 10 or more.

• Georgetown had played Villanova twice this season, and each time had won.

• The Hoyas were the defending national champions. Oddsmakers had made them 9½-point favorites. Oddsmakers are known to be a cautious lot.

• They had Pat Ewing, the college game's best player.

• And their large and sometimes abrasive coach, John Thompson, had been named the coach of the year by his brethren only the night before.

But all of this amounted to nothing.

Ed Pinckney, the Wildcats' leading scorer, had said it would take "a perfect game" to beat the Hoyas.

Even Don Larsen never pitched one as perfect.

Said the Hoyas' Horace Broadnax, in a soft and respectful tone, "They kept coming and coming."

"A tremendous, tremendous feat," said Rollie Massimino, the bouncy little Villanova coach, after embracing anyone and everyone who would permit it. "In a one-shot deal you can beat anyone in the United States."

Dwayne McClain, the quick forward, led Villanova with 17 points. He was 5 for 7 from the field and 7 for 8 from the line.

He said he knew the game was secure when he saw Harold Jensen, the sophomore, kiss Villanova's wheelchair-confined trainer, Jake Nevin, on the top of the head.

Pinckney, the 6-9½ center, outplayed the 7-foot Ewing, the player Massimino had called the best college player ever. Pinckney outscored him 16-14, outrebounded him 6-5, had five assists to Ewing's two, and grappled with him in the lane so tenaciously that, when it mattered, it seemed almost impossible to get Ewing the ball.

Later, Pinckney complimented Ewing on his play.

Gary McLain, the little guard, made each of the three shots he took, and both of the free throws, and turned the ball over just twice against as devastating a full-court press as the best defensive team in the nation could manage. In the six games of the tournament, McLain made seven errors.

And there was Jensen, the hero of the unlikely win over North Carolina, who came off the bench this time to score 14 points, making each of the five shots he took, the last of which paralyzed Georgetown.

The last of them, a 19-foot jump shot from the right wing with 2:35 left, gave Villanova a 55-54 lead that it would not surrender. David Wingate, the Hoyas' leading scorer with 16 points, here attempted to penetrate and dish off to Ewing, but a crowd quickly gathered, the pass was ill-considered, the ball came loose, and Wingate fouled Pinckney in the scramble.

With 2:11 showing, Pinckney hit both ends of the one-and-one, then Wingate missed a jump shot, Jensen rebounded, and Michael Jackson fouled him, giving Villanova another one-and-one opportunity. Jensen holed two cleanly.

That quickly, it was 59-54 with 1:24 showing, and Villanova made 7 of 10 free throws from there to keep Georgetown at arm's length. Jackson was permitted an uncontested layup with four seconds left.

Thus, a season that began with Ewing and Thompson posing with President Reagan for the cover of Sports Illustrated ended with Massimino raving in ecstasy about "the greatest thing ever to happen to me."

Thompson walked off head bowed, but made no complaint.

"Villanova won that basketball game fairly," he said. "There's no complaints to be had."

As for Ewing, he walked away with his finger raised in the "We're No. 1" manner.

"We might not have won the ball game," he said, "but I still think we're No. 1."

The record books will say differently, though.

This was a crowd-pleaser. The capacity 23,124 in Rupp Arena was strong and loud for the underdog, and had plenty to bellow about, right from the first.

Georgetown came out pressing, forced some turnovers, took an 18-12 lead, and then lost it. Despite three Ewing jams on successive possessions, Villanova regrouped, hung close with 10 points from McClain, made 13 of its 18 shots, and took a 29-28 lead into the dressing room.

The Wildcats dribbled away most of two minutes for one last shot in the half, and Harold Pressley—who scored 11 and, like McClain and Pinckney, played the whole game without relief—took it and missed it, then retrieved it and holed it. That gave the Wildcats their first lead since 2-0. Four seconds were showing.

As time ran out, Villanova's ponderous reserve center Chuck Everson put a hip into Reggie Williams, who immediately popped him. Three officials, in chaotic circumstances such as these, managed not to notice.

But Villanova sensed it could play now. It sensed something curious and magical was happening. The second half, the lead changed eight times. But always Villanova came back, until the big crowd was up and howling, except for the modest Georgetown contingent that, only two hours earlier, had wondered with good reason if the Hoyas might be among the greatest teams of all time.

Georgetown shot 54.7 percent against Villanova's multiple zone defenses, missed only 2 of 8 free throws, matched Villanova in rebounds 17-17, turned the ball over six fewer times, all in all played as solid a game as anyone could ask, and yet lost, because Villanova just kept coming and coming.

As the game wore down, a curious look came into the faces of the Georgetown players, one of absolute disbelief in what was happening to them.

That had not happened since the night two months ago, in Syracuse, when a Pearl Washington jump shot right at the buzzer had handed Georgetown its second straight loss after 29 victories. Afterward, somebody was shoving a microphone into Thompson's face, asking how did he feel.

The Georgetown coach is big enough for a motorcycle cop to hide behind and an altogether fearsome critter when he cares to be, and this was not the time to be asking dumb questions of him. He gathered his 300-pound bulk and inquired of his interrogator, in a voice throaty enough to scare hell out of an alligator, "Would you count us out now?"

"No," the man said, backing up a little.

"You're a smart man," said Thompson, whose team would play 18 more games in the season and nearly win them all.

On the final night of the season, however, it ran into a team that would not be intimidated.

'My Destiny Was Not To Be a Good Player'

FOOTBALL

By *JOHN EISENBERG*

From the Baltimore Sun
Copyright © 1985, the Baltimore Sun

Joe Don Looney lives in a wooden house with a dome on top, on a 22-acre lot at the foot of the Davis Mountains in Southwest Texas. The house has solar heating, no electricity and, currently, no running water. It does, though, have an assortment of pictures of Swami Baba Muktananda, who changed Joe Don's life 10 years ago. Call him Baba.

The house is 80 miles from Mexico, five miles from a neighbor and one mile from the nearest paved road, State Highway 118, from which you cannot see the house. The best way to find Joe Don is to look for the windmill he built to pump water from the ground. Find the windmill, find the nearest dirt road, follow it over a small hill . . .

Hello, front door. Looney, 43, spends most of his time at the house. He reads, exercises, meditates, listens to the radio, studies stars and stares for hours across a basin at the stunning, narrow peak atop nearby Cathedral Mountain. "If it was in India, it would be a holy mountain," he said, and he should know. More on that in a minute.

What he does not do is work. "I am one of the laziest suckers you will ever meet," he said. "My goal in life was always to be a millionaire by the time I was 30. When I reached 29, I knew I was not going to make it. But I figured I would go ahead and retire, anyway."

He pays no bills, eats mostly fruits and vegetables and lives off a small savings account. The money was earned 20 years ago, when he played in the National Football League, and was invested wisely by his father, Don, who played for the Philadelphia Eagles in the '40s and has been in the oil business for decades. Joe Don hopes in two years his NFL pension will kick in: $100 a month. Hello, permanent retirement.

"That (the pension) would be enough for me," he said.

Joe Don played one full year of big-time college football, at Oklahoma, and five years of pro football. He played for the Colts in 1964, his rookie season. Some think he could have been one of the greatest halfbacks ever. He was 6 feet and 230 pounds, had sprinter's speed, could catch passes, break tackles, etc. Coaches were infatuated with him.

"He had as much potential as anyone who ever played," said Sam Huff, who played and roomed with Joe Don on the Washington Redskins in 1966. "He was 230 pounds, and there was not one ounce of fat on him. All you had to do was look at him and know there was a hell of a football player if he wanted it. But unfortunately, the rest was not there—dedication, desire.

"I don't know. To be honest, I don't think he had both shoes tied."

Joe Don never fulfilled the promise he showed. He made more headlines than touchdowns. He started fights, broke curfews and disagreed with coaches. He attended four colleges and played for five NFL teams between 1964 and 1969. He fought the law, and the law won.

After spending nine months in Vietnam in 1968, his interest in football quickly waned. He retired in 1969 and began to wander. He hitchhiked, traveled around the world, used drugs, investigated a handful of religious cults and was arrested for possession of an unregistered submachine gun. He lived at various times in Hong Kong, South America and East Texas.

In 1975, he met Baba, moved to India and found peace. Today, he weighs 180 pounds, looks trim and lives in splendid seclusion because it is what he wants.

"The fact is, I do not want to have too much on my mind," he said. "I kind of want to be duh-de-duh-duh."

He does not lose sleep over his failed football career.

"I had my chances, and did not do it," he said. "I have no regrets. It was not my destiny. My destiny was not to be a good football player, but to be a famous one."

★   ★   ★

By the time Joe Don walked into the reception room at the Houston airport on April 6, 1975, he was, he said, "at the end of the rope." He had searched the world for a cure to the anger and frustration he always had felt. But his search had been fruitless.

"I was looking for a mentor," he said. "Everybody should have a mentor. I had looked hard enough. It seemed like everyone had a sect. Everyone. But I had seen so many phonies, so many sects with all their politics and hierarchies. There were always people saying, 'Well, we're the exclusive ones. We really understand Jesus.' Or 'We really understand Buddha.'

"I always said to them, 'Well, the hell with you people.' "

That day in Houston, the room was filled with people who were giving gifts to Baba. Joe Don walked up with his hands empty. "All I have for you is the love from my heart," he said, and Baba nodded. Joe Don turned to walk away. Another failure, he thought.

But then Baba spoke. "The heart is the most valuable possession," he said.

The sentence poured over Joe Don and melted him. It sounded beautiful. He was sold. The next day, his father drove him to Baba's retreat; he was touring the country at the time. As the car pulled into the parking lot, Joe Don heard sitar music. He started to cry.

"Damn, what is wrong with you, boy?" his father shouted. "These people will make you crazy."

"Crazy!" Joe Don cried. "Dad, I have been crazy until now!"

Joe Don moved to Baba's ashram in India. There were doctors, lawyers and hippies from the West and East. This was hardly the rat race. Joe Don tended Baba's elephants, meditated and spent as much time as possible around Baba.

Baba, who died in 1982 at 74, was considered one of the holiest men in India. He preached self-realization; that is, true happiness comes only when you are stripped of your trappings (possessions, friends, careers, etc.) and understand who is beneath it all. The guru gives off the energy for the cosmic pursuit simply with his presence. Joe Don fell in line.

"I chased the American dream like everyone else," he said. "But when you chase and chase and finally get to where you want to be, and it is empty, you say, 'Well, damn, what now?' Then you are open for something. I sure as hell was.

"It was not that I had always been unhappy. But I had never really been happy. Something was always missing, and I was always angry and frustrated because I did not know what was wrong. But after I had been around Baba awhile, I realized I had been happy for a whole week. Then a month. Son of a gun, I thought. Then all of a sudden, years had gone by.

"The swamis take you to who you are and say, 'OK, that's you, now you have to realize it. I will help you.' These guys are the masters of life and are in the ocean of bliss all the time. Baba is my guru. I'm a disciple. He put this all together for me. I couldn't have."

The anger in Joe Don has disappeared. "The principal of God is a mirror," he said. "What you give to it is exactly what you get back. You get what you give. If all you give is a smile, that is what you get back. What a beautiful idea."

★   ★   ★

Even today, Joe Don is a legend in Fort Worth, Tex., where he was raised. He had the looks and personality of a Hollywood star, but he had a chip on his shoulder. He barely could get through a day without starting a fight.

"When I was young, I saw so many jerks, I decided then that I was going to kick the butt of every jerk in the world," he said. "Then I realized I did not have enough years. I tried, though, for a while. I sure did."

He went to Paschal High School and played football well enough to receive scholarship offers from Southwest Conference schools. But he did not want to play.

"I was investigating," he said. "I was waiting for someone to come up to me and say, 'Hey, this is it.' "

He went to the University of Texas as a student, not as a football player, and left his mark. The same stuff. One time he walked into a fast food restaurant and over to a table where two men were sitting. "Get up," he said to one, and when the man demurred, Looney picked him up and threw him through a window at the front of the building. And on and on.

This was the operative word: Rage.

"I had a lot of frustration and anger inside me," he said. "It was unfair. This world gives value to power, beauty and athletes. I got into a bunch of fights because I wanted to be someone, but you were not unless you had a lot of money or drove a fast car. It frustrated me. I knew I was somebody. So I said, 'Doggone, I'm going to have to be a football player.' "

From Texas, Looney went to Texas Christian, but he never played football there. Instead, he transferred to Cameron Junior College, in Oklahoma. There, playing for a coach named Leroy Montgomery, he found his greatest happiness as a football player. He played on every offensive down. "It was all downhill from there," Joe Don said.

In 1962, Joe Don transferred to the University of Oklahoma. Everything seemed idyllic. That fall, he rushed for 852 yards and 10 touchdowns. He was considered one of the best backs in the country. But it all fell apart the next year. He did not get on well with some teammates. Finally, one day he punched out a graduate assistant in practice. It was the last straw.

His teammates voted to kick him off the team.

"It (the incident) happened 10 days before we played the Texas game, but they waited until after the Texas game to kick me off," Joe Don said. "They knew they had a better chance to beat Texas if I played.

"It was OK. I knew my time was coming. I could see it."

Despite his history of trouble, the next spring the New York Giants selected Joe Don in the first round of the National Football League draft. He had too much potential, it seemed. When Wellington Mara, the team owner, was asked if he had considered Joe Don's attitude, he said, "No, but I have considered his broad shoulders, his legs and his 224 pounds."

Joe Don was a Giant for four weeks of training camp. He was reluctant to learn the plays. "A good back makes his own holes," he said to head coach Allie Sherman. When Sherman asked veteran quarterback Y.A. Tittle to reason with Joe Don about the necessity of curfews, Tittle did it, returned to Sherman and asked, "Now, exactly why is it at 11 o'clock, Allie?"

Before the season, Joe Don was traded to Baltimore for defensive back Andy Nelson and wide receiver R.C. Owens. He liked Baltimore. "Joe Don respected (coach Don) Shula," his father said. But the Colts only kept him for a season. He punted and played a little halfback, but again, made more news off the field.

One night at the Civic Center, he leaped into the ring during a professional wrestling match and challenged a wrestler to a fight. Another time, he told teammates that he was going to spend the night in a cemetery in Pikesville, talking to dead spirits.

He got in serious trouble again, too. He voted for Barry Goldwater for president, and when Lyndon Johnson won in a landslide, Joe Don got drunk, kicked down a neighbor's door and punched out a man. Ultimately, he was fined $150 and put on probation for a year.

(Joe Don would vote for Richard Nixon in 1968 and for George McGovern in 1972. "I vote for men of character," he said. "If you vote for promises . . . at least men of character will say, 'Hey this is wrong' and do something about it.")

Often, Joe Don felt confused.

"I would feel real alone," he said. "The feeling would come over me and I would go off by myself and say, 'What in the hell is going on here?' I have plenty of money. I'm a good-looking guy. I'm a pro football player and have plenty of women and there is nothing wrong with my head. But what in the hell is wrong?' "

One day in Memorial Stadium, during a game against the Green Bay Packers, Joe Don said he suddenly thought he was an alien. He looked down at his body. It was covered with pads. He felt his head. It was covered by a helmet with a face mask. He looked back up and onto the field. Grown men were slamming into each other with frightening power and speed. Around him, there were 60,000 people roaring continuously. Suddenly, none of it made any sense.

"It was as if another little man had entered my head and was looking through my face mask," he said. "I sensed it. I thought I was an alien who had been put on earth, and now I was waking up for the first time, after 25 years. I was completely blown away. I went down to the end of the bench and sat there. If I had to go in the game, I could not have."

Joe Don's aggressiveness and build caught the attention of Al Flora, a Baltimore boxing promoter and trainer. He tried to talk Joe Don into becoming a professional boxer.

"He could have been a hell of a fighter," Flora said. "He was so big and strong and tough."

Flora wanted to sign him to a contract and take him to Muhammad Ali's training camp in Pennsylvania; Ali was training for his rematch with Sonny Liston at the time.

"I was going to take him up there and put him into the ring and challenge Ali right there," Flora said.

Joe Don was ready to do it.

"That was the kind of kid he was," Flora said. "He would do

anything."

Flora took a liking to Looney.

"He was lonely," he said. "No one could figure him out, but I thought I did. All he wanted was somebody to love him. He was a nice kid. He did not have one serious bone in his body."

But Joe Don's hopes for a boxing career ended in 1965, when the Colts traded him to Detroit for linebacker Dennis Gaubatz. When reporters asked Joe Don for his reaction, he said, "I think the Colts made a hell of a deal."

In Detroit, he got into more trouble. During training camp, he and his ex-Oklahoma roommate, John Flynn, wound up in a heap with a policeman in a restaurant parking lot. When Flynn was cut, Joe Don refused to practice for a day. He played little that season because of recurring headaches. The next year, he was traded to the Redskins for a draft pick after refusing to take a play into a game.

"If you want a messenger boy, call Western Union," he said to head coach Harry Gilmer.

In Washington, he roomed with Huff.

"I kept him out of trouble the whole year," Huff said. "He was like Burt Reynolds. He had the same happy-go-lucky personality, the same good looks. Women would come to our door, literally, looking for him. I would not let them in.

"He was a likeable kid. But I guess along the line Burt Reynolds got some stability in him. I don't know about Joe Don. We used to walk a mile to practice, and Joe Don would change personalities from the beginning of the walk to the end."

Today, Looney has an explanation. "The trouble was not with them, but with me," he said. "I was really rigid in what I thought. I don't know. In the '60s I think a lot of people were pretty rigid, and then you get eaten up by the whole thing. I guess I was always looking for Baba, and I made it hard for everyone else, because there was no one like him."

In 1967, he got married, had a daughter and played little with the Redskins. Once, he refused to go into a game in Cleveland. "I'm not warmed up," he said to head coach Otto Graham. The Redskins waived him in October 1967.

He went into the Army.

"I didn't have anything else I wanted to do," he said, "and to tell the truth, I wanted to see what war was like. I didn't want to shoot or get shot at, but I wanted to see it."

He got to find out. In June 1968, his unit was called up. It would go to Vietnam in a month. Joe Don went AWOL for 25 days.

"We were going to 'Nam, anyway," he said. "I told them I was going home to see my family before we left. I had two weeks of leave coming, anyway."

In Vietnam, he was stationed near the Demilitarized Zone. His unit maintained a pipeline and some tanks. He was not on the front, but several friends were killed. He says the experience changed his life.

"He was different when he got back from Vietnam," his father said. "To me that was the big change. He says his values changed. He saw guys get blown away. When he got back, it was like a 360-degree change. It was a long time before he could sleep at night."

Joe Don said, "You could let all the madmen out of the insane asylums, and it would not be worse than that war. It was bizarre. Everyone knew it was a lost cause and a bad deal, but no one wanted to take the responsibility and say, 'Hey, let's get the hell out of here.' It was a bad deal. The people in charge know nothing. Vietnam took the frivolity out of my life."

He came back and played a final season in the NFL with the expansion New Orleans Saints. But nagging injuries kept him from playing much. He retired, got a divorce and started to wander.

"The last year in New Orleans, my heart was not in it," he said. "It did not seem very important. I let my hair grow, started turning on, doing what everyone else was doing."

He and a friend went to Hong Kong for a while. He weighed 210 pounds and walked around the streets in his underwear. "I figured they would tell me if I was doing anything wrong," he said.

Soon, he began to experiment with cults. There were plenty around. One man put a blue light in his body. Another time, a friend said, "Hey, try fasting." Joe Don said, "Why not?" and fasted for 40 days.

When he returned to the United States, he fell in with a tough crowd. In 1972, a man in his house was arrested in a plot to assassinate a district judge. That was when police found the machine gun and some marijuana. Joe Don was given probation, but an investigation cleared him of any connection with the plot. "My life got real serious for a while," he said.

After that, he laid low for three years and hitchhiked around Texas, investigating cults and religions. He was aimless. He lived for a while on a family farm in East Texas. Then, in 1975, he met Baba. He was in India for three years, then returned to the United States and lived at several of Baba's retreats, in the Catskill Mountains and in California.

After Baba died, Joe Don came back to Texas. He lived on a family farm for a while. Then a friend in the state government told him about a deal in which Vietnam veterans could get land from the state ridiculously cheap. He bought the 22-acre plot for $20,000 (only $1,000 downpayment) and has built his house for about $35,000. His saving account has been depleted, but he says that is fine with him. "I'm broke, but I don't care about money," he said.

"Money was never a concern of his," his father said.

Joe Don says he is set for life.

"He seems real settled now," said Wade Copeland, a friend and carpenter who has helped with the building of the house. Joe Don would agree. "What was good for me at 17 may not be so good at 43," he said, "and I have the right to change."

★   ★   ★

Image . . .

Outside, it is dusk. Inside, the house is dark. The room is filled with the sweet smell of incense. Joe Don is pacing the floor in bare feet. His hair is flecked with gray. He weighs 50 pounds less than he did when he played football. Fasting and fruit will do that.

He is trying to make a point about what has happened to him.

"There was this man who was running hard because his shadow was chasing him and he did not like it," he said. "The man ran and ran and ran so hard that finally he had a heart attack and fell down on the ground. Then he looked up and his shadow was not chasing him anymore. All he had had to do was stop."

Joe Don stops pacing. He turns and looks at his girlfriend, Susan, a Californian whom he met in India and with whom he still spends most of his time. He breaks into a broad, white smile. No laughing. Just a smile.

The mirror.

Read My Lips

by John Sheckler of The Standard-Times. A young football star in New Bedford, Mass., gets some eye-to-eye instruction before going into battle against another youth team. The youngster is Joseph Turcotte. His motivator is Michael O'Brien. Copyright © 1985, The Standard-Times photo by John Sheckler.

Heave Hay

by Dave Kraus of the Tulsa Tribune. Nobody said it was going to be easy and Jeff Kite, a competitor in the annual Scottish Games in Tulsa, Okla., would gladly attest to that fact. The object for competitors is to try and toss a 16-pound bag of hay over a horizontal bar at different heights. Kite made it to 15 feet before missing. Copyright © 1985, The Tulsa Tribune.

Veeck Death Symbolizes End of an Era

BASEBALL

By *RON RAPOPORT*

From the Chicago Sun-Times
Copyright © 1985, Chicago Sun-Times

The year Bill Veeck sold the White Sox for the second and last time, a big party was thrown in his honor at Comiskey Park. It made him feel, Veeck said, like Tom Sawyer and Huckleberry Finn attending their own funeral.

This was a typical Veeck remark: witty, learned, self-mocking and very much in the spirit of the occasion.

Yesterday, though, the memorial service was the real thing and I, for one, am not able to laugh. Another time, perhaps.

In the last five years of Veeck's life—five years he spent out of baseball—he was anything but a lonely or bored man. He had his family, his friends, his books and his cause. No Chicago peace march was official if Veeck was not in it. No handgun-control petition was complete if his name was not on it.

But if the loss of baseball did not destroy Veeck, the loss of Veeck signified the end of something very important in baseball. His selling of the White Sox in 1980 was the end of an era just as surely as his death was.

Veeck would come into town on a smile and a shoeshine. On one shoe. He would pool a couple of bucks with his partners' money, take the door off his office so the night janitor could suggest some trades while he was sweeping up, list his number in the phone book and open for business.

Today, of course, you need shopping-center money in your portfolio to do this. Or shipyard money. Or newspaper and television station money. Baseball teams are just another takeover target for corporate America. You can no more run a ball club without $100 million at your disposal than you can run for President—and never mind your qualifications for either job.

The truth is, Veeck was smarter about running and selling a ball club by accident than most others were on purpose. What, pray tell, is William Perry, if not Eddie Gaedel, writ large?

In the early '50s, when he owned the St. Louis Browns, Veeck read that a bat manufacturer in Arkansas had gone broke and he bought up its inventory of 6,000 bats, many of them unfinished. "Come to a game and get one to use for firewood," he told the fans of his bedraggled team. "That's what we're thinking of doing." Thus did the master promoter stumble across the concept of Bat Day.

"My first full year in St. Louis, I will maintain to the end of my life, was the best job of promoting I have ever done," said Veeck, who already had set an American League attendance record in Cleveland that wouldn't be broken for more than 30 years and later would win a pennant with the White Sox.

It was a long way from moments like these to the last time I saw him, which was last summer as he lay on an inflated beach mattress in a tiny pool outside his Hyde Park apartment.

"This is my barge on the Nile," he laughed as he moved from one end of the pool to the other with two strokes. Only the sound of the Cub broadcast from a television set inside could distract him from pouring a beer or showing off the 50 varieties of flowers he had planted or slyly pointing out that one of the walls was covered with ivy.

Veeck hadn't seen the White Sox play in several years because of his feud with the team's new ownership and he had stayed away from Wrigley Field for months in protest against the new Cubs' policy of selling bleacher tickets in advance. The team's suggestion that seats would always be available for *him* just made him all the madder.

But it was no disgrace that Veeck should have ended his days as a baseball gadfly, looking in from the outside. Hadn't he spent much of his time annoying the baseball establishment when he was part of it? Why should he change just because he could no longer afford its company?

And, besides, there were indications that Veeck was beginning to feel himself well rid of the sport to which he had given his life. One of the last things he wrote was an article last October for *The Sporting News* about the trial of a Pittsburgh drug dealer whose clients included baseball players.

"It was the week of the 'rat fink,' " he said of the players who had testified about "their former friend and companion," the accused drug dealer. It reminded him of nothing so much as Sen. Joseph Mc-Carthy and the House Committee on Un-American Activities, he said. Veeck was disturbed by the use of drugs, of course. But, the biggest crime was the loss of honor.

Well, now Veeck has season tickets to see the Angels play, as Steve Goodman would have put it. But if he was an anachronism by the time of his death, his real legacy will always be alive. It would give him pleasure, I think, to know that some of us believe his greatest contribution to baseball is the book he wrote about it.

Veeck—As in Wreck is simply the finest thing ever written about the sport. This is not simply because of its unfailing good humor, but also because it is the only revealing and intelligent look inside the front office any owner has ever shared with us.

But *Veeck—As a Wreck* was something else as well. More than all the tributes from friends and dignitaries, more than all the obituaries and eulogies, it was his epitaph. Nobody ever summed up Bill Veeck's life better than he did himself. Here are the book's last lines:

"Sometime, somewhere, there will be a club nobody really wants. And then Ole Will will come wandering along to laugh some more.

"Look for me under the arc-lights, boys. I'll be back."

King of the New York Athletic Club

BOXING

By *MICHAEL DISEND*

Oliver (Gentleman Jim) Sterling, to the manor born, is a hard-charging amateur boxer at age 48. In 1982 he won the light heavyweight championship of the New York Athletic Club. He is founder and half-owner of Sterling Drilling and Production, a big company that develops natural gas and oil wells. He's handsome, wealthy and living with a young model as he struggles through a mid-life divorce. Ed (Elegant Ed) Post, a suave Italian off the Brooklyn streets, is, at age 38, a seasoned fighter. He's rich, single and a lady-killer. He is a major shareholder in Wall Street Petroleum, a much smaller oil company. The men are rivals both in the ring and in business. When the two tycoons fought in 1983, the club billed it as the "Oil Wars." In a nasty slugging match Elegant Ed defeated Gentleman Jim, although his nose was broken in the fray. The result pleased neither man. Gentleman Jim thought he won the bout but lost the decision. Elegant Ed was irked that his ring supremacy was even questioned. So as the early November date for the 1984 NYAC Night of Champions approaches, both men are preparing for a rematch.

"You don't get out of shape because you're old," says Sterling as he runs down Lexington Avenue to the gym in business suit and dress shoes. "You get old because you're out of shape." With his wavy gray hair and Irish pug nose—a face of choirboy innocence—he looks like a grown-up Campbell Kid. Sterling never walks if he can run. His body is a perpetual exercise machine. In boxing, a less skilled fighter may whip a more able foe if he's in superior condition. But the real bout here is happening in Sterling's soul.

"I'm trying to overcome Father Time," says Sterling, removing his tie as he climbs the two flights to the crowded Gramercy Gym.

"The only way to beat Ed Post is to be in twice as good condition as he is. You can let the younger guy make mistakes. Like looking at my gray hair and trying to knock me out in the first round. He'll get tired that way. Then I come back in the next few rounds with some heavy combinations and take the fight. Age has its advantages. If you look at the leader of a pack, it's usually three quarters of his life that he maintains the leadership position, able to fight off the younger competitors. He keeps all the women."

The Gramercy Gym is a grimy, no-frills throwback to the banner days of boxing. "Frankenstein scum pimps," argot for the managers and promoters who bring dishonor to the game, are banned from the premises. Fighters are protected, not exploited. Sterling, who sometimes studies Spinoza on his lunch hour, appreciates what is offered here.

In the locker room, Gentleman Jim strips and carefully hangs up his double-breasted suit. A thick mat of grayish-white hair covers his chest, but his body is muscular and well-proportioned. Even now, six weeks before the fight, he looks to be in much better shape than most of the serious young black and Latin boxers around him. After changing to worn, red NYAC sweatpants and T-shirt with the winged-foot emblem, he steps into the gym before a wall of yellowing fight posters and begins stretching exercises to loosen up his back (he slipped a disk several years ago). Because it takes an older person longer to sweat, Sterling warms up 45 minutes before putting on the gloves. As the jump rope snaps under his feet, his expression is childlike and guileless.

"Jim won every round last year," snorts Bobby Jackson, his trainer, burly man with black horn-rimmed glasses. A corrections officer at Sing Sing during the day, he wears a .38 caliber revolver under his beige smock. "I don't figure there will be any of that hometown shit. After all, both men are members of the same *club,* ain't they? Look at Jim. He's a very spunky guy with obvious drawbacks, neither of which is his heart and desire. Bad back, bad shoulder. He accepts it as part of the game. That's why he's a successful businessman. He makes something positive happen out of something negative."

After Sterling pounds the heavy and speed bags, Jackson sends him into the ring against Ronnie (Almost Heaven) Mitchell, a flashy black junior lightweight with a middleweight's punch. Gentleman Jim stalks his opponent in a dogged, almost plodding, way. His hands move up and down in a milling motion, a here's-your-licks-come-and-get 'em style. He looks like a dancing bear in a Russian circus, a dangerous 5-foot-11, 170-pound bear with an overhand right that wallops like an anchor swung on the end of a chain. Pursuing his speedier foe, he takes four punches for every one thrown, just waiting to unload that overhand bomb. When he does, "Almost Heaven" winces with pain. But Sterling is breathing hard.

"Stop with the prehistoric bullshit!" shouts Jackson from the ring apron. "Don't walk at him! Side! Side! Side! You fight quick like little suckers for speed! Don't be a millionaire! Don't be in the office! Don't be an old man in the ring!"

When the third round ends, the trainer unlaces Sterling's gloves and helmet. His face glistens with perspiration.

"I ran out of gas at the end of the last round," says Sterling. "No energy. Maybe it's my age."

"Don't worry about Eddie Post," says Jackson brusquely. "He'll be looking for an excuse to lose. He lost last time."

★   ★   ★

The office walls of Wall Street Petroleum look like a museum dedicated to the fabulous life and times of Elegant Ed Post, who just happens to be the tour guide and curator. "Call me the most eligible bachelor in Brooklyn," says Post with uncharacteristic modesty. "Don't get me wrong! I come to New York also." A lively man with immaculately coiffed black hair edging into gray, Post is constantly making acquisitions for the gallery of his days. There are framed photographs of a laughing Post (formerly Esposti) with his arm draped around world-famous fighters, a grinning Post with politicians and union leaders, a dignified Post in his current position as community mayor of Wall Street, a brave Post boxing an exhibition with five-time world champion Emile Griffith in Madision Square Garden to raise money for charity, a reflective Post with some of the 18 medals he won in Vietnam while serving as a helicopter-door gunner.

Most abundant are highlights from his 22 years of amateur boxing. There's a framed clipping from the *New York Daily News,* where he's nicknamed "Elegant Ed" for his sharp attire and style in *and* out of the ring during the 1969 Golden Gloves. Other articles cite him as a top contender and finalist in four Golden Glove competitions and a two-time competitor in the U.S. Olympic Trials. Every success and achievement is meticulously recorded. Ed Post is an overachiever. He is also a happy man.

"I run four companies!" he exclaims with delight, as if this fact has just occurred to him. "Wall Street Petroleum. Elegant Ed Productions. Elegant Ed Special Projects. And now ... Spartan Sporting Goods! I sold boxing equipment for them in college and now I *own* them! I also promote and judge fights. Other people have dreams. I make them happen. You know what the problem is? *I'm doing too many things!*"

Now Post is driving rapidly up Eighth Avenue toward Ringside, a new boxing gym near Times Square. Beside him is a bag filled with boxing equipment. "My old pal Vito Antuofermo is training there for his comeback fight next week. I'm gonna ask him to wear Spartan trunks and robe. It's incredible! Mr. Everlast watch out! I'm gonna make this a $25 million company in five years!" Post parks and sprints up the stairs to the gym. As soon as he passes through the doors, his demeanor changes, like an animal testing for any nuance of danger. All eyes turn toward the flamboyant man in the white suit, purple shirt and expensive jewelry. The boxers show subtle but unmistakable signs of deference to Ed Post, who looks like a power in the fight game.

"Champ, how much are you getting for this bout?" asks Post.

Antuofermo, the former middleweight champion of the world, seems embarrassed and doesn't reply. A teenager is taping his hands. No trainer or manager is present. Antuofermo is training himself.

"It's my first fight in almost three years," he says at last. "People don't remember I was a champion."

"You *was* a champ? You *are* a champ! The people love you!" Post leaps off his seat in the locker room and tells Antuofermo how to best manage his career. He gestures animatedly. The gestures are stiff, almost priestly, yet charismatic. He smooths his lapels, adjusts his tie knot, pulls down the back of his jacket. His gestures are the essence of a unique Brooklyn style, a classy lexicon of upwardly mobile Italian moves. That's why they call him Elegant Ed.

"It's beautiful to be a matador in the ring when a guy comes in at you like a bull," Post says later. "You twist him, turn him, give him a few jabs, and before you know it he's in the ropes! You control him. Then you do it again. You're the matador! I love the art and style of the sport. Who's the Da Vinci? Who's the Michelangelo?"

But it's next to impossible to actually see any of this, since Post is a rarity in the gym. "I was always one for light training," he admits while noting that he must shed 20 pounds for the bout. "Why knock yourself out? I'm a terrible gym fighter. What I do best is prepare mentally. I do my best thinking in the ring.

"My coach used to say you can't have women and be a great fighter. Bad for the legs. I disagree. I love calisthenics and pushups in the morning. But if a woman stays over, she asks: 'How come you're wasting your energy on the floor and not on me?' You can't win!" He laughs uproariously.

★   ★   ★

Enormous power and influence are exercised behind the walls of the New York Athletic Club, at the foot of Central Park. The dues are high. The waiting list is long. The club shuns all publicity for its boxing program. Trophies for swimming, wrestling and other sports line the walls. There are few honors visible for boxing. When NYAC ring men war in intramural matches against Hempstead and West Point boxing clubs, the fights are held only at the club. The media is never invited. Interviews with boxing instructors are discouraged. Club fighters in the Golden Gloves must identify themselves with other sponsors. Dr. Paul Scott, the gutsy 58-year-old dentist who regenerated the sport at the club, is forever being called on the carpet if there is even the suspicion that these policies are being violated.

It's hard to comprehend what stodgy purpose is intended by treating pugilism like vice. Perhaps the sight of executives, engineers and bankers testing their guts in such an uncorporate, often brutal manner disturbs club elders. Perhaps they realize that boxing, whose most ardent supporters are the very rich and the very poor, can never be a truly middle-class sport.

The fourth-floor boxing room is the most tasteful venue of its kind in New York. Above the door sits a white sculptured statue of a fisted arm. There are scores of old photographs honoring ring warriors from around the world. The wooden floors are gleaming and spotless. There are floor-to-ceiling mirrors for shadow boxing, spanking new equipment and an excellent ring.

Although the room's heyday was during the years immediately following World War II, outstanding boxers still train here. There's 217-pound Tom Gimbel, built like a walking redwood tree, the NYAC Super Heavyweight champion who made it all the way to the finals of the Empire State Games. Gimbel is vice-president at a powerful investment banking firm. Dave (the Hawk) Foxen is an executive at the New York Federal Reserve Bank and the club's 1983 junior middleweight champ. And, of course, there's Oliver J. Sterling, a restless multimillionaire with something to prove.

"More torque, Jim!" shouts one of the boxing coaches. "Accelerate! Don't unlock your back. Your swing is correct now. More shoulder!"

Sterling heads for home at the end of his daily two-hour workout. He is a lonely figure as he jogs through Central Park in the dark. He shoots an almost involuntary glance toward the sumptuous 17-room suite on Fifth Avenue where his wife and two children live. Sterling is separated. These days he lives on the other side of the park. Tomorrow he'll visit the kids as he does several times a week, despite an intense schedule. Although their relationship is cordial, negotiating the separation agreement with his wife of 16 years is clearly depressing him. She is the former Miss Israel of 1958, a stunning levantine beauty. Sterling speaks of her with respect. Of Israel also. For he is a committed Christian Zionist. He founded the American Business Council on the Mideast, a group that explains the Jewish state's case to business people. Odd stance for an energy tycoon. But Gentleman Jim is not your ordinary oil company executive.

Since 1977, when he founded Sterling Drilling with less than $100,000 in capital, the firm has experienced an astounding 58 percent compounded growth rate in drilling funds raised per annum. This has occurred despite a recession in the oil business. The company's oil and gas wells are primarily in West Virginia. The firm is involved in joint ventures with various giant utilities and other companies, including Brooklyn Union Gas, Kepco (a subsidiary of Equitable Resources), Texas Oil & Gas and Bow Valley Industries, a huge Canadian outfit. Boxing also has a big business dimension. Since 1981, Smith Barney, Harris Upham & Co. Incorporated have acted as dealer manager for each of SDPC's public programs, a relationship Sterling began with a loan officer who boxed at the club. In 1983, limited partners invested close to $30 million in Sterling Drilling Fund programs, making it the ninth largest syndicator of public oil and drilling partnerships in the U.S.

The lionhearted but shy man behind this phenomenon comes from an old New York family. Sterling's father was a well-to-do lawyer involved in real estate, oil and gas. For a while he went to the exclusive Buckley School, whose alumni include Jay Rockefeller and Franklin Roosevelt. But his first experience in hand-to-hand combat came when he was shipped off to the Fay School, a private boarding academy in Massachusetts.

"Kids as young as 6 years old were crying themselves to sleep at night," he recounts bitterly. "They were there because their parents didn't want them at home. It was a tough school with a negative atmosphere. Sort of a street scene for rich kids. If you did something wrong the masters would strike you in the face with a closed fist. One time I got knocked over three rows of seats. I was in a fight a week."

A more civilized period at the St. Marks School followed, then a fruitful career at the University of Houston, where he played football and was elected president of the intrafraternity council. He entered the Army as a private and left as a first lieutenant just before the Vietnam conflict broke out. The discipline of his boxing and the making of his fortune came after age 40.

Gym scuttlebutt has it that Sterling acquired his pugilistic avidity in the oil fields when a wildcatter accused Sterling of stealing his well site and attacked him with an ax handle. He took his lumps and bruises. A confirmed story unfolds about the time he went into the ring in Charleston just to move around with an opponent who was a Golden Gloves champion. What he didn't know was that the other boxer had made a bet that he could knock Sterling out in the first round. The champion worked him over real bad. There was blood everywhere. Jim had his nose broken, but wouldn't quit. Finally the owner of the gym stepped into the ring and stopped it. It's on Sterling's agenda to go back and find the guy. That's the kind of man he is.

"Most businessmen are intrigued that I'm a boxer," says Sterling as he jogs into a luxury apartment building near Lincoln Center. "They wonder what makes me tick. Most people are impressed. Some think it's not a very smart thing to do. Like my partners—they check me out after each bout to make sure I've got it all together. They read those articles about brain injury and then don't want me to continue. Amateur boxing is different. Brain injuries, if they occur, happen among professional fighters who are over the hill, men who can't evade punches to the head. Boxing spices up your life. It's like business: The time you put in, that's what you get out. If you stay with it everyday, you'll get a lot out of boxing without getting hurt."

Sterling jogs even from the elevator to the apartment door. Lisa opens it. She's a willowy woman with round huckleberry eyes and curly hazel hair. Her modeling portfolio is open on a coffee table.

Beside it is a volume of Chekhov plays. After they kiss, Sterling goes to the refrigerator. "Where's my cranberry juice?" he asks irritably. Lisa excuses herself, rushes away and returns with two chilled bottles. Sterling drinks them both, as he does after most workouts, and proceeds to shower and change into a fresh suit. It's time for dinner and the theater. A chauffeured limousine is waiting outside. "I think Jim's a *real* gentleman," says Lisa as the limo glides down Broadway. "I call him my 'Prince Charming.' It's totally normal for him to box everyday. Why should I complain? He's got a body like—like . . . err . . . like *uhhhh!* That's why he never hears about it from me."

"Ed has the experience and the boxing skills," says Sterling, changing the topic with a smile. "It would have been a different story last year if he were in condition. I held back then because he wasn't. Not this time."

"I want you to knock Ed Post out, to stomp him," says Lisa with the sweetest smile.

"I kind of like him," says Sterling, smiling back. "He's so full of bullshit."

★   ★   ★

Around the planet called Ed Post whirls a constellation of mentors. Some are dead, others are living.

Foremost among the dead is Post's father, Bruno Esposti, a painting foreman who worked for the government for 30 years and who died long before his son became successful. Post reverses his memory. Among the living is Major General James Hamlet, the black former deputy inspector general of the Army for seven years. Post served under him in Vietnam. The general now sits on the board of all his companies. He shocks everyone by introducing Post as his son. But his premier guide is an old former welterweight fighter from Brooklyn, Sam Markowitz, "who met them all, barring none." Post loves the still-vigorous Markowitz and consults him on a weekly basis. Markowitz is 85 years old.

Sam began boxing in the Navy during World War I. He was the junior welterweight champion of the Atlantic Fleet in 1917 and 1918. He then boxed professionally until 1926, facing the likes of Young Otto, Happy Mahoney, Hummer Hummel, Paddy Ryan, Sammy Aronson, Johnny (Dummy) Willets and Patsy Brocco. He is the embodiment of ring wisdom. "Boxing isn't bums," says Markowitz. "A man is in there fighting, fighting hard for a living. Eddie Post, he was making with the gloves a couple of times around here. I took a shine to him and put my hand on him in blessing. He's a man of character and a fella you can call a friend."

★   ★   ★

All 18 chandeliers are ablaze in Micali Terrace, a garish catering hall deep in the heart of Bay Ridge, Brooklyn. The ceiling is blue, the walls are red, the tablecloths are red. The banquet room is packed with scores of tough-looking old men and their wives. Many of the men have cauliflower ears and noses that fists have redesigned. A band is playing. It's the annual dinner-dance of Ring 21 of the Veteran Boxer's Association of Brooklyn Inc. Ed Post, the youngest and only member who wasn't a pro boxer, is there in full glory. He bounces from table to table among the grizzled ring warriors who are merrily recounting tales of pluck and skill within the roped square. This afternoon Ed's dark suit is adorned with an I LOVE BOXING button, and there is a tiny gold boxing glove in his plum-colored tie. His date, Barbara, a full-bosomed lady from Staten Island, sits alone at her table.

"As much as Ed loves women," explains Barbara patiently, "he loves boxing more. Look at the respect these men show one another. Very earthy people. What you see is what you see."

"I hear Jim's training hard," says Post as he joins the table. "He really wants to win."

"If he's tougher, you got to out-box him. If he's a better boxer, you got to out-fight him," advises a retired scrapper.

Suddenly a hand reaches out and twists Ed Post's ear sharply.

"Ouch!" cries Post. "Let go, Sam! Let go!"

Sam Markowitz, tiny but strong despite his 85 years, ignores this and leads Post around the room by his ear, making his protege bend so he's nearly doubled over.

"Stop, Sam! I beg you! Please!"

"Train!" roars Markowitz, twisting the ear. *"Train!"*

"OK, I promise! Sam! Ow! I'll train!"

Markowitz gives the ear a last twist and shoots a surprisingly fast jab at Post, who slips it. Then the little man dances lightly away, tossing combinations at the air.

"It's so embarrassing when he does that," says Post as he rubs his reddened ear. "He's the only guy alive who scares me."

But a week later, at another banquet for the National Boxing Association, Post looks the same, only worried. "I've been too busy for the gym," he says with forced gaiety. "I'm doing a half-million-dollar deal for Wall Street Petroleum that's driving me crazy. Not a big deal for Jim Sterling maybe, with 35 guys doing his programs. But big for me. Then there's the Elegant Ed Special Project stuff. *I'm doing too many things!* Hey, Vito, tell these guys how good I box."

"He had one of the best jabs and left hooks I've ever seen," says Antuofermo (who won his comeback fight handily). "Perfect like a picture symbol. Only he didn't train as he should. He used to take a girl to the gym everyday. He never took it seriously. It was just natural. I don't care how good you *were*, Ed. It depends if you're in shape."

"You better buy some Grecian Formula 16," scoffs another guest.

But Ed Post is momentarily distracted. He's spotted a tuxedoed, supremely fit Sterling and a chic Lisa across the room among a crowd of fight celebrities.

"I've got to make Jim wear my robe and trunks at the fight," he says.

★   ★   ★

Several days later, the two oilmen meet on Wall Street so Sterling can decide what color equipment Post will make for him. "I feel *fantastic,*" announces Post. "Feel my gut! Hard as a rock? Haven't felt this good in years!"

Sterling, by now in a condition extraordinary for a man close to 50, just smiles knowingly and accompanies the Brooklynite to the Wall Street Petroleum offices where he's at once given a tour of the personal museum.

"See this gentleman?" says Post, pointing to a photo of a hulking black boxer. "He's the No. 1 top sparring partner of Larry Holmes. He's got three wins and no losses as a pro, and *I* put him down."

"No kidding," snickers Sterling. "I guess I'll have to lie down and take a dive." Then he adds politely, "Very nice collection of mementos, Ed. It shows the richness of your background—how you cut across class lines, meeting famous people, champions of the world. Most inspiring."

At a busy lunch counter around the corner they get down to brass tacks.

"We're two businessmen and sportsmen who enjoy the game," says Post as he munches a turkey club sandwich. "We're champions in our own right, the way we do business."

"We intend to put on a good show and a fine fight," affirms Sterling as he gnaws on a bagel with lox. "But at the same time, you don't have to throw darts at the other guy's picture."

"Right! And when the fight's over, I'm sure we're going to embrace and say, 'Well done!' " says Post.

"Provided you're still standing, Ed. It'll be kind of hard to embrace you when you're lying down."

Both laugh loudly and a tad too long, causing other lunchers to look up from their yogurt delights and tuna melts. Sterling complains that his constant business trips prevent him from getting into the shape he wants. Post beefs about running four companies at the same time. They gingerly touch on last year's bout and find themselves with radically different versions. Tempers flare.

"This year it's a battle!" says Sterling. "For the championship of the club!"

"Correct!" snaps Post. "It's being taken quite seriously!"

But being men who keep their priorities in order, the talk turns to well sites, tax credits, available acreage and arcane provisions of the 1978 Natural Gas Policy Act. An opportunity is presented. A deal is cut.

"I'll buy you lunch on the day after the fight," says Sterling on the way out. "That way you can't order steak on me. It's very hard to eat steak with a broken jaw."

★   ★   ★

Sterling is losing time from his business, Lisa and the kids in his obsessive daily training for the fight. To make up for it, he takes the children to a concert of Ukrainian music at Alice Tully Hall. Sneaks in during intermission, that is, and dances with them in back of the hall until an usher stops the fun. Then they're off for a laugh-filled Chinese dinner. But on the weekend before the fight, he's training almost all day, running with "Almost Heaven" Mitchell around the Central Park reservoir, slamming the heavy bag and skipping rope until he's nimble as a deer. He brings his young daughter Vanessa to the club on Sunday so she can watch him spar. The girl's a fight buff.

"Almost Heaven" drives the older man beyond the limits of his endurance by throwing lightning flurries and forcing Sterling to chase him. Sterling keeps insisting on yet one more round of sparring even though he's visibly exhausted.

"Vanessa," says Sterling, as he leans against the ropes to catch his breath. "You know why this man is running around the ring? *Because he's scared of me!*"

"You're holding your left too low, Daddy," replies the 11-year-old as she towels off his face.

Three days before the fight, Ed Post is finally seen in a gym. He trains in Brooklyn at the Bath Beach Body Building and Boxing Club. It's located in an old Italian neighborhood that only makes the evening news when a delinquent debtor or loudmouth is caught napping in the trunk of a car. Over the BBBBBC front door is a painting of an enraged giant ape wielding a 1000-pound barbell above a skyline of Manhattan. Inside, a man named Fingers concocts special health-food drinks behind the counter.

"General Hamlet is in the hospital!" says Post as he comes rushing through the door. "My $500,000 deal still hasn't come through! My trainer's brother just died! I can't believe this is all happening now! *Too many things!*"

After changing into spiffy fight gear, the role of flab around his waist is unmistakable. His arms seem to have no muscle definition. He can hardly sustain a rhythm on the speed bag. On the reflex bag he appears absurd. His sit-ups are accompanied by tortured moans. He looks so pitiful that other boxers stop to help him. Soon he's surrounded by fighters showing him such elementals as foot placement and the proper way to throw a punch. His sparring is ineffectual. He seems to have forgotten everything. "Who the hell is this guy?" asks a smirking weightlifter. "He's totally out of shape and he can't box for shit."

After the workout is over, Post is dejected. He drives to a hangout called the Del Rio Diner and orders a tunafish platter but doesn't eat. He even neglects to flirt with the waitress.

"The thing I don't get," he says at last, "is that I've spent my whole life trying to cage the animal and become a refined person. Sterling is trying to change from being a refined person into an animal. Why? I went to a tech high school so tough that when Murray the K came there, he said, 'In this school you either walk like a man or you don't walk at all.' I fought everyday. What can Jim Sterling know about that?" He picks listlessly at the tunafish. "The animal has to come out of the cage. I've been wearing these suits and ties too long. Tomorrow I'm going back to that school and I'm gonna walk around. I still got 72 hours."

Sterling comes to a nearly empty Gramercy Gym two nights before the fight. He does 10 rounds of shadowboxing and some bag work. His punches are thunderous. His speed is at an optimum level. But he still wants to do more.

"I wish I was in better condition," he says. "Part of it may be age."

"You're in the best shape Jim Sterling can be in," says Bobby Jackson. "At this point, either you're in shape or you're not. Either your head's together or it's not. Either you've boxed or you haven't. Either you're ready or you're not."

Sterling asks if he can spar just one more time.

"No!" says Jackson. "That's anxiety. You want to wear a belt *and* suspenders."

"I feel great," says Sterling hesitantly.

"So you feel great!" explodes Jackson. "Is that a sin? Stop messing with your head. Post will either drop on the mat or quit on the stool. Then you'll be known as the big bully of the New York Athletic Club. No more Mister Nice Guy. Don't you dislike this guy at least a little bit?"

Sterling lifts his finger a trifle.

"Mess up his nose with jabs! Keep the pressure on the belly! Drop him!"

★   ★   ★

On a cold November evening, the NYAC sixth-floor gymnasium fills quickly with more than 500 people. There are many beautiful women. Fighting males always draw beautiful women. A light crowd of cigar smoke hovers in the air as millionaires, chairmen of the board, politicians and brokers sip whiskey and savor the irresistible anticipation that precedes public combat. There are five bouts on the card for this Night of Champions. The light heavyweight fight between Elegant Ed and Gentleman Jim is scheduled last and is billed as the "Return Battle Royale."

Just before the first bout, Sterling climbs through the ropes of the specially erected raised ring and begins to shadowbox. His face is rhapsodic but the eyes are hard, intent. Ed Post is nowhere to be seen. Finally, a few minutes later, he comes running into the gymnasium carrying a paper bag. In it are Sterling's new robe and trunks. Post has been stuck in traffic.

"I didn't think you were going to make it," said Sterling, back in the locker room. "You missed the club photographer."

★   ★   ★

An oil tycoon, almost 50 years old but in superb condition, climbs through the ropes wearing a shimmering blue satin robe with Gentleman Jim on the back. He dances lightly round the ring, listening to the roar of the crowd. Younger club members resembling fraternity boys on a tear hoist their cups and bray at every opportunity. Older men ponder Sterling quietly. Many know that he has trained nearly two hours a day for the last eight weeks in preparation for this bout. Bob Jackson, a gruff bear also in blue satin, stands in his pupil's corner.

Another oil tycoon enters the ring wearing a red, white and blue satin robe with Elegant Ed on the back. Post also dances around, shadowboxing lightly. He looks surprisingly fit, loose and ready. His godson, Michael Ringle, is in his corner. The men were wearing safety helmets and 12-ounce thumbless gloves. They have had a taste of immortality and the hunger remains. The referee touches gloves. The bell rings.

Round 1: Sterling the aggressor chases Post. Both fighters shoot left jabs. Post misses with a right. Post fires left jabs, one after another, into Sterling's face. Sterling attacks with a hard overhand right, knocking Post backward. Post throws a weak right hand and misses. They circle each other warily. Then it's Post with a hard left into Sterling's face. Once again. And again the jab. Sterling charges. Post steps to one side. Post shoots another left into Sterling's face. A sudden heavy combination by Sterling. Post falls back. Then Post resumes the jab/hook attack. He's found Sterling's range.

"You're going knockout crazy!" booms Bob Jackson in Sterling's corner. "Go under! Make him pay! The body! The body! When he drops his hands, *then* go for his head."

"Remember Brooklyn!" Michael Ringle snarls as he dips Post's mouthpiece into the water bucket. "You got to win it for Brooklyn!"

Round 2: Sterling charges across the ring but Post sidesteps and sticks him with the left jab. Sterling pursues but Post circles him, all the time throwing the left, measuring him with the flicking jab. Sterling is frustrated. He can't break through. He lands with a looping left and then desperately wallows into Post, his body lurching from side to side. He's off balance. Post fires hard with both hands. Hooks. Jabs. Combinations. Sterling is shaken. He steps back. Post steps in and lifts his right for the knockout punch. He looks at Sterling. He doesn't punch.

Round 3: Sterling opens with his most potent charge of the night. Post is driven into a corner. Slips away unhurt. Post throws a hard right. Sterling charges again. Post shoots a brutal left and then a right cross into his face. A bell ends the fight.

As the referee announces Post's unanimous victory, hoisting his right hand in the air, Sterling stands quietly alone. For a few moments he looks utterly abashed. Then he sees his children in the audience and blinks his eyes. He composes himself. Boxers don't fear physical pain, but they dread losing. Such are the perils of dream, the exigence of Father Time. A fighter accepts this also. Gentleman Jim crosses the ring and embraces Elegant Ed.

★   ★   ★

A boisterous fight crowd descends to the club Tap Room. Red-checked tablecloths, hanging lanterns, rude waiters, lots of polished wood. The noise level is high. When the video replays go on, Post and Sterling watch their bout together. They are cordial and solicitous to each other. Members of the same club. Two rich men who earn their living by drilling into the earth.

"What did I do wrong?" asks Sterling to the guests at his table. "I want to fight him again."

"I think they're trying to discourage Jim here because of his age," Bobby Jackson says. "It was close—I'm not saying he won, but it was close—if he had the body attack."

Four beautiful women are dining with Elegant Ed. The champion is euphoric. The women listen raptly to his every word. Between bites he gestures with his knife and fork. The women gaze at his hands. As members and their guests start to leave, Post leaps from his meal and puts his arm around Sterling. He pats Jim's back. He squeezes his biceps. He adjusts his tie.

"Say, Jim," says Ed, "I'd like to buy you lunch next week. Anything you want. As you may have noticed, I had steak. I finished my meal. Chewed very well."

Valvano Should Think This One Over

COLLEGE BASKETBALL

By *MIKE LITTWIN*

From the Los Angeles Times
Copyright © 1985, Los Angeles Times

Jim Valvano was born to the fast lane. Rocco and Angelina's little boy Jimmy hit the ground running, and he never found a good enough reason to slow down, much less stop.

He coached North Carolina State—the little team that could—to an NCAA basketball championship two years ago, wisecracking every step of the way, and it looked as if he had finally gotten where he wanted to be. Not Coach V. He never broke stride.

Sure, he was a famous basketball coach. But why stop there? There were more jokes to tell, more money to make, an empire to build.

So, Coach V became a cottage industry unto himself.

He published Jim Valvano's Italian Cookbook. He does weekly and daily radio shows. In the middle of this basketball season, he somehow found time to be TV analyst for a game between Indiana and Illinois, far from Raleigh, N.C. It isn't unusual for him to stray from home, however. He's a big name on the lecture circuit, dispensing jokes and motivational techniques to corporate executives.

Too much, you say. Well, it's his life and his fast lane and his need to stay in the race.

And whether or not he knows the meaning of the word burnout, Coach V is no dummy. He knows he needs more than a sparkling personality to keep pace. He needs to win basketball games, too.

To win, of course, you need players. To acquire these players, coaches often compromise their principles. At least those coaches who have principles.

Which brings us to Chris Washburn.

Chris Washburn is a young man from Hickory, N.C., who grew

up to be a 6-foot-11 wonder, a basketball player to make a coach's eyes go round and his stomach to growl. But Washburn was a troubled young man, in and out of mischief. He attended three high schools, playing great basketball and usually making terrible grades. His last high school was one that has traditionally catered to athletes who needed to improve their grades enough to get into college.

Washburn scored a total of 470 on his Scholastic Aptitude Test, just 70 points above the minimum. That put him in the lower 3 percent of all prospective college students who took the test.

Some schools stayed away, figuring Washburn was not a candidate for scholastic honors. North Carolina, Duke and Wake Forest— all traditional basketball schools in the state of North Carolina— stayed away.

Coach V wanted him, however. He needed him.

According to a story in Sports Illustrated, N.C. State sent Washburn scores of letters over a period of years, sometimes daily. Coach V and his staff were relentless in their pursuit, which was anything but trivial. Love, they say, is blind. So is lust. Coach V wanted Chris Washburn. Finally, he got him.

It didn't matter that the average freshman at N.C. State scored 1,030 on his SAT. It didn't matter that Washburn was not in the running for any good-citizen awards. He could play basketball.

You know what happened. They loaded Washburn's schedule with easy courses—history of American sport, composition and rhetoric, sociology of the family, public speaking—and kept him out of academic trouble. But they couldn't keep him out of other kinds of trouble. He was allegedly caught shoplifting on the team's preseason trip to Greece. On September 20, he was convicted of assaulting a woman on the N.C. State campus, and got a 30-day suspended sentence and a $25 fine.

Finally, on December 22, he was charged with second-degree burglary for taking $800 worth of stereo equipment from a student's room. He was kicked off the team and later pleaded guilty to three misdemeanor offenses. He was sentenced to three days in jail, ordered to perform 320 hours of community service and was put on a five-year probation.

So, who's to blame?

There is Valvano, whose cynical recruitment of Washburn is nothing to joke about.

There is the N.C. State chancellor. Nobody with a 470 on his SAT gets into a college without the chancellor's knowledge and acquiescence.

There is the system, which encourages this form of behavior from coaches and chancellors. It encourages schools to cheat by making it easy. It sets standards for admittance so low as to be without meaning.

Valvano is a great one for paying lip service to the ideals of college sport. He tells you how important his players are to him, how important the university is to him, how important integrity is to him.

But, in this case, all we can see is how important Jim Valvano is to Jim Valvano.

Of course, a lot of coaches would gladly have taken Chris Washburn. Bob Knight wouldn't have. Dean Smith pursued him early, but then stopped. There are others—voices in the wilderness.

During the last recruiting season, Walt Hazzard badly wanted a local high school star for UCLA. But UCLA administrators, in the aftermath of the Billy Don Jackson case, have raised their academic standards for athletes, who must also be students. At a time when qualified students are being turned away at UCLA, the administration turned Hazzard down. Let other schools, other coaches, bend their principles.

Washburn wants to come back and play, and Valvano says he is considering what action to take. What is clear is that Washburn can't simply be put back on the team. Take away his scholarship, make him take legitimate classes, see if he stays out of trouble, see if he belongs at N.C. State. Give him the rest of this season and all of next to work on being a respectable student.

If he passes that test, then maybe he can return to the basketball team. If Valvano really cares about Washburn, that's the least he'll do.

There is something more important than winning basketball games, after all. There are standards. Coach V needs to slow down long enough to learn that.

Tom's Still Terrific!

BASEBALL

By *PAUL ATTNER*

From The Sporting News
Copyright © 1985, The Sporting News

If nothing else, Tom Seaver prides himself on controlling his emotions. The Thinking Man's Pitcher never loses his cool on the mound, nor forgets the task at hand.

But even Seaver couldn't quite cope with the electric atmosphere surrounding his quest for the 300th victory of his career. After attempting for days to portray things as just another shift at work, he walked into Yankee Stadium on August 4 and became as nervous as a raw rookie.

"My emotions were like I was pitching the first day in the big leagues," Seaver said. "You get sick to your stomach, you feel lousy, you have headaches. I'm just glad I don't feel that way before every start."

But this, of course, wasn't just any start. It was Hollywood of long ago, where the vanquished hero returns to the scene of his conquests and wins the day. "Storybook," he had called it.

OK, so Seaver was in a Chicago White Sox uniform pitching in Yankee Stadium instead of wearing the Mets' colors in Shea Stadium. But the emotion and significance of the moment was lost on no one in attendance, including Richard Nixon, who sat in a sky suite and cheered along with the crowd.

Seaver, twice discarded by the Mets, the team he led to the 1969 world championship, all but filled the Yankees' park on what was also Phil Rizzuto Day. Cheers of "Let's Go, Mets" broke out occasionally and Seaver's every appearance on the field before the game was greeted with ovations. Tom Terrific had come home to carve another niche in his storied career.

"If not Chicago, then I couldn't think of a better place to do it than New York," Seaver had said earlier in the week. In the days before the game, he said he would try to maintain a normal routine.

On Friday, he stayed at home in Greenwich, Conn., mowed the lawn and did other household chores. On Saturday, there was a quiet family dinner. The plan on Sunday was to eat breakfast, get in his car "and go to my job, like I always do."

But he couldn't sleep Saturday night and he had gotten up twice in the wee hours. When he arrived at Yankee Stadium, where so much baseball history has been written, when it sunk in that he was back in New York, where he always will be remembered as The Franchise, the man who made the Mets, when it sunk in that his goal for so many years finally was at hand, he couldn't wait to get going, to get it over with.

It was almost a foregone conclusion that Seaver would win the game. What other pitcher of his era performed better in pressure situations? Before, he would do it with smoldering fastballs; now he used craftsmanship and a sackful of pitches. But the result is the same.

He is 40, in his 19th season. The White Sox picked him up last year to be their fifth starter. Yet, this season, he leads the Sox in innings pitched, in ERA, in games started and in victories. He is not like Early Wynn, who held on past his prime before reaching No. 300 in 1963. "A doctor told me 10 years ago I could pitch till I was 45," Seaver said. "I've got no reason to think he isn't right."

But on this day, he had more urgent thoughts. With a strike looming two days ahead, Seaver wanted to win No. 300 right away. As he had zeroed in on his quest, he'd been holding mass press conferences in each city he visited. But it was becoming a circus, and he wanted the sideshow to end.

In victory No. 299, against Boston on July 30, he had been sloppy, giving away a 4-0 lead before the White Sox rallied in the 10th inning to gift wrap a 7-5 victory. He had been lucky, and he knew it. But the next day, when he got in his light running and throwing despite a downpour in Boston, one could tell that luck wasn't going to be a factor in his next start. The determination that characterizes Seaver's career was taking over.

So much has gone into that career, which he never really expected. Seaver enrolled at the University of Southern California to become a dentist, not a pitcher. Instead, he has drilled steady holes in the record books.

He is only the 17th pitcher to win 300 games. He ranks eighth in career shutouts (61) and he's fifth in strikeouts (3,499) and fourth in ERA (2.80) despite playing on teams with a composite record around .500. The seasons have flashed by quickly, but the grind has been kind to him. He remains boyishly handsome, the perpetual cherub. He's a bit thicker in the middle, sure, but energetic enough to still look forward to pepper games at the ball park with his White Sox buddies.

Everything that made Tom so Terrific in the beginning hasn't been eroded. He never really was a wide-eyed innocent, anyway, even if he loves to get to the park early to chew tobacco and work the New York Times crossword puzzle. After all, it was Seaver who notified the commissioner's office in 1966 that there seemed to be a big mistake happening in his life. He couldn't sign with Atlanta and take his $50,000 bonus because he still technically was a college player whose season already had begun. Yet the NCAA had turned around and declared him ineligible. So the commissioner, William Eckert, took the names of teams interested in signing him (Mets, Phillies, Indians), put them in a hat and held a drawing.

Since then, there have been many glorious moments. The world championship season of 1969, when Seaver transformed a woebegotten franchise into a winner with a 25-7 record that brought him the first of his three Cy Young Awards. He and wife Nancy are the All-American couple, with their own TV show and their own endorsements and a poodle named Slider.

He threw a no-hitter for Cincinnati against the Cardinals in 1978. In 1969, he had a perfect game until the Cubs' Jimmy Qualls singled with one out in the ninth. There was a 19-strikeout masterpiece against the Padres in 1970, ending with 10 strikeouts in a row. In his first All-Star Game appearance, as a rookie in 1967, he ended the game in the 15th inning with a strikeout.

There were low points as well—most notably the battle with a sore rotator cuff in 1982, when he was 5-13 for the Reds and thought his career might be over. That was followed by his emotional return to the Mets in 1983, when he was the opening game pitcher in Shea Stadium.

Then, there are memories of the two unfathomable departures from the Mets. How could a franchise be so nearsighted, so out of step twice? Did the Red Sox discard Ted Williams? Did the Yankees cut loose Mickey Mantle?

If Seaver was looking for revenge, he has gotten it many fold. After the first departure in 1977, his innocence gone amid battles with club Board Chairman M. Donald Grant and New York columnist Dick Young, Seaver watched from Cincinnati as the Mets unraveled. Attendance tumbled, performances deteriorated and finally the team was sold. He was brought back in 1983 by the new owner, Nelson Doubleday, ready to finish off his career in a Mets uniform. But another blunder, when he was left off the Mets' protected player list in 1984 and snatched up by the White Sox, brought more shame to his old team.

So now, Seaver likely will pitch one more year and finish his career in Chicago. He remains a proud, sensitive, introspective man, yet a piece of him stays buried in the past. It may not be a coincidence that after 1977, Seaver never again won 20 games, even if he continued to pitch, for the most part, terrifically.

"I'm not going back with the idea of getting any revenge," he said a few days before going after No. 300. "I have some very, very good memories of New York and its fans. When I left New York (the last time) it was an honest mistake. There was no animosity leading up to the point where I was unprotected. Nelson Doubleday called me and apologized and told me he hoped I got to 300 real soon. It's not anything where I'm trying to show anybody up."

But Seaver realizes that in the hearts of baseball fans, he always will be a member of the Mets. He recalled a recent trip to London with his family, when he went to dinner at a branch of a New York restaurant. He was told it would be a 90-minute wait. Then he pointed to a poster on the wall, showing Tom Seaver in a Mets uniform. "I was seated in a minute," he said.

"Will I always think of myself as a Met?" said Seaver. "I'm not sure. Funny, when I first came up, I thought I'd never last this long to be identified with any team. But I still can pitch well, that's very important. I don't feel old. I still get satisfaction out of pitching and winning, and that keeps me going.

"Mechanically, I'm still strong. I haven't lost my mechanics. And all the work with weights I've done over the years has paid off. I remember in 1967, when I showed up at my first training camp carrying a 10-pound weight, I was almost laughed out of the clubhouse. Now you go into any clubhouse and you see a whole expanse of exercise equipment."

Seaver's winning style attracted fans, who saw him as an embodiment of the newly emerging modern-day athlete. He was perfect for the Big Apple: articulate, photogenic, good-humored and clean-cut enough to keep out of the gossip columns, yet independent enough to become a union leader. But his baseball intelligence has made him just as appealing to purists.

Long before the zip left his fastball, he was thinking about location and change of speeds. Discuss pitching with him and you'll get involved in the theory of relativity and the four parts of the proper throwing motion and the use of the major muscles of the lower body —things that Dizzy Dean never discussed over a barroom beer.

That intelligence has allowed Seaver to age so gracefully. He'd love for you to believe that his fastball now resembles a powder puff. But any pitch that still arrives at home plate occasionally at 90 mph isn't a hitter's delight. Still, he no longer is the sinker-slider-heater pitcher of his youth. A change-up that took him 10 years to develop and a curve that only recently became effective are now prominent parts of his repertoire. Mix in the ability to vary speeds and spot everything he throws, combine it with 19 years of knowledge and the result is a perplexing puzzle for any batter.

"He's a master of changing speeds, running the ball, cutting the ball, jumping the ball," said White Sox catcher Carlton Fisk. "He has a sense of what to do and when to do it. It's almost like he is reading the batter's mind. There aren't many pitchers who have that feel, that sense. Really, when the game gets the toughest, that's when he's at his best. He uses everything. Every pitch is different. He has a fastball, but he may throw it at five different speeds, so it's really five different pitches."

There is no artificial trickery, even if Seaver has made concessions to age. He may lift weights and throw during the winter, something he never did at 25, but he doesn't toss up any knuckleballs or spitters. Batters know what pitches to expect, but locating them is another matter.

Just ask the Yankees' Dave Winfield. In the eighth inning of victory No. 300, Winfield represented what would be the last major roadblock for Seaver. By then, the White Sox had overcome some atrocious early-inning baserunning to take a 4-1 lead as Seaver kept the Yankees subdued with his change of speeds and control.

The go-ahead run was driven in during a four-run sixth by shortstop Ozzie Guillen, a rookie from Venezuela who had bounded up to Seaver during spring training and told him he would end his 300th win with an unassisted double play—and then keep the ball for himself. By game day, Guillen had changed his mind, telling Seaver he'd get the game-winning hit instead.

But now Seaver faced Winfield, the man who passes these days for Mr. Yankee. Seaver had retired 10 straight before Bobby Meacham got New York's fourth hit of the game to start the eighth. Ken Griffey forced Meacham and Don Mattingly singled, bringing up Winfield. Seaver, who would throw 146 pitches, started off with a slow curve for a strike. Then four fastballs, all nibbling at the corner, ran the count to 3-and-2.

In his youth, Seaver would have reached back for a 95-mph fastball. But a 40-year-old pitcher knows better. "You know he is going to be aggressive," he said of Winfield. "You try to take advantage of that aggressiveness and feed off it if you can."

That's what Seaver calls the gray area of pitching, the difference between pitching and throwing. "I never considered myself a thrower," he said.

He threw Winfield a tantalizing change-up, knee high. "I used (catcher) Carlton Fisk's feet as my target," said Seaver. Winfield swung and missed to end the inning. Seaver trudged wearily off the mound.

Between innings, Seaver's younger daughter, Anne, leaned over from her seat next to the White Sox dugout and spotted her dad. "Three more outs," he told her. "Good," she replied. "Then we can go home and go swimming."

As Seaver walked out to start the ninth, the crowd rose and applauded. Each pitch carried with it the kind of tension and emotion normally reserved for pennant races. Dan Pasqua led off with a single, then Ron Hassey became Seaver's seventh strikeout victim and Harold Baines made a leaping grab in right field to retire Willie Randolph.

Seaver, in a rush to end things, walked weak-hitting Mike Pagliarulo on four pitches. Fisk and pitching coach Dave Duncan, acting as the White Sox manager because Tony LaRussa had been ejected in the sixth inning, hurried to the mound.

They had made a similar visit in the eighth. Both trips were characterized by Seaver as "a kick-the-pitcher-in-the-rear" pep talk. Looking at Fisk, he realized, "I didn't have a prayer in hell of coming out." Seaver was exhausted, but only pinch-hitter Don Baylor stood between him and No. 300.

"If you aren't going to get yourself up for one out in that situation, you're never going to get yourself up," he said. Baylor hit the first pitch, a fastball to left for the final out.

Seaver bent over at the waist and smiled. Then he spotted Fisk, ran toward the veteran catcher and leaped into his arms. He embraced his tearful wife, daughters Sarah and Anne, then his father and father-in-law. In the clubhouse, his teammates doused him with champagne. "You are wasting $50," he said with a laugh.

The Yankees presented him a silver bowl to honor the day, even as Owner George Steinbrenner paced the New York locker room, livid that his team was finishing on the wrong side of history this day.

Eighteen years ago, Seaver beat the Cubs, 6-1, for his first major league victory. Now he had No. 300. For those who believe in omens, the final score of 4-1 matched his uniform number, 41.

"The only thing is, how did George know (I'd win 300)?" said Seaver with that high cackling laugh of his. He looked at the bowl. "He didn't put the date on. I'll have to do it myself."

Then he added, "I really couldn't tell what (stuff) I had to work with. One of the few times I felt like this was in 1969 when I almost pitched the perfect game against the Cubs. It was as if I was levitating on the mound. I felt I controlled my emotions, but I really couldn't feel the ball coming off my hand like I normally could."

Seaver should have a free ride into the Hall of Fame. But he says that 300 victories is now what he wants to be remembered for. Consistency is his choice, the fact he has 111 more career victories than defeats (300-189), the fact that "every time they put the ball in my locker, I went to the mound."

He will wait until the off-season to reflect more on the accomplishment. "Perhaps in November, when I'm out to dinner with my wife, I'll be able to savor and appreciate it," he said. "Then I'll pour my heart out to her."

But for one sentimental day in New York, baseball fans poured their hearts out to Tom Seaver. It was a trip down memory lane that neither will ever forget.

Steps of True Grit

GENERAL

By *BUCK JOHNSON*

From the Chattanooga Times
Copyright © 1985, the Chattanooga Times

The anxious husband watched as the plane's door swung open and the steps were wheeled into place and locked in its opening. The wheelchair was at his side. It had been several days since he had wheeled his wife to the plane that had taken her to a clinic in Pennsylvania, but he had already resigned himself to the fact that the trip would do little to check the ravages of multiple sclerosis. His wife would never walk again.

"Do I have to use that chair?" a woman asked the stewardess.

"Are you sure you can walk?" answered the woman in the uniform of the airline.

"With the help of God and that man," she said, pointing toward her husband, "I think I can."

The pilot and co-pilot came to watch and be near the trembling woman as she began descending the portable stairway to the ground.

She took a step and muttered, "Thank you, Lord."

Another step. "Thank you, Lord." With each step, she looked to the heavens above Lovell Field and said, "Thank you, Lord."

By the time Ernestine Noel got to the bottom step, tears were streaming down Roy Noel's face and he said, "Don't tell me there ain't a God somewhere, because you are a walking example."

Despite her battle with multiple sclerosis and 26 trips to the hospital, Ernestine Stephens Noel has been walking ever since that tearful reunion with her husband 13 years ago.

But, there's more to the lady who showed true grit that day. Neither the stewardess, the two pilots nor anyone else who watched that scene would ever have guessed that those trembling legs once carried Ernestine Stephens to a national basketball championship and to the brink of Olympic stardom.

The scene changes to a different time in a different setting, to the days of the Great Depression in the little hamlet of Monroeville in

South Alabama where Charles and Harriet Stephens raised 10 children. It was not the best of times for anyone, especially a black family with 10 children.

Charles Stephens, age 94 now and still going strong, was the patriarch of a special clan with high priorities that helped it overcome the devilish disadvantages of the era in which it lived. He was a machinist, had his own shop and provided for the needs of his family. When Sunday came, it was a day of rest and worship. The horse and wagon was brought out and, with Harriet at his side up front and the 10 children in the back of the wagon, the Stephens family headed for church.

"I worked only a half day when I was growing up," Mrs. Noel said last week as she reminisced about those days of growing up in South Alabama. "I remember walking down the street and meeting a lady and asking her if she needed someone to clean her house. She told me to come on and I did, but Daddy heard about it, got out the horse and wagon and came and got me. He told the lady I wouldn't be back."

There in the Noel's cozy cottage on Dorsey Street were pictorial reminders of Monroeville, including the little frame schoolhouse where the 10 children attended the first nine years of their school life. Charles Stephens didn't require them to be educated—he demanded it, and the result was that eight of the 10 graduated from Tuskeegee Institute. The other two could have, but decided high school was enough. The year 1949 was their banner year in which four of the children graduated from Tuskeegee and another from high school.

It was from the four college graduates of 1949 one picks up the story of Ernestine Stephens and her sister, Harriet.

"We graduated from high school in April 1945," said Mrs. Noel, "and Daddy enrolled us in Tuskeegee in May. I was only 15, Harriet was 16 and we were scared to death because we had never been away from home and it was 144 miles to Tuskeegee. My brother, Willie, took us up there on the bus and told them if we came home, the family would just send us back. He asked us what we planned to study and I told him I didn't plan on being anything, but he entered us in physical education."

If they didn't already know, the young women of Tuskeegee learned in a hurry what work means. Ernestine and Harriet spent much of their time around the gym, cleaning the dressing room or swimming pool or helping with the uniforms. The one thing they didn't give much thought to was basketball.

"Well, I had played only one time in my life before going to Tuskeegee," she remembered, "and that was in the ninth grade on May Day. We were outside on a dirt court. The boys used one basket and the girls used the other."

Coach Amelia Roberts announced that tryouts for the Tuskeegee team would be held. A position on the team was a prestigious one because it would provide much travel and play against the best college teams available.

"Harriet and I could almost communicate with each other without saying anything," said Mrs. Noel. "We were sitting in our room and just got up and went to the tryouts." (Harriet was a guard and Ernestine a forward.)

When they arrived at the gym they learned there were 391 girls competing for only three openings on the squad, but two of those openings went to the Stephens sisters and Ernestine still can't believe it.

"First," she said, "we were freshmen and that was a no-no. We were from Alabama and that was a no-no because of the out-of-state recruiting, and we were sisters and that certainly was a no-no. We knew we were not going to make the team, but when Coach Roberts posted our names we just looked at each other, then ran and hugged her."

Ernestine Stephens embarked on an athletic journey that probably would have taken her to Olympic competition in London had she not aborted it herself. She did not find the glory then that women athletes do now in college sports. She did find two-week trips on a rickety bus to black colleges in Tennessee, South Carolina and other Southern places where black women athletes were practically ignored by the press regardless of their ability.

The amazing fact is that Tuskeegee never lost a game during the four years the Stephens sisters played on the team. Even the powerful New Orleans Xavier team could not beat Tuskeegee.

"One year we won a game, 1-0," said Mrs. Noel. "Our captain, Hattie Turner (from Glendale, Ohio) was fouled and she made the free throw."

There were no conferences for the women athletes, but word somehow got around that they did have talent. A promoter, in 1946, conceived the idea of bringing together the best college women's teams at New York's Madison Square Garden to play for the national championship. Tuskeegee was invited along with the University of Chicago, Xavier, South Carolina State and Wilberforce of Ohio. Tuskeegee was scheduled against Wilberforce, but got a forfeit when the religious school decided the tournament was against its principles.

"We played Chicago for the championship," said Mrs. Noel as she rolled the miniature gold basketball the champions received in her fingers. "All I remember is that I was scared stiff and scored 20 points. From the noise it made, I think there was a big crowd, but I was too scared to look toward the stands."

By then, her coach was Romania Peters and it was a happy and honored team when it arrived back in Tuskeegee.

In the meantime, Maj. Cleve Abbott, the school's athletic director and track coach, saw something in Ernestine Stephens that might help his track program. He had taken money from the track and field fund to finance the women's basketball program.

"I wasn't interested in track, but Major Abbott told me to get out there against the high jumpers," said Mrs. Noel, "and I went. They put the bar at three feet and I said to myself, 'Oh, my God! I'm out right now.' Well, I had jumped a lot of barbed wire fences back home, taking a short cut on the cows, so I went for it. That first day I cleared 5-3 and could have jumped higher, but I was tired."

Chasing the cows home was part of the everyday life for the Stephens children. Ernestine's daily chores included milking two cows in the morning and pulling parsley in the afternoon to feed the hogs. "One hog bit me," she said with an impish grin, "and I bit him back. I screamed and he squealed."

Track was just another athletic endeavor for the natural athlete of the Stephens clan. Tennis was another.

"I played tennis in Texas once and didn't know my opponent," she remembered, "but I do remember she beat the daylights out of me."

The opponent was Althea Gibson, who later became the only black woman to win the Wimbledon championship.

Ernestine and Harriet Stephens were on the Tuskeegee track team two years and became inseparable. Ernestine remembers finishing second in her first track meet to a girl named Greene from Tennessee State. That became a pattern, Greene first, Stephens second and the silver medal from a meet in Fort Worth, Tex., was on the table last week as Mrs. Noel told of her athletic career.

"I ran against Wilma Rudolph in the 220," she recalled, and said she defeated the girl who would become another of our greatest Olympians. "We called her Antelope. She would reach down and grab some grass and put it in her mouth and grunt as she ran. With that sound behind me, you think I'm going to let it catch me?"

Then came the trials for the 1948 Olympics. "Harriet and I went to Ann Arbor (Mich.). When she didn't make it, I withdrew. My sister and I had never been separated. I told them I had a twisted ankle and I just didn't want to go to the Olympics, so I returned to school. The Olympics were in London. Wasn't I stupid?"

Alice Coachman, a teammate, did go to London and brought home a gold medal.

"We were a team," said Mrs. Noel. "Alice and I didn't work against each other. But, she was better than I because she practiced. She worked at it. I didn't."

Graduation time came at Tuskeegee, a day that brought special significance to Ernestine Stephens because of Roy Noel, a young man from Charleston, Miss.

"At 5:30," she said with a smile, "I married Roy, and at 7:30 I was graduated. We left that night and came to Chattanooga and stayed with Mrs. Alma Spence. She took me under her wing and showed me how to be a wife."

Mrs. Noel became a physical education teacher in the city school system, a job she held in elementary schools here for 11 years. Her marriage to Noel has also produced four children—Roy Jr., Charlsia,

Maria and Deborah—and seven grandchildren.

Harriet also became an educator, and today is in New Jersey serving as director of a school for the educable mentally retarded.

How was a story that has been kept hidden by a modest lady for nearly 40 years brought to light? It happened about a month ago when Carlyle Elliott was approached at Martin-Thompson Co. by a woman who handed him a tattered school letter, a "T," and asked him if he could have it restored to its original condition.

"Boy," exclaimed Elliott, "your boy has been pretty rough on this."

"That's not my boy's," said Ernestine Noel. "That's mine."

Elliott immediately called Sally Worthington, whose sewing magic restored the letter, free of charge to an unsung athletic heroine of yesteryear.

There are a lot of memories stored in the little cottage on Dorsey Street, many of them reaching back to the dusty roads of Monroeville. The family photos and the memorabilia of athletic success hold special places in the heart of Ernestine Stephens Noel, but none can compare with that day when she turned away from her wheelchair and walked down the steps from the plane into the arms of a loving husband.

The fight against multiple sclerosis continues, but she uses her influence to help others stricken with the disease. Once she noticed a woman in a wheelchair constantly staring at the floor. She walked over to the lady and said, "What are you looking for? There's nobody down there but the devil. Look up at the Lord." The lady looked up.

And a radiant smile broke across the face of Ernestine Stephens Noel.

Please Don't Feed The Bears

PRO FOOTBALL

By *KEVIN LAMB*

From Sport Magazine
Copyright © 1985, Sports Media Corporation

MONDAY

The Chicago Bears' defensive meeting room is rocking like a substitute teacher's classroom. Players are arguing with coaches. Passions are primed. There is cackling from the back.

The coaches are showing the film of yesterday's victory at Tampa Bay. Gary Fencik wants to know why he didn't get credit for an assisted tackle on that last play. He touched the ballcarrier, didn't he? Well, yes. But he was on the ground when the tackler drove the ballcarrier into him. Fencik, legitimately the team's leading tackler, laughs. Nice try.

Stats are at stake. Unlike offensive players, defensive players have subjective stats. Coaches decide who made the tackles and sacks, the assists and hurries. It's not always cut-and-dried. But the contract clauses providing bonuses for those stats are black and white.

At least the players have waited until the meeting to argue. Against Minnesota last year, when the Bears sacked Archie Manning 11 times, they argued right out on the field.

"I got him."

"No, I got him."

The Bears, in fact, are in perpetual argument. From the yuppie club president to the survivalist trainer, this is a team of clashing personalities and aggressive behavior. But it is also the best team in football in 1985, and that makes conflict colorful.

"They want a bunch of cookie-cutters," says Dan Hampton, the defensive tackle, referring to NFL muckity-mucks. "They want people to say, 'This guy studies his plays. He goes home. He eats

Dinty Moore beef stew. He watches *M*A*S*H* until 10:30, turns out the light and goes to sleep.' This team doesn't have those prototypes."

All NFL teams have their characters. What makes the Bears different is that their characters aren't covering kickoffs. They're the stars. Jim McMahon and Walter Payton, Hampton and Fencik and Steve McMichael. In a perfect world, these people wouldn't get along.

Mike McCaskey—George Halas' 42-year-old grandson and now the president of the Bears—is a refreshing individualist himself. He likes diversity, even dissension. This summer, after the Bears drafted 314-pound defensive tackle William Perry in the first round, defensive coordinator Buddy Ryan called Perry "a wasted draft choice" and a waste of money. "In a lot of organizations, you make that statement, you're gone, period," says Mike Ditka, the head coach. "And in some organizations it can be tolerated."

It is tolerated on the Bears, in large part, because McCaskey likes a bubbling pot. "It's a delight more than a tolerance," he says. "One of the joys of running a professional football club, compared to other businesses, is there's greater room for colorful personalities."

By 2 p.m. all the players have left Halas Hall, the Bears' headquarters in plush, suburban Lake Forest. Besides rehashing yesterday's game film, all they do on a Monday is limber up their sore muscles and treat their injuries. They won't start practicing for next Sunday's game, at San Francisco, until Wednesday.

It's a big game. The Bears are undefeated; the 49ers, defending Super Bowl champions, are struggling. The Bears lost the NFC championship game at San Francisco last year. It was a bitter defeat. Ditka expects this game could figure in determining the home sites for this year's playoffs.

"I don't know what it'll be like around here January 15," he says, "but, boy, it's got to be nice."

TUESDAY

Game plans for San Francisco are ready by midafternoon. The offense is going to pass. A lot. Ditka still seethes at the memory of the 49ers' eight-man fronts when the Bears lost, 23-0, last year. McMahon was injured then. Now he's not. Now he's the NFL's leading passer.

The defense wants to make Joe Montana take more than his usual two seconds or so to throw the ball. It will confuse him with multiple coverages, which it uses every week. It also will bump the receivers at the line. If the cornerbacks can slow down the receivers a split second, that might be enough time for the rush men to reach Montana. Simple.

It's the players' day off, but middle linebacker Mike Singletary comes to pick up the game plan. He always does. If he weren't so sincere, Singletary might be too serious to take seriously. As it is, his teammates call him the playing coach. But they can't always contain their laughter through the end of his Hey-Now drills.

Singletary leads a Hey-Now every few weeks at the end of pre-practice stretching exercises. He's a minister's son, and the drill sounds like a revival meeting. Every time Singletary says something, the other players respond, "Hey now!" Singletary's lines don't rhyme. They have no cadence. Last week some of them went, "Five years ago, we were not much good," and "Now we're 4-0" and "We're going to beat Tampa Bay."

"I'm sure even Mike thinks it's hokey," wide receiver Brian Baschnagel says. "But it does get practice off to a rousing start."

Singletary's intensity has had teammates shaking their heads since he joined the Bears in 1981. The players called Singletary "Tasmanian Devil" at first, then changed it to "Samurai," which better suggests the attack noises he makes on the field.

Payton hunts on Tuesdays. He's serious about it. The Monday before he broke the all-time rushing record, he told reporters, "The only thing I'm looking forward to now is getting out there with the bow" and hunting the next morning with Roland Harper, his former Bear running mate. Payton can hunt in his backyard, which is bigger than some ZIP codes. Out of season, he can use the 80-foot shooting range in his basement.

In honor of breaking the record, Payton brought his linemen gifts. Expensive wristwatches are such a cliche. Instead, he gave them top-of-the-line Browning shotguns, engraved with the particulars of the historic game.

One of those linemen is Mark Bortz, the left guard. He collects guns and is a military historian. He is trying to round up Bears players for a survivalist weekend next spring at one of those camps where teams shoot dye pellets at each other in the wilderness. Bortz says the linemen and Payton are all for it. "We've already picked out who we want to shoot," he says.

Bortz would like strength coach Clyde Emrich on his team that weekend. Emrich also has a gun collection, only his isn't designed for four-legged creatures. Bortz likes to kid him about waiting for the next Civil War. "Clyde likes to talk about the range of fire he's got from his condo," Bortz says. "He's got high-powered rifles, practically cannons. Who's he going to take on? The Romans?"

WEDNESDAY

Today is the first day of full workouts. The defensive players are meeting on the field. They're walking through assignments. Sometimes they walk roughly. Buddy Ryan is in charge, and he keeps everybody on edge. He considers it high praise to say, "Not all bad." At a meeting before the Tampa Bay game, he said, "We've got to do something about this Swiss-cheese defense. It's got holes in it and it stinks."

Ditka conducts the offensive meetings. The units are rarely together, except at special-teams meetings from 9 to 9:30 and when they practice against each other. They meet separately at 9:30, and again before practice begins at 1:20. The regular practices on

Wednesday and Thursday—the week's longest—last until 4.

Both Ditka and Ryan are more outspoken than most NFL coaches, and their differences sometimes crash through the closed doors of staff meetings. Besides the Perry bickering in August, they have squabbled over a number of issues involving defensive players and strategems. When the Bears forced five turnovers but allowed 445 yards at Minnesota this season, Ryan said, "We used too much zone"; Ditka said he was glad to see all the zone coverage, which makes turnovers easier.

Ryan has as much independence as any assistant coach in the league. One of the reasons is that Ditka is secure enough and smart enough to distinguish strong opinions from insubordination. He could have replaced Ryan last year or this year, but he recognizes he has a good coach. "He has great rapport with his people," Ditka says. "Our people believe in his system and find ways to make it work."

This afternoon McMahon's wife brings his children to Halas Hall. His daughter is 2, his son not quite 1. As he carries his daughter into the locker room, he whispers loud enough so reporters will hear, "Let's go see some naked boys."

Later, he comes out for a television interview. A chaw of tobacco makes his lower lip the size of a shot glass. The eyeslits in his sunglasses are no wider than a pencil. The hood is up on his bright-blue rain jacket, and a sweatband is outside the hood.

McMahon is in his public uniform. He does need sunglasses to protect his eye from bright TV lights. When he was 7, he stabbed it with a fork, trying to untie a knot. He could wear plain old Foster Grants, though. He could look, well, normal.

But then people might think he's just another pretty-boy quarterback. That would be enough to make him puke. He cultivates his antihero image. As his friend, wide receiver Ken Margerum, says, "He likes to be disgusting on purpose, just to get a reaction out of people." But his contempt for convention and authority in general is very sincere.

"That's why he's a great quarterback," Margerum says. "Defenses have all these computer printouts of what you're going to do on first-and-10 and second-and-long and third-and-3, and Jim just goes against all convention of what he's supposed to do. A lot of big plays go to a completely different receiver than the one that was planned. You can't defend that."

McMahon has never been far from authority's thumb, growing up Catholic and going to a Mormon school. At Brigham Young, he says, "I was on probation my whole time." This week, a Utah writer asked him for his fondest memory at BYU. "Leaving," he said.

He has learned that shocking people turns the tables on authority. He has learned to do that by drinking conspicuously, as when he arrived at Halas Hall with a can of beer the day he was drafted, and by dressing outrageously. He sometimes wears a T-shirt with lots of bears on it. They're in a circle, in pairs, making little bears.

THURSDAY

Yesterday was interview day for the opposing coaches, and in today's papers you can almost feel Ditka and 49ers Coach Bill Walsh trembling. Walsh said the Niners "fear for our safety" against the Bears. Ditka said he didn't know if he wanted to show up Sunday, either. Today he walks into the press room and announces, "The game's been canceled. Mutual fear."

Dan Hampton is depressed. He has a sprained ankle and might not play. *Hampton,* who played 23 days after arthroscopic knee surgery two years ago.

He had his third operation on that knee last February, and he was downright embarrassed at the rehabilitation schedule that had him coasting into training camp. But he's learned not to force things. "After five knee operations, it's time I realized I'm not bulletproof," he says.

Hampton and McMichael are the scourges of the offense at practice. McMichael is the one most apt to get into a fight. "He goes full bore all the time," says center Jay Hilgenberg. "If he gets by you in practice, he'll turn around and laugh at you. Then you block him and you smile and he kicks you in the shin."

Still there is palpable respect and even affection for the offense by the defense. When the Bears were losing 32 of 51 games from 1980 through mid-1983, that wasn't the case. Defensive players taunted offensive players. They considered the offense a handicap.

This is a close-knit team now. "This team doesn't show its closeness by hugging and kissing," says McMichael. "It shows it by sarcasm."

Hampton is more lighthearted at practice than McMichael. He likes to play the 30-second clock. When he thinks the offense has been huddling too long, he says, "Hey, McMahon. While we're young."

Meetings have finished and Payton is at the receptionist's desk—answering phones. "The more you can do," he says.

Rain has soaked the field behind Halas Hall, so practice is at a public park half a mile away. Walking there, Payton stops to sign an autograph for a woman driving a pickup and hitches a ride in the trailer. Under a shelter at the park, he meets an elderly man. He extends his hand and says, "Hi, I'm Roland Harper." He visits two spectators on the sideline and offers to determine which one has a wider umbrella.

Payton is Mr. Loose. He's the one who set off firecrackers in the racquetball court. He's the one who dipped the morning doughnuts in some of the trainers' paraffin wax to make them look glazed. The trainers also have something called artificial fat tissue, which they use for padding players' hands. It feels like rubber, looks like cheese. Payton puts it in players' sandwiches.

He goes back to the field and gets William (The Fridge) Perry to run a goal-line drill. Perry is the ballcarrier. Perry offers some tackling advice. "Lock 'em up," he says, meaning to grasp hands behind the ballcarrier. Payton's barely reach. "Lock 'em up?" Payton says. "I'm just trying to get you out of bounds."

All this occurs while the special teams are practicing. There is still time for Perry to practice fielding punts.

FRIDAY

Singletary tells Ditka that the Bears will shut out the 49ers, no question. He thinks the game plan is that good.

Practice is shorter on Friday, concentrating on short-yardage, goal-line and two-minute situations.

Today's cartoon features a bear and a California gold rusher playing chess. The bear is taking the gold rusher's quarterback with his linebacker, which he calls "Big O," the name Otis Wilson has tried to get Ryan to call him, instead of "55."

It was drawn by the Halas Hall superintendent, who has been a commercial artist and does not look like a superintendent. He wears a bow tie and pince-nez glasses, sports a cookie-duster mustache and rides a motorcycle. He reads philosophy and classics. He often pushes his broom with a Walkman around his ear, probably tuned to the public radio station. His name is Richard McMurrin.

McMurrin posts a cartoon nearly everyday. Payton was the subject of one of his best last year. Payton had just broken the rushing record and just been given a very expensive sports car by the company whose shoes he endorses. Payton and the car were in the background. In the foreground were the offensive linemen with smiles of utter appreciation, saying "Walter gave us T-shirts." The T-shirts advertised Payton's shoe company.

When the Bears had a quarterback controversy two years ago, Payton said that wasn't the problem. "We could put Dick the janitor back there," he said, "if everybody else did their job."

At the next practice, McMurrin was in uniform. At quarterback.

Hampton is back at practice, as is defensive end Richard Dent, who has been nursing a hip pointer. Their only problem now, says Ryan, is "sunburned bottom lips" from pouting when he said they wouldn't start. Ryan's problem has been getting a pass-rush without blitzing.

"I think teams are afraid of the piranha effect with us," Hampton says. "They're afraid if we get one or two sacks, we'll smell blood and go crazy. They say, 'We'll throw interceptions. We'll throw into coverage. But we're not going to give up a sack.' "

Ditka would rather not hear his players denigrate the opposition. But, he says, "I think a certain amount of cockiness, being assured and feeling good about it is not a bad thing."

"If you're running with a pack of scared dogs," says McMichael, putting it differently, "everyone is going to be scared. But if you're running with a bunch of mean ones, all the dogs are going to be mean."

SATURDAY

On the flight to San Francisco, a surprise appetizer is served. It's

alligator from a Tampa restaurant. Ditka and General Manager
Jerry Vainisi have eaten alligator there before their last three games
in Tampa, all victories. It's a little bland.

Today's workout is short, with special-teams work and the offense and defense picking up loose ends, working on tricky forma-
tions and other possible problems. At the hotel the players will meet
as a group, watch a special-teams film and break up for offense and
defense meetings. Ditka talks to the whole group. He makes more of
an effort to keep the players loose than to wind them up. That's partly because a coach who has broken his hand punching a locker after
a game can stir players up without much effort. But it's also because
he knows people play better when they're not tight.

"We made some horrible mistakes in practice Wednesday,"
Brian Baschnagel says. "But we corrected them and went on. He
didn't make us run any more. In the past he would have yelled and
screamed all during practice and at the end he'd say, 'Get on the line
and we're going to run until we drag.' "

Ditka has a reputation for being oppressively intense. In fact, he
gives his players and staff a lot of slack. He was a defiant player
himself, the tight end who once said George Halas "throws nickels
around as if they were manhole covers."

"I played hard," Ditka says. "I was outspoken and I was an individual and we (the Bears of the early '60s) had a lot of them."

Ditka surprised some of his bosses by installing a players council,
entertaining weekly gripes from five designated representatives. He
acknowledges that it is risky letting football players have a long
leash. "That's why when teams start losing, you see them go to more
rigid schedules," he says. But he believes, at least for now, that it's
even riskier to throw a harness on strong personalities.

"Another coach might have wound his team too tight for a game
like this," McCaskey says. "Our practices were loose, but tense."

SUNDAY

Payton is pinching butts, throwing rolled-up socks, keeping the
pre-game atmosphere light in the locker room. He ignores the players who prefer to put their game faces on quietly. He used to be one of
them himself, lying under the training table to concentrate on the
battle.

The players hadn't talked during the week about their bitterness
toward the 49ers. But they remembered a feeling that the Niners had
been a bit too haughty in victory last year. Now Ditka has wallpa-
pered the locker room with newspaper clippings from that game,
appropriately underlined.

One line they remember particularly: "Next time bring an offense." None of the 49ers had said it. It was a writer's line. But athletes don't split hairs over who's the messenger.

Rarely does a game plan come to life so vividly. The Bears pass
on their first five plays and take a 7-0 lead after 2½ minutes. They
lead, 16-0, after 16:05. Seventeen of their first 24 plays are pass plays.

The defense checks the receivers at the line, just as planned, and sacks Joe Montana seven times, the most in his career. McMichael is his shadow. It is only the fourth time a Walsh team doesn't score an offensive touchdown. The 49ers get their fewest yards and first downs ever under Walsh. The score is 16-10 for the whole third quarter, but the game is never close. It ends, 26-10. "We brought an offense," Ditka says.

Running out the clock, the Bears put Perry in the backfield for the first time in a game. The 49ers had put guard Guy McIntyre in the backfield against Chicago last year, but only as a blocking back. Perry carries the ball twice. He gains two yards each time, topping the 49ers' second-half rushing yardage by one. "Grass and smoke and chinstraps were flying," Payton says. The linemen say they're thankful Perry didn't fall on them.

In McMurrin's Monday cartoon, McMahon will be handing off a cheeseburger to Perry. The caption: Big Back attack. Ditka talks in days to come about using Perry at tight end for a flea-flicker.

"I just wanted to see if he could run with it," Ditka says after the game. But he remembers McIntyre.

This is still an up-from-hungry team. Despite its cockiness and its general respect as the league's best team, it goes into games with the desperate mean streak of an underdog. "We all have the feeling that if we slip one game, it's all going to come crashing down on our faces," Bortz says.

Baschnagel, on injured reserve, notices the emotion even from the coach's box. "When things aren't going the way you like them to, you can feel that anger inside," he says. "That's why when something happens, small as it might be, it triggers that momentum, and when we get going it's difficult to stop it." That's no surprise, though. If Ditka's coaching philosophy can be reduced to one sentence, it is "Put a chip on your shoulder in July and leave it there until January."

But for now, they put the chip aside. They are elated. The film room will be rocking again tomorrow.

Hold On There!

by Ted Kirk of the Journal-Star Newspapers. Nebraska running back Doug DuBose got past the Colorado defense, but not without paying a stiff price. Impeding DuBose's progress in an unusual manner is Colorado's Kyle Rappold. Copyright © 1985, Ted Kirk.

4,192: The Emotion

by Terry Bochatey of United Press International. The impact of the moment was too much and the camera was there to capture the tears after Cincinnati Player-Manager Pete Rose collected career hit No. 4,192, breaking Ty Cobb's all-time record. Copyright © 1985, Terry Bochatey, United Press International.

Evert Wins Record Sixth French Open

TENNIS

By *JOHN FEINSTEIN*

From the Washington Post
Copyright © 1985, the Washington Post

Once in a great while, sport becomes very special. The timing, the scene, the athletes, even the fans, are in the precise alignment. Everyone involved senses they are part of something magical.

Today, Chris Evert Lloyd and Martina Navratilova produced one of those special moments. For almost three hours they dueled in the French Open final, their emotions on display for all the 16,500 enthralled fans in Stade Roland Garros.

When it was over, when Evert somehow had come up with the final burst to win the championship, 6-3, 6-7 (4-7), 7-5, the two friends and great rivals hugged each other and pushed backed tears of exhaustion and pride that both had every right to shed.

For Evert, her sixth French championship, a record for women, might have been her most gratifying. A year ago here, she was humiliated by Navratilova, 6-3, 6-1, in a final that lasted barely an hour. She wondered then if perhaps she could beat Navratilova ever again.

But at Wimbledon in July, Evert played a tough first set before losing. At the U.S. Open in September, she won the first set and felt she should have won the match. In February, she finally beat Navratilova in a Virginia Slims tournament in Florida.

But this was special. This was a Grand Slam final. And, from the beginning, on a chilly, windy afternoon, Evert sensed she could win.

"There were times when I started to get disheartended because I would get a lead and then it would slip away," she said. "Once, I might have given up mentally in a situation like that against her. But today I just kept telling myself to hang in because I sensed that she was nervous, too."

Navratilova, clearly nervous early in the match, kept coming back. She was down, 3-0, in the first set and came back to 3-all. She was down, 4-2 and 15-40, in the second set and came back to lead, 5-4. She had a set point in that game, but Evert saved it. Evert broke to lead, 6-5. Navratilova broke back and won the tie breaker.

Finally, during the memorable 67-minute final set, the two women took turns climbing from the mat.

"It was one of those matches that seemed like it would go on forever," Navratilova said. "It was a shame someone had to win, and I would say that even if I had won. In tennis, though, you don't play to a draw."

For a long time today it seemed that might be the best solution.

Twice, Evert served for the match. Twice, Navratilova broke. Throughout the third set, Evert had chances to build a comfortable lead and each time Navratilova came up with an answer.

In the end, though, just when it looked as if Evert was through, drained by the tension of two hours and 52 minutes of sustained drama, she produced the magic shots. It was Evert, down, 0-40, while serving at 5-all in the third, who made two near miraculous shots to save the game. And it was Evert who hit two winners, one crosscourt at 30-all, the other down the line on match point, to finally get the victory she wanted so much.

"When I hit the last winner down the line I was really proud of myself," she said. "I never gave up, and when I finally got to match point I went for a winner and I hit it. I had held my emotions in for so long that I really kind of let go."

She let go with a joyous shriek, her arms raised over her head, her shoulders slumping in relief, her eyes sparkling with happiness.

"That was about as dramatic a match as I can ever remember playing in," she said.

Navratilova agreed. "We've played so many great matches over the years but this being a Grand Slam final and all the tension it had, it had to be our best," she said.

That's saying a lot. They have played 65 times, almost to a draw, Navratilova winning 33, Evert 32.

From the beginning it was apparent there would be no repeat of last year's rout. Evert, saving game points each time, won the first three games. Navratilova argued several line calls, shook her fist after good shots, threw her head back and searched the cloudy sky for help each time she missed.

"I didn't play as well as I expected to," she said. "What I did today I did mostly on heart because my game wasn't at its best."

At the start, Evert's game was about as good as it gets. She consistently was hitting backhand winners, making Navratilova's every advance to the net an adventure.

Evert ended the first set with a second-serve ace, when Navratilova guessed down the middle and Evert served wide, followed by a crackling forehand crosscourt on set point. The score was 6-3 and the crowd, firmly behind Evert from the start, was ecstatic.

Navratilova began the second set by blowing a 40-0 lead and was broken when Evert raced in for a drop volley and slugged a forehand winner down the line.

But Navratilova hasn't won 11 Grand Slam titles without a good deal of grit. Behind and struggling on a day when she didn't have her best stuff, she willed herself back into the match.

Trailing, 4-2, she faced two break points at 15-40 that probably would have ended the match had Evert converted either. Navratilova responded with two superb serves.

She saved the game with one of her patented, lunging backhand volleys on Evert's backhand. Navratilova then broke for 4-4 with a crisp backhand winner.

A moment later, serving at 4-5, Evert faced set point. She took a deep breath and slammed a backhand past Navratilova.

Evert won the game with a solid forehand volley and, when she broke Navratilova with yet another wonderful forehand, the match was on her racket.

Not for long. Navratilova, attacking on every point, broke for 6-all. Navratilova won the tie breaker, 7-4, aided by a double fault by Evert. Now, the noise from the crowd was a murmur. It sensed Evert's chance had come and gone.

"After I lost the tie breaker I had a talk with myself," Evert said. "I said, 'Chris, stop holding back. Play loose. Play like you were playing in the first set when it was early and you were just hitting out.' "

Instead of fading, Evert again took control. She won the first game of the third set with a gorgeous drop shot and broke coming in behind a backhand to hit a tough volley that Navratilova ran down, but netted.

It was 2-0, Evert. Serving for 3-0, she had three game points. One of them produced the longest rally of the match, but none produced a point for Evert. She made two errors and Navratilova had the game.

Evert promptly broke back and had two points for 4-1. But, after five deuces, Navratilova won the game with a backhand winner. When she held at love for 3-all, Navratilova seemed in control.

Navratilova had a break point in the next game but netted a forehand passing shot, dropping her racket in disgust as the ball hit the tape. Evert saved the game with what seemed like her millionth winner, a forehand past Navratilova's futile lunge.

Evert broke again to lead, 5-3, running down a volley and whipping a forehand crosscourt. Navratilova, guarding the line, never moved.

For the second time, Evert served for the match. For the second time, Navratilova overpowered her, breaking at 15, snapping an overhead to end the game. Quickly, she held at love and just as quickly Evert faced 0-40 at 5-5.

"Right then, my chances to win the match on paper were zero,"

Evert said. "But I played some good shots."

"I wasn't thinking straight," Navratilova said. "I should have attacked her and I didn't."

Evert saved break point one when Navratilova hit a backhand long. She saved break point two with another perfect backhand. She saved break point three on the most remarkable point of the match. It ended with both women at the net, hitting reflex volleys at each other. Finally, Evert fought one off her body and it went right at Navratilova, who netted it.

Stunned, Navratilova stared at the ball for a moment. "Nine times out of 10, I win that point," she said. "Nine times out of 10."

A moment later, Evert held to lead, 6-5. "By then I was really working on myself to end it," she said.

Finally, she did. With the crowd gasping and screaming on every shot, Evert got to deuce, hitting a perfect forehand lob that Navratilova reached, but lobbed long.

Evert took one final look around and hit two shots for history. The first was a forehand that screeched crosscourt. Navratilova lunged, got her racket on the ball, but pushed it past the base line.

Roland Garros was bedlam. Navratilova missed a first serve. She hooked in a second. Evert returned, Navratilova chipped a backhand and came in, looking for Evert to go crosscourt with her backhand one more time.

"I had gone crosscourt so much I thought it was the right time to go down the line," Evert said.

In her dreams, she will always see that shot. Navratilova never had a chance. Evert scorched the ball two inches above the net and three feet inside the base line and the side line. For the 17th time she was a Grand Slam titlist. At 30, she had won the longest French Open women's final ever played in a match that will stand as one of the greatest ever played.

"If I had lost after having so many chances I would have been very depressed," Evert said. "But to come back after what happened last year and win this way, it's a great feeling."

Navratilova said, "It was one of the most incredible matches you can ever imagine. It had about everything."

Truly, it did. As the two women mounted the steps to the victory platform, the fans rose in tribute. Together, holding their trophies, Evert and Navratilova stood basking in one of those moments to be remembered and treasured for a lifetime.

Players Betrayed Tanner's Trust in Them

BASEBALL

By *BRUCE KEIDAN*

From the Pittsburgh Post-Gazette
Copyright © 1985, Pittsburgh Post-Gazette

Baseball never made a better marriage than Chuck Tanner and the Pittsburgh Pirates. They were born for each other—the man from New Castle and the franchise from the big city down the road.

How sad it had to end this way. The relationship in tatters. The air thick with acrimony. The memories bittersweet.

It was finished, without question. Once they had soared together to the heights of rapture. Now they were only handcuffed to each other. A contract was all that remained between them. It had to be broken, for the sake of them both.

In the end, after nine years, he felt betrayed. And he was right. But who had betrayed him? Tanner blamed the leaders of the corporate-municipal coalition that is in the process of purchasing the franchise from the Galbreath family. But it was not the new owners who wielded the knife.

He had hoped to be the knight in shining armor, riding to the rescue of the franchise he loved. He had prevailed upon friends to pledge financial support to the undertaking. Together they would buy the Pirates, wringing from the city the financial concessions that would make such an undertaking realistic. His friends would buy the team, and he would run it for them.

It was a pleasant enough fantasy. But a lifetime devoted to baseball had not prepared Tanner for the pitfalls of the political arena. Forces beyond Tanner's ken were at work in that arena. Alliances had been forged, promises made, markers called in. The last thing the power structure wanted was the distraction of a field manager turned White Knight.

He could not be ignored. He had too high a profile. But he could be discredited. A meeting was arranged. Very preliminary. Very private. When it was over, there was a carefully worded leak to the news media. Every inquiry was a "demand." Every concession sought was more ruinous than the next.

Tanner was outraged. He should not have been. This was not baseball he was playing. This was another game, with a different set of rules. He was simply out of his league.

The real betrayal took place years earlier. And it took place in his own clubhouse.

Tanner's single greatest strength as a manager has always been his relationship with his players. Most managers know when to make a pitching change. Most know when to play the infield back, when to signal a pitchout or order a suicide squeeze. Tanner knows all those things as well as anyone. But he has always had another dimension, one that set him apart.

He is baseball's Great Motivator. In every smoking ruin, Chuck Tanner sees the fires of redemption. In every run-of-the-mill athlete, Chuck Tanner sees the seeds of greatness.

"Believe in them," he says, *"and they will believe in themselves. Expect the best from them, and they will give you their best. Treat them like men, and they will act like men."*

It is the Tanner Method. It would not have worked for the late Danny Murtaugh. It would not work for Dick Williams or Billy Martin or Gene Mauch or a hundred others. But it is the style that fits Chuck Tanner, and he can no more change it than he can stop believing that every defeat is a prelude to victory.

It is a style he brought with him to the major leagues. In Hawaii, he won the Pacific Coast League pennant with a collection of discarded veterans and notorious troublemakers who looked more like the Dirty Dozen than a baseball team. *"If you can't play for Chuck Tanner,"* the players said, *"you can't play for anybody."*

He believed in himself and he believed in miracles. In Chicago, he attempted to harness the prodigious talents of the outlaw Dick Allen and transform them into a White Sox pennant. In Oakland, he attempted to work in harmony with the insufferable Charles O. Finley, then owner of the A's. They were impossible tasks. He came astoundingly close to succeeding at both of them.

In Pittsburgh, he won a pennant, then a world championship. He did it in part by being a smart tactician. But he did it also by being patient and tolerant. He did not demand that his players walk the way he walked or talk the way he talked or conform to an elaborate set of regulations. It was often said that he had 25 sets of rules for 25 players. In fact, he has only one rule: *Come to the stadium prepared to give 100 percent of yourself from the opening pitch of the game until the final out.*

He does not believe in curfews or dress codes. He believes in people. He believes in his players. And if Chuck Tanner was betrayed, it was his players who betrayed him.

He believed in Dave Parker, who dissipated his talents with cocaine and brought pushers into the clubhouse.

He believed in Dale Berra, who hid his cocaine use behind a facade of lies.

He believed in Bill Madlock, who stopped caring and stopped trying and brought no leadership to the role of team captain.

He believed he could rekindle the competitive fires in George Hendrick. He believed he could coax John Candelaria into being a great pitcher again. He believed in them even when nobody else did anymore.

Dave Parker betrayed Chuck Tanner. Dale Berra betrayed him. And Bill Madlock. George Hendrick. John Candelaria. And too many others who proved unworthy of the trust he placed in them.

He will manage again. But it may be that his methods do not work anymore. Maybe the drugs and the long-term contracts and the selfishness in baseball leave no room for a man like Chuck Tanner. If that is so, it is a damning indictment of the game.

Former Player Cleans Up the Gym

BASKETBALL

By *SAM HEYS*

From the Atlanta Constitution
Copyright © 1985, The Atlanta Journal-Constitution

Sammy Drummer hopes he's never asked to sweep the basketball court. Having to clean the backboards with Windex is embarrassing enough.

"Sometimes before a game we have to go over and wipe down the backboard," he says. "That brings back old memories. I say, 'Why am I up here?' "

Drummer played basketball for three colleges and now is cleaning for one.

Five years ago Drummer was one of Georgia Tech's finest players ever. Now he is 28 and a janitor at Ball State University in his home town of Munice, Ind., earning $13,228 a year. He wears a ring of 40 keys on a belt loop and worn-out leather Converse basketball shoes on his feet.

"I sit back now and I think about the way things turned out, and at times tears just pop into my eyes," he says. "It's a funny feeling."

Drummer's story is that of a college athlete who didn't get his degree, didn't make it in the pros as he had dreamed he would and has little to show for the four years he spent in college except a scrapbook of memories.

"He was used. They just used him until they were done with him," says Drummer's high school coach, Myron Dickerson, of Drummer's college years. "It's ironic that Ball State wanted Sam as bad as anybody and now he's back over there. He's made the circle."

His case is not an isolated one. "The circumstances are typical almost to being a composite of what happens on the average, to black athletes in particular, and to white athletes to some extent," says Dr. Harry Edwards, a professor of sociology at the University of California at Berkeley who testified this summer before a Senate sub-committee investigating the academic integrity of college athletics.

A study by the National Collegiate Athletic Association released this summer revealed that only about half of the athletes who entered major universities on athletic scholarships in 1977 graduated within six years. The study included 6,804 athletes at 206 participating institutions in the NCAA's Division I, which includes the majority of America's largest colleges.

"What this means," says Edwards, "is that these Division I schools are running plantations and the kids are not getting educated. As long as there is an endless supply of 20th century gladiators being created in the black communities of this country by parents who are blindly orienting their children to become athletes, why should these schools be concerned about what happens to any particular black athlete?"

Dr. Doug Conner, executive director of the American Association of Collegiate Registrars and Admissions Officers, believes some athletes have not graduated because they "major in eligibility."

"One of the problems has been that athletes could go to college and could just take courses to keep themselves eligible but not necessarily work toward any kind of degree," he says.

Drummer majored in industrial management at Georgia Tech and needed approximately two more years of academic work to graduate when his athletic eligibility expired in '79.

He was admitted to Tech from DeKalb Community College in '77 despite having no algebra in high school or college and scoring only 500 total on the Scholastic Aptitude Test, with 400 being the minimum and 1600 the maximum.

"He is certainly not typical of the ones (athletes) we get," says Dr. Joseph Pettit, Georgia Tech president. "We've got a different coach now and a different athletic director. I'm not saying we might not take a Sammy Drummer, but we are certainly putting education way out front. Our overall policy is to try to get students who can get through. He was really not a very good prospect academically from the start. I think our standards are somewhat higher now.

"I think a young fellow like that takes his chances. We certainly have to tell him that maybe only 1 percent ever get into the pros. I think that's really terribly unfortunate. A student with those kind of scores comes with a disadvantage."

Drummer was behind in school before he ever started. Growing up along the dirt roads of Bolivar County in the Delta country of northwest Mississippi, Drummer didn't enter school until he was 10. Because of his age, he was placed in the third grade.

After his first school year, his mother moved the family to Muncie. "I didn't want to raise my children in the South like I was raised," says Elizabeth Drummer, who had supported her family by chopping and picking cotton. "I knew if I stayed down there, they'd have to do the same thing. I wasn't about to let them work in no field."

Drummer was placed in the fifth grade in Muncie, perhaps because he was two years older than most fourth-graders. He therefore missed three of the first four grades of school.

Basketball became Drummer's life in Indiana, as he no longer had to be satisfied with shooting a balled-up rag at a five-gallon can as he had in Mississippi.

He could dunk a basketball in the seventh grade, and when he injured his knee in the ninth grade and was placed in a hip-to-ankle cast, he still practiced shooting, even in the snow. He would often play until 3 or 4 a.m. on the court next to the public housing project where he lived with his mother, three sisters and brother.

In high school Drummer was bused across town to Northside, an upper-middle-class school with a 10 percent black enrollment. In a state where high school basketball is a major event and in a city where rival Central High had won more state championships than any Indiana school, the 6-foot-5 Drummer was possibly Muncie's most famous citizen.

"He was a popular kid. He wasn't a bragger or showoff or troublemaker or anything like that," says Dickerson, his Northside coach. "He'd do anything to play basketball."

To play basketball, Drummer had to remain academically eligibility, and that was a struggle.

"School was hard because I was having so much problem with the little stuff, stuff that I should have learned in earlier grades but didn't even know," he says. "If it wasn't for basketball, I wouldn't have gone as far as I did in school. But basketball kind of gave me a boost and made me try hard.

"I wanted to learn. I really didn't want to be dumb all my life."

When Drummer was in the 11th grade, his English teacher, Barbara Pugh, realized that he didn't know that letters had specific sounds. So she bought a phonics workbook designed for children learning to read and worked with him during her free time. Drummer's reading improved and by the time he was out of her class, he was reading on a fourth-grade level.

Both teachers and students would work with Drummer individually. "You'd have to sit around after class," he says, "and sort of like take class all over again."

"He'd stay after school and a lot of teachers would be willing to help him. I mean really help him," says Sonny Burks, a Muncie policemen who moonlighted as a security officer at Northside and became a friend and adviser to Drummer.

Asked if Drummer was "socially promoted" through high school, Northside principal Owen Lemna replies, "Sam was a young man who was friendly and had a smile on his face. He got along with people, he was courteous, he was pleasant. You can draw your own conclusions from that."

Needing a 2.0 grade average to receive an NCAA scholarship,

Drummer graduated from Northside in 1975 with a 2.13 average of a possible 4.0. He had not received a college-preparatory education, however.

Six of Drummer's 37½ credits were in industrial arts and eight were split among art, typing, physical education, health and driver education. His science was limited to physical science, he had no foreign language and his seven semesters of English were spent in "reading lab," an individualized program for students unable to read at grade level.

Drummer scored only 210 on the verbal half of the SAT college board and 290 on the math half, with 200 being the minimum on each half. But because of his basketball ability, he received scholarship offers from—depending on the newspaper reports—more than 200, 300 or 400 colleges. He was ranked among the top five high school basketball players in the U.S.

His recruitment became an ordeal he wanted to run away from, often hiding upstairs when recruiters came to his door. "It was a mess, I mean a mess," says Drummer. "I didn't have no one to sit down and tell me what it was all about. All I knew is I had all these coaches coming in from all directions."

Drummer signed a Big Ten letter-of-intent with Indiana but later changed his mind. "I don't think I could have played ball there," he says, claiming he only signed with Indiana to get other recruiters off his back. "Indiana never mentioned no help books-wise, and I knew I needed help."

Although Indiana did offer tutoring for its athletes—just as most colleges do—Drummer eventually signed a scholarship with Gardner-Webb College, a small Baptist school in Boiling Springs, N.C., although he would change his mind about entering that school also.

Gardner-Webb assistant coach Roger Banks had become a father figure to Drummer, their relationship having started when Drummer was in the ninth grade. Banks, for 15 years one of the Southeast's most successful recruiters, had first seen Drummer play on a Muncie playground and had befriended him. He became the only person Drummer trusted during his recruitment.

"I thought he (Banks) was really interested in helping me," says Drummer. "I just got so hooked to him, attached to him, I don't know how to say it. I never really met no one like him. He helped me out with lots of things, advice and everything."

"Sammy was like family to us," says Banks, 39, now living in Newland, N.C., and working as regional director of Jim Barfield Inc., an insurance and employee-benefit company.

Drummer would later babysit for Banks' children and be tutored by Banks' wife, and even now Banks often uses the pronoun "we" when talking about Drummer's career.

"Nobody during Sammy's recruiting process knew of his insecurity academically," says Banks. "Sammy had a lot of pride and he didn't want anybody else to know he had those kind of (academic) problems. And nobody else that recruited him really cared (about those problems). He was too good a player."

When Banks left Gardner-Webb during the summer of '75 and was hired at Austin Peay University—a small state-supported school in Clarksville, Tenn., that had recently developed a strong basketball program—Drummer decided he too would go to Austin Peay. Because he had not yet enrolled at Gardner-Webb and because Gardner-Webb belonged to the National Association of Intercollegiate Athletics and Austin Peay to the NCAA, Drummer was able to receive a scholarship at Austin Peay and play that season.

Drummer planned to major in physical education at Austin Peay and about half the classes he took as a freshman were P.E. courses, according to Banks.

Drummer averaged 16.7 points per game as freshman at Austin Peay, but when the season ended and Banks got a better-paying job at Georgia Tech, Drummer decided he would follow Banks to Atlanta.

Because of NCAA rules, Drummer could not transfer from Austin Peay to Georgia Tech without sitting out a basketball season. So he instead transferred to DeKalb South, where he did not have to miss a season, because it's a junior college and not under NCAA jurisdiction. That season he was named player of the year by the National Junior College Athletic Association, averaging 28.9 points and 13.8 rebounds a game.

To play for a senior college again, according to NCAA rules, Drummer had to graduate from DeKalb South. He totaled the necessary 90 credit hours for graduation by transferring approximately 40 hours from Austin Peay and attending DeKalb South for four quarters. Again, he had his choice of colleges, but he chose Tech to remain close to Banks.

"I told Sammy he would never graduate from Georgia Tech," says Banks, "but once he came out of Tech and into the pros, we'd get him in school somewhere else and he'd get his degree even if it took 10 years."

"Sammy was a weak student for Georgia Tech," says George Slayton, academic adviser to Tech athletes. "He had a good attitude and he went to class well but he was a very, very weak student. I am sure he felt totally out of place, because he wasn't up to the other students in academic ability. His background was very weak, but he tried at least."

Although Drummer was a junior in athletic eligibility when he entered Tech, he was able to transfer only about half his previous credits so, academically, he was the equivalent of a late freshman or early sophomore.

Asked if Drummer was put at a disadvantage by being admitted to Tech, his former coach, Dwane Morrison, says, "We were honest with every youngster that came in, telling them that it was difficult. But we were also honest in telling them the tutoring was available."

While Drummer remembers few courses he took at Tech, Banks remembers him taking some textile courses and Slayton remembers him taking some courses that he did not need as an industrial management major.

"We had to give him some free elective work because he didn't have the background to go into all the required courses he needed," says Slayton. "Sometimes you have to give the athlete things that don't count toward graduation to keep him around and give him a chance to get his feet on the ground."

As a basketball player, Drummer had no such adjustment problems. He was All-Metro Conference as a junior in 1977-78 and, as a senior, led Tech to its best record (17-9) of the 13-year period from 1972-1984. His career scoring average of 22.3 points per game is the second highest in Tech history.

Following his senior season, Drummer dropped out of Tech and awaited the annual spring draft of the National Basketball Association, where the minimum salary in 1979 was $35,000 per year and the average salary was $170,000. But instead of being a first-round draft choice—as he was predicted to be before his senior season—Drummer was not selected until the fourth round, by the Houston Rockets. They released him after a summer tryout camp, shattering his only lifetime goal.

"I didn't ever want to come home," he says. "I wanted to go off and melt or something."

Drummer had tryouts later in the summer with the San Antonio Spurs and Kansas City Kings but he was cut by them also.

Many pro scouts and coaches felt Drummer, at 6-5, was too small to play forward and not a good enough ball-handler to play guard. And wherever he tried to play, he carried the tag of a fourth-round draft pick. If he had been a first-round choice, he would have been virtually assured of making a team.

Banks believes Drummer was hurt by playing at Georgia Tech, where Morrison's deliberate offense did not showcase Drummer's running and jumping ability, only his excellent shooting skills.

Banks—who left Tech to become an assistant coach at the University of Georgia before Drummer's senior season—says he made a mistake in "placing" Drummer at Tech.

Finally, in the fall of '79, Drummer got a job with the Harlem Globetrotters. He signed a $35,000 contract, but in only four months he had gone from basketball stud to basketball clown.

Then in November 1980, during his second season with the Globetrotters' international team, Drummer, along with teammate Rickey Brown, was arrested in Sao Paulo, Brazil, for possession of marijuana and cocaine. Drummer contends that he was "set up" by a group of Brazilians hoping to obtain a payoff from the Globetrotters and that the cocaine and marijuana were planted in his hotel room. Drummer says he has never used cocaine and only smoked marijuana in college.

Although he was never convicted, Drummer was fired by the Globetrotters and, after spending two months in a Sao Paulo jail, was deported to the U.S.

His future as a pro player—in the U.S. or Europe—was suddenly very dim. "There wasn't any opportunity from there on," says Banks. "There was no way you could explain it (the drug charges)."

Moving in with Banks, Drummer took a construction job in Athens. "That's something I never figured I'd be doing," he says.

Banks did get Drummer a tryout with the Hawks in the summer of '81 but he was released. Later that year Banks got Drummer a tryout in Belgium, but he didn't make that team either.

Afterward, Drummer went back to Muncie to live with his girlfriend.

Unable to find steady work in Muncie, Drummer spent a year putting roofs and siding on houses and cutting trees, to sell for firewood. He got his job at Ball State (18,000 enrollment) almost two years ago when the supervisor of custodial services, Jim Frazier, made a deal with him. "He said if I played basketball on his (industrial league) team and we won the league, he'd hire me," says Drummer. "We went 13-0."

Drummer's nightly duties include dusting, sweeping, cleaning bathrooms and labs, picking up trash in vending areas and locking up as many as a dozen buildings at the end of his shift. University Gym is one of his buildings.

Driving a van with mop buckets hanging in the back, Drummer gets a call on his beeper when a janitor is needed in his area: A professor has locked his keys in his office, there's a water leak, someone has gotten sick. "You be doing something important," says Drummer, "and some student drops a pop and you have to run over there to clean it up."

Although he smiles as often as ever, Drummer says he is bitter about the way his life has turned out. He says that if he could do it over, he would stay at one school. "Transferring so much," he says, "they (the pros) might have wondered, 'What kind of guy is this?' "

Drummer had looked forward to taking care of his family financially by playing in the NBA but says he doesn't earn enough money even to marry his girlfriend, Rosemary Bailey. She has four children by a previous marriage, a fifth by Drummer and another by Drummer on the way. He has thought about working two jobs, as well as completing his degree at Ball State.

Banks believes Drummer really would like to have a college degree. "I don't think he would have paid the price to sit in class and be humiliated over and over again if he didn't," says Banks.

Drummer hasn't talked with Banks in 1½ years and has lost contact with all his other former college coaches and teammates. He says he hasn't heard from his former agent, Jack Manton of Cumming, since the arrest in Brazil.

Drummer plays basketball once a week in a Muncie industrial

league at his old junior high school, plays in pickup games at Ball State on his days off and would like to switch to the morning work shift so he would have more time to play basketball. He is unable to relinquish the dream completely.

"I haven't given up. I love the sport too much to give up just like that," he says. "I sit back and watch and deep inside of me I know I should be out there. I would like to give it one more shot."

It's not a dream Drummer necessarily holds for his children, however. He tells a story about his girlfriend's 9-year-old son, who loves to play basketball. The boy recently brought home a report card with two F's on it. Drummer was upset: "I told him, 'I'm not that smart, but I'd rather see y'all learn something than be like I am now.' "

My Life With The Redskins

PRO FOOTBALL

By _GEORGE STARKE_ with _RANDY RIELAND_

From The Washingtonian
Copyright © 1985, Washington Magazine Inc.

Joe Gibbs came right to the point.

"We don't want to cut you because you've done a lot for the organization," he said. "So we'll let you retire."

My 13-year career with the Redskins was over. I was in shock. When Joe Bugel told me he wanted to see me up in Gibbs' office that Tuesday, I thought they were going to tell me I was going on the injured-reserve list. Having played in the National Football League for that long, I certainly had enough injuries to qualify. That's what they would have done in George Allen's days when a player was near the end of his career. They'd carry you on the injured reserve your last year so even though you might not play, you wouldn't suddenly be without an income. That way you'd have time to reorganize your life. But the Redskins don't do that anymore.

I wasn't angry or bitter. I was just numb. It's funny; I had seen a lot of players end their careers, and I always could see it coming for them. But not for me. It's something you can't prepare yourself for.

Instead of going to Tampa Bay with the rest of the team for our last preseason game, I went to stay with some friends in New York. I had to get out of town. I had absolutely no idea what I was going to do. One day you don't have to go to work anymore; that's not easy at any age.

Bill Bradley described it well in his book. He said it's like you die twice. There you are in your '30s, and just like that your life as an athlete is over. You have to get your affairs in order. And people start to talk about you in the past tense.

One of the hardest things is that your relationship with the guys on the team changes. The day you leave you're never again part of the team. Sonny Jurgensen has a story about that. He says that a week after he retired, he and his wife went out to dinner with a group of the guys from the team. Afterwards he said to Margot, his wife, "Did that seem strange to you?" And she said, "Yeah, there's something different. You're not a part of those guys anymore."

The guys may look at you the same way and talk to you the same way, but an emotional link has been broken. They have a common purpose, a common goal, and even though you were a part of it a few days ago, you aren't anymore. It's a very strange feeling.

You miss a lot of little things, things you take for granted. For 12 years I went into the locker room and turned right and there was my locker. So the first time I went back to the locker room after I retired, I walked in, turned right, and saw that my name was gone. Then I saw Riggins had taken my locker. I was there to work out, so I piled my stuff on top of Riggins'. I couldn't imagine using another locker. When John came back into the locker room, I told him, "My stuff's in your locker." And he said, "You've come a long way. You can call it my locker."

What he didn't know was that I had to practice saying it.

★   ★   ★

One of the ironies of my lasting so long in the NFL is that I was never that crazy about football. I never considered myself a big tough guy, and I thought the violence was unnatural. My first love was basketball. My second was swimming.

But the football coach drafted me back in tenth grade at New Rochelle High School in New York. He grabbed the back of my trunks as I was diving into the pool and said, "Starke, football practice starts upstairs."

I didn't even know how to put the equipment on. But I ended up being a high school All-America. The reason was that I was big *and* quick. Most of the other linemen were just big.

I could have gone to college almost anywhere. The offers were incredible—money, cars, guaranteed admission to graduate school for me or anyone else in my family, dates with the cheerleaders. But I would always ask the same question: What if I decide to quit football? They would hem and haw, then finally say, "Well, we'd have to take it all back." I just couldn't imagine going to college with that hanging over my head, that I would have to play football, which I still wasn't nuts about. Besides, I felt big-time college football wasn't so much fun. The recruiters from those schools would look at you like you were a slab of meat. They would stare at your legs, stare at your arms. It was so dehumanizing. That wasn't how I wanted to play football.

So I went to Columbia University, where they didn't have football scholarships. I was easily the biggest guy on the team, but I made a deal with the coach that I would play tight end if I outran the other receivers. I outran them all. Of course, this was Columbia, so they weren't exactly the cream of the crop.

Still, George Allen drafted me in 1971, the year he jumped from the Rams to the Redskins. He called and asked if I could play anything else; the Redskins didn't need tight ends. I said, "I don't know, maybe tackle." He said, "OK," then click, he hung up the phone. The next day he drafted me in the 11th round.

When I got to camp, the first thing I heard about George was that no rookie had ever played for him. He didn't like them, I was told. That was bad enough. But on top of that, eight veteran tackles were competing for three spots. It was terrifying and exhilarating. Here I was, coming out of Columbia, I had never considered myself a football player, and suddenly I'm playing against some of the biggest, meanest sons of bitches I had ever seen. I lasted two weeks.

Hank Stram, then the coach of the Kansas City Chiefs, picked me up. I made it through the preseason before I was cut, but he told me, "I like you, kid. You're going to make it in this league. I want you to hang around and work out, and as soon as someone gets hurt, I'll put you on the club." That was back before I knew football was a business, so I believed him.

I stayed around and worked out every day. Every time someone would get hurt, I would go to see Hank and say, "Now coach?" and he would say, "Not now, George." After about six weeks I went to him and told him I didn't have any money. He said we might be able to work out a deal.

He said he could arrange for the organization to lend me $300. Stram was also the team's general manager and could do just about anything he wanted. But he told me he didn't know if the organization would go along with the loan and that one way of convincing them to do it would be for me to sign a contract to play for the Chiefs the following year. That was illegal; a player not under contract can't, during the season, sign with a team for the next year. But Stram told me he would keep the contract in his desk drawer and pull it out when it was legal. I needed the cash so I signed. I ended up working for 11 weeks before I realized the Chiefs weren't going to call me up. So demoralized and without having played one pro game, I retired from the NFL.

Then the Dallas Cowboys, of all teams, came knocking. I was living in this out-of-the-way place with a woman I had met when a stranger showed up at our door. He said he was from the Cowboys and that they had been looking all over the country for me. He said Stram had been telling people he didn't know where I was.

I told him I had retired from football, but he insisted on taking me to dinner, which was a good idea because I hadn't been out to dinner for a long time. I had no intention of getting back into pro football. Then he offered me a $500 cash bonus if I signed with the Cowboys. That did it. I wanted to go home for the holidays, and I needed the money. So I signed. This contract, unlike the one in Hank Stram's desk drawer, was legal because the season was over.

Stram was beside himself when he found out about it. He

couldn't push it, though, because he knew the Kansas City contract wasn't any good. For years after that he wrote me, asking for the $300 back.

The next year I tried out with the Cowboys as a tight end, competing against a rookie, Jean Fugett, whom I became good friends with. He won. I was cut again. But five minutes after I was released by the Cowboys, the Redskins signed me and I left for the long drive to Carlisle. By the end of the year, 1972, I would be getting ready to play in the Super Bowl against the Dolphins.

★   ★   ★

I came in as the youngest guy on the oldest team in football. The Redskins back then were Charley Taylor, Billy Kilmer, Richie Petitbon, Lenny Hauss, Chris Hanburger, Diron Talbert, Verlon Biggs, Ray Schoenke, Bill Brundige, Ron McDole, Jack Pardee—a bunch of tough, crusty veterans who could figure out five ways to beat you and five ways to help you beat yourself. They were guys the rest of the league said were too old, too fat, too slow, or too much trouble. And they were too old and too slow. But they also were the meanest and the smartest.

I grew a lot by playing with them, by being around men with limited abilities who overcame their limitations. Like Pat Fischer, a little, slow, white cornerback who still managed to be one of the best in the league. Or Larry Brown and Lenny Hauss, two of the toughest men I'd ever seen, both playing with their legs all banged up.

I learned that you have no limitations unless you place them upon yourself. And toward the end of my career, when guys like the Hogs, who really are very talented, came along, I tried to share a little of that history with them. Because I had seen guys with nothing, guys all beaten up and taped together, go out and win. That's what makes greatness. I'm glad I was able to hang around until the Redskins won the Super Bowl in 1983. It was like a little bit of the old guys was still out there on the field.

More than anyone, George Allen was responsible for the Over-the-Hill Gang's playing way over their heads. He was the master motivator, also a tremendous defensive strategist. Had he possessed the offensive skills of a Joe Gibbs, he would have been unbeatable.

But he was, above all, a motivator. The thing you have to remember is that by the time they get to the pros, football players have heard every kind of pep talk you could imagine. And the Over-the-Hill Gang was the oldest team in football, so they had really heard it all. Still George would always come up with some new scheme every week.

One that stands out came the week before we were to play the Dolphins in 1973. This was the year after we lost the Super Bowl to them, so George really wanted to win badly. There we were at the Monday-morning team meeting, and George comes in and sits down. "Forget the game this week," he says. "I don't want you guys out on the field. I don't want their guys out on the field, either.

"I don't like Don Shula. So it's going to be him and me at the 50-yard line. And we're going to battle it out, winner take all."

We're sitting there, wondering what he's leading up to, and then, his voice rising, he says, "To show you how serious I am, I've been gettin' ready for this battle." Just as he says that, the door bursts open and in comes Jhoon Rhee, the karate expert. Turns out that George has been taking karate at night. So Jhoon Rhee brings out these boards, and George stands up and announces, "I'm going to do this to Shula." He turns around, and just like that he breaks a board. Then another board. Then he tells us, "I've never broken three boards, but this is Shula week, so I'm going to break three boards." So he whacks the third board and smashes his hand. I mean blood is going everywhere, and we're sitting there thinking, "What is this guy doing?" And he just shoves his hand in his pocket and says, "Dismissed."

Another time he got Mike Hull, a special-teams player, to come back and talk to us the day after George released him. This guy's been cut, his career's over. It's the most difficult and painful time of his life, yet George gets him to come back in and tell those of us who still had our careers how he felt about losing his. "It doesn't matter what you do," Mike said, "you should always do it with your mightiest heart." Then he broke down and cried. That phrase "your mightiest heart" stuck with me. For years, when I was getting ready for games, I would think back on it.

Allen was great, a real players' coach. He never talked much to me, though, because I was an offensive player. George was so defensive-minded that he was very uncomfortable around offensive players. It was like they had some disease he would catch if he touched them. But he made his defensive guys feel they could do anything.

Joe Gibbs, by contrast, isn't much of a motivator. He's the master strategist, at least offensively. For defense, he relies on Richie Petitbon, who was one of Allen's generals. Gibbs comes across as the brainy professor, although he's grown with the job and is a little more comfortable around players than he used to be. But he has to have a team with leaders, a team that's self-motivated. That's why he was very fortunate in coming here to a team that had veterans who were used to winning, who knew what it takes to win. Joe came up with the strategy, and in 1982 he took us to the Super Bowl.

★   ★   ★

Remember the big Billy-versus-Sonny quarterback controversy? It was so much media hype; they were close friends. On the field, though, they were very, very different.

Billy was one of the most intense players I've ever seen. His intensity in the huddle was such that he would bite your face off if you messed up. He didn't care how big you were. And when he got sacked, he'd scream at these big defensive linemen, "F--- you. We're going to kick your ass all day."

He wasn't the most skilled quarterback, so he had to get everything out of himself to do the job. He didn't seem to throw the ball; it's more like he willed it downfield. And sometimes he would get so emotional, so intense, that he would call plays we didn't have in our playbook. None of the guys, not even the big linemen, had the nerve to tell him he had called the wrong play. We'd just improvise.

This happened over and over during one Monday night game against the Cowboys. The game had gone into overtime, and Billy's getting all excited, calling these plays we didn't have. Finally, we get down to the 1-yard line and he simply says, "Sweeney, I'm comin' over you." Which meant he was going to run a quarterback sneak over Walt Sweeney, our guard.

The only problem was that we didn't have a quarterback sneak. But we figured out the blocking, Billy goes in for the touchdown, and we win the game. After that, "Sweeney, I'm comin' over you" became a favorite line around town. The Redskins, to this day, don't have a quarterback sneak and if they did they wouldn't run it much because Joe Theismann's one of the worst in the league at it.

Now, for Sonny, football was like a stroll in the park. He was always cool and confident and was the best quarterback I've ever seen. A classic Sonny story: 1973, the same game against the Dolphins that George Allen had smashed up his hand for. George never liked Sonny, probably because he didn't like offensive-minded ballplayers and Sonny was the ultimate offensive player. But Billy wasn't having a good game, so near the end, when we're deep in the hole, George sent Sonny in.

Sonny hasn't played in weeks. He trots into the huddle, then gets down on one knee. He pulls up a blade of grass, sticks it in his mouth, and says, "We're down six points. We have 96 yards to go. We got 50 seconds left. There's really only one question we have to address in this huddle: What are we going to do with the extra 20 seconds?"

Sure as hell, Sonny whips us down the field in 30 seconds, we score a touchdown, and win. That was Sonny. The game held no mystery for him. He made you feel, "The Dolphins are no big deal. This 96 yards we have to go is no big deal." That was his style. Joe Theismann couldn't say something like that in the huddle. It would sound ridiculous.

In truth, quarterbacks are seldom the real team leaders. They're glorified in the media and in the eyes of high school cheerleaders everywhere. But usually quarterbacks aren't tough guys, and out on the field the tough guys are the ones you rally around when things aren't going well.

You need someone to take charge out there because a lot of things can go wrong on the football field. Talk about crises. Football players have to be crisis-oriented. It's fourth down and 25 to go, 10 seconds are left, and you have to block a defensive end who looks like a werewolf. That's a crisis. Or with 80,000 people in the stadium and millions more watching on TV, you make a mistake and you know they're going to replay it 10 times in slow motion and every old lady from Bristol, Conn. to Santa Barbara will know the right tackle's a bum. That's a crisis.

★   ★   ★

When you get right down to it, playing football is an unnatural thing to do for a living. Unless you're psychotic, the concept of once a week getting into a fist-fight with somebody you don't know is really a little strange. I would drive through Rock Creek Park on the way to the games, and it would be a beautiful fall morning. People would be strolling along the Potomac or riding their bikes or playing with their kids, and I'd be driving to get into a fight. It was violence by appointment.

You have to learn how to get yourself prepared to do that. If you don't, you'll be hammered because you know the other guy will be prepared. Getting psyched up in high school is easy; by the time you're a pro, it's different. It's your career and you have to find ways to make your adrenaline pump. You have to learn how to trick yourself into being mean.

Everyone has their own way. Pete Cronan used to yell and scream; he had a very violent way of getting himself ready. But most guys are very quiet about it. They're also very superstitious. They never vary their routines. Everybody knows what John Riggins is going to do before a game. He gets a shot of B12. Riggins is from the old school, the days when B12 was considered a kind of legal amphetamine. Now everyone knows that's not true, but it's important to John. Probably at some point in his career somebody gave him a B12 shot and he had a good game. The funny thing is that Riggins hates shots. We'd hear his yell from the trainer's room and know he'd had his shot. It was time to go to work and kick ass.

I had my own superstitions. I would always come into the locker room a little late, put on my uniform in the same order, sit the same way in the same chair, get taped by the same trainer. And I'd think about great, tough, courageous people I had known. They didn't have to be football players, just people who I thought were dedicated. I would imagine they were watching me and I didn't want to let them down. It was a very private thing.

I would always click in by the time I walked out on the field. One time, though, I clicked into game mode without realizing it. I was in a movie theater watching North Dallas Forty. And there's this scene where John Matuszak is getting himself pumped up, pounding his fists together, pounding the lockers. Matuszak is a very big, very mean boy and I was watching what I knew really was his personal form of preparation. I had played against Matuszak, and as I watched him getting ready I start thinking I can't let him go out on the field being more intense than I am. So I clicked in. I stood up in the middle of this theater and started yelling, "Matuszak, you son of a bitch, I'll kick your ass." My date pulled on my arm. She thought I'd gone nuts.

I didn't realize what I was doing. It was like this other person had taken over.

Some guys do a lot of talking on the field. They talk in the huddle, they talk on the line, they talk to other players, they talk to themselves. Usually the guys who talk the most are the ones who aren't sure of themselves. They're nervous. I knew I was getting too old when I started talking too much.

The Redskins offensive and defensive linemen seldom talk, except for Mark May. Some guys, especially linebackers, do it to get themselves pumped up. Linebackers make noise; they have to keep up their emotional intensity because they don't know if they'll be covering a halfback on a pass or taking on a giant guard. Some defensive backs talk a lot, too, mainly to wide receivers. They want them to think too much, to flinch at the wrong moment because they're worrying about getting hit. Wide receivers don't talk much at all. They don't want to seem like they're paying attention to what the defensive backs are telling them. Their way of answering is spiking the ball when they score a touchdown.

Still, despite all the action, there's surprisingly little talk on the field. Here's an example: For 12 years, two games a year, I played across the line from Too Tall Jones of the Cowboys. For about 75 plays a game, our faces were a foot apart. These were some very emotional games, too; one time he split my helmet right down the middle with his fist. But in all that time, in all those intense moments, we never exchanged a word, with one exception. The year we won the Super Bowl we first beat Dallas in the NFC championship game. And at the end of the game Too Tall said, "Good luck, you deserved it." That's it. One sentence in 12 years.

Still, I don't have any doubt that if I were stranded in Dallas without a place to stay, I could call Too Tall and he'd invite me over. Without exchanging a word we developed a relationship on the field.

★   ★   ★

You're expected to do a lot of things on a football field that your better judgment tells you not do. Take kickoffs: You're supposed to go running down the field at top speed for 40 yards and then smash into another guy running at you. It makes no sense, which is why just about everyone cheats. The times that I did it, I would always turn away or flinch at the last second before I ran into somebody. The coaches tell you, "Don't slow down, don't slow down, don't slow down." And you're thinking, "My knee, my career, my life." And they'll carry me off and get someone else out there, and the coaches will tell him, "Don't slow down, don't slow down, don't slow down."

When he was here, Rusty Tillman was one guy who could do it. He would throw his body into the three-man wedge, and I would wonder how he kept from killing himself. Otis Wonsley is another. But there probably aren't five guys in the league who can do it. When you're running full-speed at someone, it's a strange moment of truth.

Blocking punts is another unnatural act. They expect you to throw your face and body into someone's leg as he's kicking. Even

Rusty, who was like a madman on kickoffs, couldn't block a punt. Only person I knew who could do it was Billy Malinchak. He would pick the ball right off the guy's foot. But most people figure they're going to get kicked in the face, so they turn away at the last second. I've never seen anyone get kicked in the face, but you can't escape thinking it. Even if you know how bad you'll look on the films, you're still going to pull away. That's why, even when you see guys get in there cleanly, they rarely block the kick.

I'm amazed at some things people could do. Think about being a 180-pound wide receiver going over the middle, stretching for a ball, and knowing that a 240-pound linebacker is going to smash into your ribs or face. I've seen Frank Grant and a lot of other guys get their faces broken going over the middle. I wouldn't do that for all the money in the world.

You never dwell on injuries, because you can't worry about things that you can't control. If you start worrying too much, you should think about doing something else for a living. But it really is a spooky feeling to see someone get hurt.

I don't ever remember consciously thinking, "That could be me," but that has to be what makes you feel so uneasy. It has to be the reason players move away from injured players. It has to be the reason coaches whisk them away so they're out of sight from the rest of the team.

The worst thing is to see the film of someone getting hurt. When Jeff Bostic hurt his knee last year, we almost raced through the film. That's the last thing you want to see in slow motion. To watch a guy's knee get twisted or buckled—that gives you goose bumps. Players are superstitious. They don't like to hang around injured players. It's almost like you're afraid of catching something from them.

That's always been true. One thing that's changed, though, is the attitude about playing hurt. I think of guys like Lenny Hauss, Jack Pardee, Diron Talbert, who would play every play, no matter how much they were hurting. They would never leave the field, never complain. Many times they would fix broken fingers out on the field. And they wouldn't let you leave the field unless you couldn't walk. Now a guy gets a hangnail and he doesn't go out on the field for two weeks.

One big reason I lasted so long is that, first, I didn't get hurt that often, and second, I would play when I was hurt. Diron used to tell me, "If you want to play a long time, never leave your hat on the field." He meant that you should never leave the field. If you let somebody else out there, they might find you can be replaced. The key is getting them used to seeing you out there.

★   ★   ★

Football can be a wonderfully complex chess game built on elaborate strategies. But you'd never know it based on what you hear from television announcers. There really is a whole other game happening on the field from the one you see on TV. Announcers like

Pat Summerall and Frank Gifford haven't played for so long that they're years behind the strategies.

Sometimes they just make up things. For example: How many times have you heard an announcer say, "The quarterback just called an audible"? All teams have elaborate ways of disguising the few times they do call audibles at the line. Usually the defensive players don't even know when it's done. So how do the guys in the booth know? They don't. They just make it up. They also tend to focus on a great catch or a nice run, but they don't give you much information on what's really happening on the field. Like how an offense can attack a particular defense; why a defense works against one team and not another; how a series of plays have been calculated to set up a particular run. Most broadcasters just focus on a specific play, without putting it into the context of what has led up to it. I think fans want to be more aware of the chess game.

The media also tend to make a big deal about players who don't deserve all the attention. There are some truly impressive players in the league, guys like Walter Payton and Howie Long. But then you have guys like Mark Gastineau or Lyle Alzado, who really aren't that impressive but are built up by the media all the time. They're made into heroic figures because they're colorful.

Maybe it's hard for me to be objective about this because it was my position, but some great offensive linemen never get the credit they're due. Hardly anyone could name two members of the Dolphins' offensive line, but Dan Marino is on the cover of every magazine in print. Say for 75 plays of a game an offensive lineman does exactly what he's supposed to do; he blocks the player he's supposed to block. But say his man makes two sacks and he gets called for holding twice. That's all the announcers will focus on, and every old lady from Bristol, Conn., to Santa Barbara, Calif., will think he's a bum.

Announcers can do a lot to your reputation. Earlier this season, Hank Stram came right out and said Joe Theismann was having problems because he was over 35 and that when quarterbacks reach that age they hit the wall and no longer have the courage to stay in the pocket. He said it definitively. That's just not true.

But people start to believe it. Even coaches and general managers start to believe it if they hear it or read it enough. A negative image is created. And maybe a few years down the road a general manager may not take a chance on you because he remembers something he read about you years ago.

That's one reason ball players don't trust sportswriters; they can write things that directly affect your career. I'm not just talking about hurting your ego; I'm talking about helping you lose your job. We've got mortgage payments and car payments just like everyone else.

Writers tend to look for headlines or a controversy, regardless of the consequences for the players or the team. And because this is a political town—which makes it boring by definition—there's pressure to come up with something big every day. It's that push for headlines that makes athletes reticent, that makes them respond in pat phrases.

Let's say when I was playing, a writer had asked me how I felt about playing against Too Tall Jones the next week. The honest answer might be, "He's not that tough as a pass rusher and he plays the run fairly well. He's impressive to sportswriters because he's so big and he's a Dallas Cowboy." The next day the Dallas papers would say that George Starke said Too Tall Jones was a wimp. That writer would be making Sunday a long day for me.

In some ways I think a writer would rather have you lose because a negative story is easier to write than a positive one. You can't write so much if Joe Theismann has a good day. But if he has a bad day, you can bring up Cathy Lee Crosby or all the television he's doing or all the time he's spending at his restaurant.

Or it's like if John Riggins gets drunk at a dinner. Every paper in the country would be all over him. But if John had been given some award, it would have been a minor item. Part of the problem is that people like to read about fallen heroes.

Another example is all the stories about players' using cocaine. It's a false issue. Personally, I don't think most people care if a player uses cocaine or not. The media are just laying on it to sell papers.

In fact, football today is drug-free compared to what it used to be like. When I first came up, amphetamines were part of the game. The older linemen would come up to me before a game and say, "Are you OK? Do you need anything?" For a while I didn't know what they were talking about. In one game when I first started playing, I looked across the line at this guy and he had no pupils. That was scary. Then I looked and saw this linebacker chewing on his moustache and jumping all over the place. He couldn't stand still.

One reason I never took speed to play is that I never could forget how that guy looked without any pupils. It scared me. Plus my ego wouldn't let me think that I had to use speed to beat somebody. It never made you a better ball player anyway. It was just a way to get you in the mood to hit somebody. And once players realized it wasn't in their best interest to use it, they stopped.

★　　★　　★

Offensive linemen never had any notoriety. That is, until the Hogs. I'll take some credit for that. I just didn't want to be as anonymous when I left the game as I was when I came in. Now people wear Hog shirts and Hog snouts and actually talk about offensive linemen.

It started in training camp before the 1982 season when Joe Bugel, the offensive-line coach, looked down at Russ Grimm in a four-point stance, and seeing his belly hanging down, said, "You look like a hog." A week later Bugel came out on the field with these T-shirts with hogs on them, and he says, "We're going to call ourselves the Hogs." You have to remember that this was training camp, which is dull and monotonous. You'll do anything to break the monotony. So when the tight ends said they wanted to be Hogs because they block, too, we had a little ceremony and voted them in.

The media picked up on it, and because we were having a great season, the Hogs started getting attention. We became synonymous with the Redskins' success. Next the wide receivers came up with "the Fun Bunch." Originally, it was "the Buck-Naked Fun Bunch" because they met in the shower, but the media just picked up "the Fun Bunch."

Anyway, through that season all that existed was the name "the Hogs"—no T-shirts, no posters. After the Super Bowl, though, I thought, "Why don't we make some money out of this?" and told the guys that if they each chipped in $500, I would form a corporation and handle everything. I figured if anyone was going to make money off this, we should be the ones. So I formed a corporation called Superhogs and registered the name "the Hogs." And we began marketing Hog products to a town hungry for Hog paraphernalia.

Then we created the "Hogs' Night Out" poster—that's my living-room furniture in it. We posed in the tuxedos because it was time to upgrade the image of offensive linemen. Quarterbacks are always stylish, wide receivers are always described as gazelles, but the image of linemen was big, dumb, grubby guys. Our image was important, I said, so after that every time we ate together, we would come downtown in limos and in our tuxedos.

The first dinner was at the Palm, and the place went nuts. The Hogs, the waiters, and the customers sang the night away. And thus was born "Hogs' Night Out," a tradition I hope they continue. Eventually, we went national—a story in *Sports Illustrated* and a McDonald's commercial with the Baltimore Orioles. And we became the most famous offensive line in NFL history.

The whole thing was a radical idea. Individual agents might get commercials for a player, but never before had a group of players marketed themselves.

★   ★   ★

George, what's wrong with the Redskins?

That's all I heard during the first part of the season. Everyone was looking for some easy answer, some insight that would explain why a team with so much talent was having so many problems. It's never that easy to explain.

Recently, I read something about men in combat. This veteran wrote, "People don't fight for the flag. They don't fight for Mom. They don't fight for their country. In combat, you fight for your buddies." Football's a lot like that. You don't play for the money. You don't play for the city of Washington. You play for each other.

You develop this intense bond. If it doesn't develop, you'll never have a great team. The big difference between a good team and a bad team is that on a bad one you just have a group of individuals out on the field.

Sometimes the problem goes all the way through an organization. Every year you hear how good the New England Patriots are going to be. But they never go anywhere. I think it's an attitude problem that goes to the top of the organization. First, you can't have a constant turnover in coaches; you can't constantly be in transition. You also need to have an owner who the players feel gives a damn about them. How can you play for a guy like Robert Irsay, the owner of the Colts? The flip side is someone like Art Rooney of the Steelers. He's a great owner. When Joe Greene retired, the Steelers gave him severance pay, which is something teams didn't have to do back then. It meant something to the other players.

I always felt Washington has had one of the best organizations in football. That's why we had only one losing season in my 13 years here. When George Allen was coach, he pretty much said to Edward Bennett Williams, then the owner, "I'll give you a winning team. You pay the bills and stay away." George didn't want him hanging around the sidelines or bringing friends through the locker room to show off his "boys."

Jack Kent Cooke likes to get more personally involved with the team. I think to some extent his ego has gotten caught up with the team. He likes to brag that the Redskins will do this and that they'll do that, and when they don't, he takes it as a personal affront.

The team also has a leadership problem. "Scrappy," Larry Kubin's nickname, is gone. Mark Murphy is gone; so is Joe Washington. And, without patting myself on the back, I was one of the leaders, too. You need players whom the other guys can lean on when things aren't going your way during a game. Coaches can't do that. You don't have the same kind of relationship with them.

During the first couple weeks of the season, after the Redskins had lost to the Cowboys and the Eagles, I kept reading that the Redskins couldn't win without George Starke. It was very flattering for two weeks. By the third week it started to bother me.

So one day when I was out at the stadium working out, I told some of the guys, "Look, enough is enough. I'm tired of reading this. You must *really* be tired of reading this. Go out and kick someone's ass. It's time for somebody else to come forward."

I never planned on being a leader. I had never been a captain of anything, going back to high school, and I ended up being one of the captains of a Super Bowl team. I grew into the role, as did other Redskins who had learned how to win with the Over-the-Hill Gang.

Someone will come forward on this team. But it does have a different chemistry from the team that won the Super Bowl three years ago. That was a team of destiny. I know that sounds like a cliche, but it really was. Most people don't have an opportunity to be part of something great, but that was our time. It was a magical season. Everything came together.

By the time we got to the Super Bowl, it never occurred to us that we would lose. The amazing thing is that we ran the same play over and over in that game and the Dolphins couldn't stop us. It crushed them psychologically to see that we didn't feel the need to trick them. We dominated the game like no offensive line ever has.

The next year we made it to the Super Bowl again, but we lost to the Raiders. I still think we had the best team in football, but the whole year was a struggle. The magical quality wasn't there anymore.

★   ★   ★

The other day I was riding in an elevator, and a woman looked over at me and said, "Are you a football player?" After a pause, I said, "No." "Well, you should have been," she laughed.

Life after football has taken some getting used to. I don't miss playing much. But I do miss being part of the team. And I miss the image. It's nice being larger than life. You hear all this hype about yourself for years, and it's hard not to believe it.

But you have to reflect on what you really are. In my case, I know at least some of my success had to do with being in the right place at the right time. I played with some great players and on some very good teams. It means a lot to me to be able to say, "I played with Sonny Jurgensen," or "I played with Larry Brown."

I was lucky enough to span several eras of the Redskins and when I look back on my career, it's a kaleidoscope of different images. Starting out with George Allen and the "Over-the-Hill Gang"—some of the most courageous men I've ever known—and ending with the Hogs, maybe the best offensive line in the history of the NFL. There are certain plays I can visualize: Riggins' touchdown run in the Super Bowl; Billy Kilmer beating Dallas in overtime on the quarterback sneak we didn't have in the playbook; Kenny Houston stopping Walt Garrison on the one-foot line in a big game against Dallas, maybe the best defensive play I've ever seen.

Another special thing about having played in Washington is that in this town it's hard not to feel important as a football player. Football has winners and losers, it's black and white, and against a backdrop of the grayness of politics, the Redskins have more appeal than they might somewhere else.

Another good thing about playing in Washington is that it's a town that is often polarized between blacks and whites, Republicans and Democrats, conservatives and liberals, but the team can be a unifying force. It was great to be part of a group of men who can bring people together on Sunday who hated each other on Saturday.

I really believe there's nothing in this town that more directly affects people's lives than the Redskins. Not even the President. People were proud when the President ordered the Navy jets to bring back the Palestinian hijackers. The Redskins are capable of making people feel pride like that every week. It's a great feeling to affect people like that.

When you have a good day, it's almost like the whole city smiles. How can you beat that?

Hagler Puts End to Brawl And to Hearns in Third

BOXING

By *RICHARD HOFFER*

From the Los Angeles Times
Copyright © 1985, Los Angeles Times

They met immediately in the center of the ring Monday night, with all the elegance of a head-on collision, and thus released the held breath of about 16,000 fans. And for the next 10 minutes, the collective gasp resounded, soaring into the night sky above the outdoor arena. Who could believe what was happening? Had two men, ever, responded to their calling with such commitment, with such self-confidence?

Marvelous Marvin Hagler, whose fierce, bald head would soon run red, had for this night abandoned the sweet science, had refused to employ the master boxing skills that had won him the undisputed middleweight championship. Instead, he stormed into the long right arm of Thomas Hearns, the super-welterweight champion who dared challenge him, either unmindful of his own personal safety or disparaging of Hearns' well-documented offenses.

But did Hearns box in return, did he use his foot speed to spare his body from the shorter boxer's inside digging? He matched Hagler's nameless bravado and he traded until he had no more to offer, until his long legs betrayed him, until Hagler bombed him on the top of the head with a lurching, overhand right, sending him reeling to the floor, soon flat on his back.

The most anticipated fight in three years, a fight that guaranteed the two champions a combined $11 million minimum, was over, with referee Richard Steele waving Hagler off, supporting a dazed Hearns against the ropes until Hearns' handlers could arrive and carry him off, like a gunnysack. Boxing's two best fighters had finally resolved all questions—age vs. youth, height vs. might, you name it—and just 2:01 into the third round. It was over. And the 16,000 people, rhinestoned-celebrities and cigar-smoking cognoscenti, in their bleacher seats atop some asphalt behind Caesars Palace, remembered to breathe.

It was quite possibly the most remarkable three-round fight in ring history. Certainly it was the most unexpected. Hagler, 30, figured to extend Hearns, 26, if he could, piling up points with the body shots while defending his shaven head, carrying the fight into the late rounds when his celebrated endurance might make a difference. Hearns' strategy was simple and oft-stated. Taller at 6-1, by nearly four inches, he was going to knock Hagler out in three, using the well-leveraged right hand that long ago earned him the Hit Man mystique, that earned him this fight in fact with the sudden dispatch of legendary Roberto Duran, the man Hagler could not finish.

It didn't work out that way Monday night, a warm night with small breezes moving the pennants atop the bleachers. The night began as a cultural affair, with the slight undercard interrupted by seemingly spontaneous applause. It's Jack Nicholson. It's Muhammad Ali. It's Bo Derek. It was strictly Las Vegas, and even the entrance of the two warriors, Hearns to the Michigan fight song, Hagler to a curious military march, seemed only to divert the crowd's attention, perhaps until Magic Johnson or Sylvester Stallone was identified.

But the community of celebrity was quickly engrossed in what developed. It was hard not to be.

Hagler, who weighed 159¼ for his 11th title defense, admitted his surprising rush afterward. It was a terrorist mission, strictly, only one he expected to return from. "I figured I had to take punches to get some," he said. It was a calculated risk; few have ever taken more than a few punches from Hearns, 159¾, and stood to return them.

But Hagler, whose long residence in obscurity was possible only because of unbelievable self-confidence, fully expected Hearns' cannons to be small bore, the Hit Man's 34 knockouts in 41 previous fights notwithstanding. There had been some thought, anyway, that Hearns had lost some punch as he moved from welterweight to super-welterweight and now to middleweight. Except for the devastating knockout of Duran last year. That was hard to discount.

But Hagler was right. Hearns could not hurt him, not badly anyway. In that firestorm of a first round, when it was almost impossible to tell one salvo from another, Hearns did connect with a wicked right uppercut. And certainly Hagler was stunned. Yet he did not yield an inch, and before that round was over, he had backed Hearns into the ropes and used his strength to keep him there. The suffering Hearns simply could not box out.

The second round was no less active. Hagler worked his concussive magic on Hearns' nervous system. He hit him with a right hand and a left hook and began to unravel the wiring that kept Hearns' legs steady. In the final 20 seconds of that round, Hagler pinned

Hearns against the ropes, hurting his midsection, hurting it even worse than Sugar Ray Leonard did in their showdown here four years ago.

There was something strange about Hearns in that round, even though he grinned and still bombed back. He seemed to stand in Hagler's way long after he should have removed himself from fire. His legs weren't working.

Throughout all of this, there was the continual threat of stoppage, by the ring doctor of all people. Hagler, whose brow is studded with scar tissue as well might any man with a 61-2-2 record, bled openly. There was a cut high above his right eye, deepened with each round. But the blood ran down the bridge of his nose and though frightful did not obscure his vision. Anyway, most of it seemed to get sopped up on Hearns' shoulder, where Hagler occasionally rested his head to dig to the liver.

The third round belonged to Hagler altogether, although a time-out to inspect Hagler's cut did pose a threat to his domination. Hearns' right hands, though sharp, were no bother otherwise; Hagler suffered them gladly. Then, after ring physician Dr. Donald Romeo gave his permission for more violence—he simply asked Hagler whether he could still see—the overhand right by Hagler. There were two lesser blows, but they were not required. Hearns was on his way down. Falling back and to the side into the ropes.

Steele looked at him, after Hearns hauled himself up before the count, and called it off, making it a three-round TKO. "He was not responsive," Steele said. "I didn't have to ask him questions—I knew he had enough. His eyes were glazed and his legs very wobbly. By the second round, Hagler's punches were really telling on him."

Neither fighter had that much to say after the fight. Of course, Hagler hadn't been saying all that much before the fight; he doesn't talk for just the fun of it. But even in his brief comments, he seemed suddenly charismatic, no longer the working stiff who piled his trade with the flamboyance of a union dockworker. A knockout can do that to personality.

Yes, he wanted to prove something by beating Hearns better than Leonard had. He did. Yes, he said he knew he was on his way after the second round, because "he looked tired going back to his corner. I could tell he was hurt." He said his confidence grew, for that matter, after the first round, when Hearns "threw everything but the kitchen sink." And he could catch it.

Hearns, meanwhile, was generous to Hagler afterward and admitted it was Hagler's fight, certainly not his; he doesn't ordinarily brawl. Why did he allow himself to get sucked into that kind of fight? He shrugged. "I had to protect myself," he said.

He hadn't, it wasn't possible. Hagler's determination—to be the greatest fighter today—was such that he would have walked into a lumber saw to achieve his dream. And Hearns, though no less determined, was not as many-bladed as other fighters had found him, as he himself had thought.

Of course, there was immediate talk of a rematch, though they are never as prosperous as that first mysterious fight between two great fighters. But that surely is a long time coming, as anybody could tell who saw Hearns supported against the ropes, looking into a distance you just can't imagine.

In the World Series, Any Buddy Can Be a Hero

BASEBALL

By *TONY KORNHEISER*

From the Washington Post
Copyright © 1985, the Washington Post

Biancalana. Doesn't that have a nice lilt to it? Go ahead. Divide it into syllables and say it out loud: Bi-an-ca-la-na. Sounds like a crisp, white wine. Excuse me, but might I have a bottle of Biancalana, please? Buddy Biancalana. That's a great name, isn't it? You want to know his real name? Roland Americo Biancalana Jr. How can someone named Anthony Irwin Kornheiser not root for someone named Roland Americo Biancalana Jr.?

You know, it hasn't always been easy on the Biancalana Bus, no sir. Buddy hasn't exactly been Kansas City's answer to Honus Wagner. In his brief major league career—156 games over slivers of two seasons and chunks of two more—Biancalana's batting average is .194, a nifty number for a weekend bowler, but more or less underwater for a major league baseball player. This season, he jolted the old horsehide at a .188 clip. Numbers like that tend to make a brief career briefer. Excuse me, but have you considered getting a day job?

When players slam long home runs, they say they dialed 8 (for long distance). Biancalana had to dial 0 and ask for an outside line just to dial 9. When Pete Rose broke Ty Cobb's record, David Letterman, who first showed his baseball savvy by calling Terry Forster "a fat tub of goo," began the Buddy Biancalana Watch, telling people how many hits Buddy needed to catch Pete in case they wanted to plan ahead. Let's put it this way: if you're thinking of visiting Hawaii anytime in the next 35 years, book the trip.

So guess what?

With hitters such as George Brett, Willie McGee, Tommy Herr, Willie Wilson and Lonnie Smith to choose from, who do you think has

the best on-base percentage of any regular in the World Series?
Biancalana.

(Well, now that you mention it, maybe one glass, thanks. And a breadstick.)

Eight for 16. Fifty percent. Four hits, four walks.

"We've been pitching Biancalana like he's Babe Ruth," groused Whitey Herzog.

And if you find that hard to believe, how about this? The battle of shortstops in this World Series matched Biancalana against Ozzie Smith, which was sort of like matching Pablo Picasso against Earl Scheib. Not that Buddy isn't a good fielder, he certainly is. But Ozzie may wind up in Cooperstown, and Buddy may wind up in siding. So not only is Biancalana hitting 270 points higher than the Wizard of Ahhhs, but with the same number of fielding chances, Buddy is 18 for 18, and Acrobatic Ozzie has one error.

Cue Dom DeLuise: "Surprised?"

Buddy, baby, talk to us.

"Am I surprised?" Biancalana said, repeating the question and grinning. "I'm not going to say I'm surprised, but I'm pleased." Looking out at all the reporters who had gathered around his locker after Thursday night's game in St. Louis, he said, "*You* guys are surprised. Maybe the Cards are surprised. Maybe my manager is surprised. I'm not."

Can you do a back flip?

"I can do a somersault. I'll save it for Game 7," Buddy said, giggling and having a heck of a time. "I'm feeling real good about myself now. I'm having a good Series, and it feels good after the way people got on me during the season. Don't misunderstand me, it was justified—my numbers speak for themselves. But I took this as a second chance after the year I've had, and I may have opened some eyes and shut some mouths."

At 25, he still looks young enough to be carded, and when he took a small furtive sip of the beer he was holding, he might have been a teen-ager from an S.E. Hinton novel. Except that far from feeling alienated, Biancalana felt more secure than ever. "I don't think it can feel any better than this," he said, thinking it over. "I guess maybe I could hit a home run to win a game." He laughed. "Maybe that's in the cards for the sixth game." Everywhere he looked, all he could see was blue sky and candy. "It's been very satisfying. It's going to be a nice winter to walk around in, if we win the Series."

And if the Royals didn't, could he still enjoy the walk?

"Yes. As of now, yes I could."

As of now—and believe me, I never thought I'd be writing this—Buddy Biancalana is in the hunt for the car. And he knows it. "I thought about it a little before the Series—could it *possibly* be me? But to be honest with you, it crossed my mind (Thursday) when I got on three times."

Wouldn't it be something if he won it. How long do you think it would take Letterman to call and invite him onto the show? Fifteen seconds?

"I'd go," Biancalana said happily. "But I'd need some of you guys to write me some lines. I'm not very creative."

Dick Howser, who has to be almost as happy at Biancalana's blossoming as Biancalana is, was in another room, delightedly telling people that the key move in turning Biancalana from beep-beep to boom-boom was batting eighth in this DH-less Series. "They're pitching around him to get to our pitchers," Howser said jokingly.

And so it was asked of Howser if Biancalana is this good moving up one spot in the order, when are you going to bat him cleanup?

Howser laughed. "Not within the next two days, I can assure you."

May I propose a toast then to Kansas City's new star. This, Buddy, is for you.

Caught in the Act

by Matthew McVay of the Seattle Times. Seattle Mariners short-stop Spike Owen holds up the evidence and then adds insult to injury by balancing himself via Otis Nixon's body after tagging out the Indians outfielder on a steal attempt. Copyright © 1985, The Seattle Times.

Concentration

by Dave Kraus of the Tulsa Tribune. Union High School pitcher Tracy Cashel is all arms and legs as she concentrates on her wind-up during action in a girls' softball tournament in Broken Arrow, Okla. Copyright © 1985, The Tulsa Tribune.

John Galbreath

GENERAL

By *ROY McHUGH*

From the Pittsburgh Press
Copyright © 1985, the Pittsburgh Press

You are shown first of all the gleaming bric-a-brac on the mantelpiece, the golden cups side by side, the golden figurines, the tangible prizes other than money, and more to be cherished than money, the things that highly successful racehorses bring to their owners.

Chateaugay and Proud Clarion were such horses, both Kentucky Derby winners, Chateaugay in 1963, Proud Clarion four years later. John Galbreath owned them. Roberto was such a horse, the English Derby winner of 1972, and he is earning his keep for Galbreath as a tireless companion to brood mares.

Do they remember these things back in Pittsburgh? Horses don't count for much in Pittsburgh, where John Galbreath is known to the average citizen as a man who got skyscrapers built and who sank a lot of money in a baseball team so that various .250 hitters could live like racehorse owners themselves.

Galbreath looks up at the mantel. He points out the trophies in the middle of the row, the place of honor, Chateaugay's and Proud Clarion's flanking Roberto's. "Only place in the world you'll see that," he says, being factual rather than boastful, for without any question it's the only place in the world, there on the mantel under the brown-shingled roof of The Residence, his fieldstone and cedar ranch house with oak trees all around it on the Darby Dan Farm in Ohio. Winning two Kentucky Derbies and also the English Derby remains unique in the annals of the turf.

Winning the English Derby was the start of his friendship with Queen Elizabeth, really. She envied him for it. Racing is the sport of queens as well as kings, but only commoners have won the English Derby. Queen Elizabeth's horses finish among the also-rans.

"Did you ever hear the story about the Queen coming over here and carrying on?" Galbreath asks. He is smiling; *lese majeste* doesn't worry him. At 88, one is perfectly free to take liberties. In any case, there's a bond between Galbreath and the Queen.

"The way I got to meet her, have you heard of Walter Annenberg?" Past his fractured rhetorical question, certain that Annenberg's renown as a U.S. ambassador to England has spread to the most ill-informed, Galbreath races on. "A hell of a fellow. I admire him more than anybody I know. He said to me, 'John, I'm going to put on a party.' "

It was to be a party requiring a guest list tailored to Annenberg's notion of company fit for a queen with a special interest. Rule No. 1: No politicians. Rule No. 2: Someone in the crowd who could talk about horses. Nominated, Galbreath flew to London.

That he should hit it off with the Queen was in the cards. They talked about horses for two solid hours, Galbreath astonished at the range of the Queen's knowledge. Somehow the name of Roberto came up. The Queen expressed a desire to breed a mare to the famous ladies' man. Her wish was of course Galbreath's command. "You can't turn the Queen down, you know." You can charge her a stud fee—for Roberto the standard price is $225,000—but it would not be good form. Galbreath was "more than pleased" to observe the code.

There are two Darby Dan farms. Darby Dan in Ohio, near Columbus, is on land that used to be called the Darby Plains. It's where the Galbreath racehorses are weaned and broken and trained. They are bred at Darby Dan in Kentucky, near Lexington. The Queen sent a mare to Kentucky. With Roberto's cooperation, it eventually gave birth to a colt. Not long afterward the announcement went out that the Queen planned to visit America.

Coincidence? Maybe. The Queen has certain official duties. "But no one can ever make me believe that she didn't come over to see her foal," says Galbreath with a twinkle in his eye.

On the day of her arrival at Darby Dan in Kentucky he was waiting. She had an escort of 50 policemen. The Queen handed Galbreath a package and in it was a picture of herself, "about the loveliest thing I've ever seen," Galbreath says. He turns to a woman in a white starched uniform, white stockings and white shoes, a sort of all-around major domo named Jean Justice, and asks her to bring the Queen's gift to the sun porch, where he is having his morning coffee. The full-length photograph, elegantly framed, shows Elizabeth every inch a monarch.

The Queen in real life—and we are now at the crux of Galbreath's story, the part about her carrying on—is a human being, an individual, "a delightful, charming person." She toured the Darby Dan grounds; she saw Roberto; she saw her mare.

"And then I said to her—just kidding; I knew why she'd come—I said to her, 'As long as you're here'—innocent as a baby, you know—'would you like to see your foal?' Well, she walked right up to that foal and put her arm around its neck. And do you know what she did then? I give a dollar to anyone who can tell me. Only four people have guessed. Four dollars it's cost me for a hundred dollars worth of fun. Do you know what she did?" Galbreath is laughing. "She kissed that darn foal on the nose!"

★   ★   ★

In a 1955 Fortune magazine article Galbreath is described as "unpretentious." The Pittsburgh Press, in 1969, described him as "a remarkable man whose deeds and personality have had curiously little impact on either baseball fans or the public in general."

After the seventh game of the 1960 World Series, when Bill Mazeroski's home run beat the New York Yankees, the door of the Pirate clubhouse was closed for a few minutes to the sportswriters. Through the mob came Galbreath and his bodyguards. The door opened briefly for Galbreath alone and as he hurried on in, doing his best to be unobtrusive, a reporter angrily shouted, "Who does that guy think he is?"

Galbreath has never wanted attention. He is not one who longs to be stared at on the street, to be fawned over by maitre d's. Three kinds of people own baseball teams: descendants of the game's pioneers—and there are fewer and fewer of those because it is almost impossible to make a living in baseball any more—faceless conglomerate managers, and rich men yearning for celebrity. John Galbreath is none of the above.

Tom Johnson thinks he knows why Galbreath bought the Pirates in 1946—bought just a piece of them, actually, because Frank McKinney's share, and even Johnson's, were larger. It was not his idea that the franchise would turn a profit. Rather, he considered it "a valuable thing to have for his Pittsburgh contacts," says Johnson.

They were contacts, for the most part, with U.S. Steel. Galbreath had been taking company-owned mill towns off the hands of the corporation, renovating the houses and selling them to the steelworker tenants at down payments as low as 10 percent. He had put up a mill town from scratch and named it for Ben Fairless, U.S. Steel's chairman of the board. In the 1950s Galbreath was to build the U.S. Steel-Mellon Building in Pittsburgh and in the 1960s the U.S. Steel office tower on Grant Street.

He did all this from Columbus. The president of a baseball league, the American Association, also lived in Columbus. George Trautman by name, he introduced Galbreath to McKinney, an Indianapolis banker who had heard that the Pirates were for sale. Galbreath and McKinney agreed to buy them—the purchase price was $2.5 million—and realizing the need for a local partner they brought in Johnson, a lawyer McKinney had met in Washington during the war, when they worked for what now is the Pentagon. Bob Hope at the time was a minority stockholder in the Cleveland Indians, so McKinney, as a sort of lark, proposed that the Pirates offer stock to Bing Crosby.

With Crosby aboard, there were four principal owners. McKinney at first called the shots. At what exact point it became clear to

Galbreath that McKinney's true interests were with the minor-league team in his home town is best known to Galbreath, but the Pirates seemed to be spinning their wheels. Always intolerant of aimlessness, he paid a visit to McKinney in Indianapolis. "We were sitting in his car, by the side of the road," Galbreath has recalled, "and I said to him, 'Frank, you buy me out or I'll buy you out.'" Galbreath did the buying out.

He was now in control. A year ago, Galbreath summarily replaced the man who'd been training his horses. Galbreath doesn't second-guess the people in charge of his racing stable. He doesn't give orders. His son Dan doesn't second-guess or give orders. "If we're dissatisfied with the results we're getting," said Dan early this summer, "we don't tell the trainer how to train. In the first place, we wouldn't know. And it's the same with the baseball team. We're in the real-estate business and we have our own decisions to make. We hire the best guys we can find and let them run things—as long as we're happy with what they're doing."

They were not at all happy with what Harding Peterson was doing, so they fired him last May as general manager of the Pirates, a team overburdened with high-priced players who had failed to deliver. On Peterson's watch, the Pirates had won a pennant and World Series. Their head man was more lenient with the best guy he could find to run things in 1951, Branch Rickey.

Galbreath in his business dealings is unequivocal and direct. Branch Rickey, in all of his dealings, was intricate and roundabout. The paradox is that, according to Tom Johnson, Galbreath in the beginning "idolized" Rickey. Both were Ohio country boys and fraternity brothers, Delta Tau Deltas, Galbreath at Ohio University, Rickey at Ohio Wesleyan. Running things for the Dodgers—the Brooklyn Dodgers—Rickey had made a series of trades with the Pirates and had burglarized them—"taken our pants off," as Tom Johnson puts it. He appeared to be the genius who would soon have the Pirates going places.

But then in each of his five years as general manager they finished either last in the National League or seventh when there were only eight teams.

Rickey's operation in the context of the 1950s was expensive. The Pirates lost money. Rickey, meanwhile, was working hard to organize a third major league. Galbreath "saw through him, saw what he was up to," says Johnson, but toyed with the thought of extending Rickey's contract. In the end, Rickey left, and Joe Brown moved up from New Orleans in the Pirates' minor-league chain.

Called out of retirement after Peterson's departure, Brown says of Galbreath, "He permitted me to make my own mistakes—or to be right." Brown was right just often enough to keep Galbreath happy for 20 years while the Pirates were winning two World Series, the same number of pennants and five Eastern Division championships. Then in 1979, Harding Peterson's fourth year, they did it again: They won the World Series.

And still the losses piled up. The figure given out is $18 million since 1970, when the Pirates made the switch to Three Rivers Stadium from Forbes Field—"and I think that would be on the low side," says Johnson. When Warner Communications bought 48 percent of the Pirates, Johnson unloaded his 30 percent, selling out to the Galbreaths, who had long ago acquired most of Bing Crosby's stock. Johnson is not a man of unlimited means. He said to the Galbreaths, "Gentlemen, I cannot put up dollar for dollar with you. Don't expect me to throw fresh money into the fiery furnace."

The Galbreaths, for all their wealth, were being scorched by the fiery furnace themselves. It took a lawsuit against the city, settled out of court, to free them from the cost of managing and maintaining the stadium, but attendance kept dwindling, salaries kept going up. The flames in the furnace leaped higher.

There came a day when Dan Galbreath, since 1969 the Pirates' president, went to his father and said, "Dad, these losses are staggering. We haven't been able to turn on the city or turn on the fans, and the Warner people are ready to sell their stock. I think it would be a good opportunity to sell the whole team."

And John Galbreath answered, "I agree."

The Galbreaths are reticent about the non-financial reasons for their wish to be relived of the Pirates. It never thrilled them to be employing a lot of coke sniffers, if that was the case, but they recognize the connection between drug use in baseball and the widespread social and cultural changes of recent times. As for the belief that they considered themselves misunderstood and unappreciated in Pittsburgh, perceived as carpetbaggers from out of town and doomed to constant unfavorable comparisons with a civic monument like Art Rooney, the owner of the Steelers, nothing in their demeanor suggested it. All they have ever said—wistfully—is that they'd like to see bigger crowds at Three Rivers.

As it happens, John Galbreath was neither popular nor unpopular in Pittsburgh. Ordinary people were hardly aware of him. The same was true of the press.

On one of the occasions this summer when Dan Galbreath answered questions about the sale of the team, his father walked into the conference room ahead of him and started talking to a small group of reporters. The younger ones didn't know who he was. Interrupting an anecdote, television crewmen passed between Galbreath and his audience to hook up their microphones. Then a man from the Pirates front office began to introduce Dan. Irritated at last, Galbreath broke in on him. "May I complete my story?" he asked. The abashed front-office man stepped aside.

Some years back a reporter inquired of Galbreath if he paid as much attention to baseball as to horse racing or Ohio State football. "Make no mistake about it," he said. "My real love is the real estate business. Nothing means as much to me as sitting across the table from a man who has just bought a house, knowing I have made it possible for him to own a little bit of our country."

The way it turned out, enabling others to own a little bit of the country has enabled Galbreath to own larger bits. The Darby Dan Farm in Ohio, 115 acres when he bought it half a century ago, has grown to 4,200 acres. Galbreath would make a deal with the owner of an adjacent piece of property. Let me buy your farm, he would say, and you can live on it free for the rest of your life. As the magazine writer who labeled him unpretentious observed, his watchword could very well have been: Simple solutions to complicated problems.

Printed on the back of Galbreath's business card is a maxim of Ralph Waldo Emerson: "Don't ever despair, but if you do despair, work in despair. Don't ever quit." When Galbreath went broke during the Depression, he did not for a minute despair. He got himself back on his feet by selling millions of dollars worth of foreclosed property for the banks, insurance companies and savings and loan associations that were stuck with it. He persuaded large blocks of property owners whose holdings were unencumbered to put them up as security and buy houses, later sold at a profit. It was one of his simple solutions. Like unloading the Pirates, the simplest solution of all.

★   ★   ★

Born in the Ohio village of Derby—and how is that for an omen? —Galbreath was the son of a farmer and the grandson of a Methodist minister. He worked his way through Ohio University by waiting on tables and developing film. Something else he developed, unexpected in the light of his bucolic origins, was a taste for playing polo. His success in the real estate business quickly made it affordable, and when a nag he had bought for $100 won a race at a county fair, he switched from polo ponies to thoroughbreds.

Routinely, Galbreath put in 14-hour days, not infrequently keeping appointments in Pittsburgh, New York and Cleveland between dawn and dusk and flying home to Columbus for dinner. Now that he approaches his tenth decade, his pace is not as frenetic. He goes to his office in Columbus as usual—the John W. Galbreath Co. occupies two whole floors of a building he added to the city's skyline, one of eight in the last 20 years—but doesn't get there until "late."

In other words, 9 a.m.

For an octogenarian who in 1984 had two severe heart attacks, Galbreath appears to be fit—somewhat diminished in stature, one assumes, but maybe not. He was never a physical giant. Dan Galbreath, although taller and huskier than his father, is in many ways a chip off the block.

One on one, they are warm, open, friendly, hospitable people, the father more spontaneous than the son. If John Galbreath had been as accessible and gregarious as Art Rooney is, he would have the same reputation for affability. He is simply too busy to display the common touch he possesses. Says Tom Johnson: "Let's put it this way: John is interested in the little guy, in helping people out, but he works at the top echelon."

Exactly. Galbreath is comfortable with crowned heads, with heads of state and even with heads of religions. When his wife, the former Dorothy Byron Firestone, was in better health, they entertained the likes of Princess Margaret, Princess Michael of Kent and Aly Khan. Presidents stayed with them, notably Gerald Ford. "And we've had a couple of others," says Galbreath, groping for the names.

"Ronald Reagan?"

"No, not Reagan . . . Oh, it'll come to me. You know who I mean. . . ."

"Nixon?"

"Nixon. I've had some wonderful guests. And the one I think I enjoyed more than anybody I've ever met, outside of two or three presidents, was Dr. Norman Vincent Peale. Pastor of the Marble Collegiate Church on Wall Street. He's a fellow who can entertain you even in his sermons. One of the finest men living, Norman Vincent Peale."

Galbreath has an arrangement with Ford, the most unforgettable center who ever played football for the University of Michigan, to be a guest at Darby Dan on the weekend of the Michigan-Ohio State game in Columbus if Ford expects Michigan to win. Regardless of how he is betting on the Kentucky Derby, he's invited to that, too, every year. Galbreath customarily has a horse in the Derby and until recently he was chairman of the board of directors at Churchill Downs.

Ford's bedroom in The Residence is over an artificial stream piped under the house. Its source is the Big Darby Creek, which winds its way through the farm, and it makes a charming picture from the quaint wooden bridge that leads to the front door of The Residence. Until Galbreath disillusioned him not long ago, Ford talked ecstatically about the pleasures of getting back to nature, of being lulled to a sound sleep by a sure-enough babbling brook.

The Darby Dan landscape is scenic: rolling hills, stands of trees, shady lanes, corn fields, wheat fields, horse barns and bluegrass, fences like the ones in Kentucky, the rails horizontal, painted white. Among the regular tenants of Big Darby Creek are a pair of swans. With mud, leaves and branches they have built a nest on a barren little island. Wild ducks and geese frequent the creek.

"Prettiest sight you ever saw when the mama's in front and the papa's behind and all the little babies in between," says Galbreath.

Once when 200 honkers from Canada landed on the water, Galbreath was warming himself in front of the fireplace. Dan, in the next room, saw the geese through a window and excitedly called to his father. The Residence happens to be a split level and as John reached the head of a flight of five steps, almost running, he slipped on the polished floor, tumbled all the way down and broke a leg.

Today there is no trace of a limp. He firmly resists coddling. When Jean Justice attempts to deny him a second cup of coffee on the sun porch, he overrules her, declaring, "It won't hurt a thing, woman." At the office, his role is to be a sounding board, an adviser, for which guilt persistently gnaws at him, because Dan, "loaded down with work," is "traveling all over everywhere."

"All over everywhere" takes in Hong Kong, where the Galbreaths are adding to the 99 huge condominiums they have built there. It is Dan who keeps the family's eight-passenger jet on the go, taking off from the Darby Dan airstrip. The swimming pool, tennis courts and nine-hole golf course are used about as often as the seats in the upper deck at a Pirate home game.

Dan relaxes by shooting bighorn sheep. His father's career as a slayer of wild game is in the past. On the walls of Darby House, the building in which the Galbreaths do their really large-scale entertaining, are the mounted heads of animals John has killed on African safaris—a rhino, a hippopotamus, its vast mouth agape, a cape buffalo (dangerous and fierce), all kinds of antelope. His tiger, realistically stuffed, is the first thing you see when you go through the door.

That anyone so susceptible to the cuteness of baby ducks and geese should have it in him to amass such a collection might seem at first blush to be out of character. Still, common wisdom has it that the American enterpreneur is by instinct a huntsman. Nor do the Galbreaths only depopulate. Between 40 and 50 acres of Darby Dan Farm have been convented into a game preserve. Buffalo from the plains of the West and horned beasts from Africa graze behind tall wire fences. There are zebras and ostriches, wild turkeys and peacocks, leading the same pampered lives as the racehorses in their pastures of timothy.

Dan, the scourge of bighorn sheep, is an amateur ornithologist. He calls his house Tree Tops and has filled it with paintings of birds. Dan's sister, Mrs. James W. Phillips, uses the third Darby Dan house, Gay Chateau, as a summertime residence. Explaining the name—Chateaugay turned around—Dan seems embarrassed. "Twenty years ago," he says, "the word 'gay' had a different meaning."

Year by year the world changes. Nothing remains the same, including a city's affection for its baseball team. Darby House, where Bing Crosby sang for his supper when the owners of the Pirates and their friends got together, contains all the relics—the World Series trophies, Roberto Clemento's uniform, Willie Stargell's uniform.

Clemente and Stargell. Could they have been John Galbreath's favorite ball players? Clemente in particular? "Well," Galbreath says, "he stayed at my house. . . ."

Galbreath is a man who hates to be pinned down. Don't ask him to choose between Roberto, the racehorse he named for Clemente, and Chateaugay or Proud Clarion. There are memories Galbreath doesn't classify.

He turns to a picture on the wall—Mazeroski in the act of hitting the Home Run. Still at the plate, Mazeroski has completed his swing. The photograph shows the Yankee pitcher, the Yankee third baseman, the Yankee shortstop and the Yankee left fielder. It shows the red brick wall just behind the left fielder, the scoreboard and the clock.

Galbreath has a question, his question for every visitor. "Where's the ball?" The ball is a speck of white against the sky over Forbes Field, but where? Even without glasses, Galbreath can find it. He points a finger. "One inch above and one inch to the right of the clock."

Again it's October 13, 1960, when Pittsburgh's heart belonged to the Pirates, and the time is forever 3:36 p.m.

Northern Star: The Great Alaska Shootout

COLLEGE BASKETBALL

By *JOHN SCHULIAN*

From the Philadelphia Daily News
Copyright © 1985, Philadelphia Daily News

Dreams are for chasing. Where they lead you may depend on something as unpredictable as how hard the wind blows.

Up here, it must blow like the devil, for the average Alaskan dream is as big as Mount McKinley. People don't worry about winters cold enough to freeze the ears off a moose, or about how that same moose may collide with a speeding Blazer and send it skidding into eternity. The risk is nothing compared to the reward everybody is sure lies behind the next glacier.

It was that way with gold, it was that way with oil and it was that way with the Great Alaska Shootout, even if the Shootout doesn't seem like such a gamble anymore.

Face it, you can still conjure up visions of bushy-whiskered sour-doughs desperately panning for their fortunes, and even if the Trans-Alaska Pipeline is pumping black gold 800 miles from the north slope down to the port of Valdez, it still seems impossible. But an eight-team college basketball tournament? One that begins Friday with a field including Villanova's defending NCAA champions and North Carolina's heirs-apparent? One that was Patrick Ewing's collegiate launching pad, brought a call from Eddie Sutton as soon as he landed the Kentucky coaching job, and will have six of this year's games broadcast everywhere ESPN can reach?

As sure things go, making a success of Shootout ought to be no more difficult than finding hamburgers at McDonald's. And yet, just eight years ago, there was no Shootout, no $30-million Sullivan Arena to play it in and hardly even a basketball program at the University of Alaska-Anchorage. There was just a coach and athletic director named Bob Rachal who made conversations stop and heads turn as soon as he blew into town.

"God, he was a big, good-looking stud," says Lee Piccard, Alaska-Anchorage's vice chancellor for campus affairs. "He was just born 100 years late, that's all. He really belongs on a riverboat on the Mississippi, with a white hat and a string tie and a deck of cards."

For Bob Rachal was a gambler and a dreamer, and when you think of him now, which almost no one in Anchorage does, you realize how perfect he was.

Not for the Mississippi.

But for Alaska.

★   ★   ★

He was imported from the Lower 48 by a chancellor whose Kentucky roots had provided many a lesson in the quickest way for a school to make a name for itself. "I guess they have basketball in Kentucky, don't they?" Piccard asks with a sly smile.

And after this chancellor got everybody squared away on the pronunciation of his savior's name—Ra-shall, not Rakal or Racial or anything like that—he started blabbering about how one day UAA was going to play UCLA and Notre Dame and every other powerhouse he could tuck in a dog sled. Naturally, the local reporters, being inquisitive sorts, called UCLA and Notre Dame to ask about this, and the reply they got in both cases came in the form of a question: What the hell is UAA?

The only person this failed to upset was the person you might have expected it to upset the most.

"The thing you had to understand about Bob Rachal was that he'd had cancer," Piccard says. "It hit him pretty young, too—21, 22, something like that. And I guess that after you've been threatened with dying, you aren't going to be threatened by much else."

So Rachal got on the phone and started booking games with Stanford and Southern Cal. Never mind that UAA was a Division II school that had only recently severed itself from the two-year Anchorage Community College. Never mind that the Sourdoughs, who would later change their nickname to the Seawolves, had always played teams with no names at all. Never mind that there was nary a dime in the basketball program's budget for such calls in the first place.

"I'll tell you what that sucker Rachal would do," Piccard says. "He'd go to a pay phone and call those other athletic directors collect, and he'd always do it when he knew they wouldn't be there. You know, at quarter to 8 in the morning, when there's only a secretary around. And he'd ask if they would call back when they came in."

What is it Robert Stone wrote in his novel *Dog Soldiers?* Unusual circumstances demanded an unusual hustle? Whatever, you get the idea of the kind of hustle Rachal had. And the beauty of it was, it worked. No one ever realized he was being snookered, and UAA, with maybe 600 full-timers among its 4,500 students, had a schedule to be proud of.

But Rachal wasn't finished. He served notice of that before the first game he ever coached up here. The Seawolves were opening the 1977-78 season against the University of Alaska-Fairbanks, a team they had never beaten, a team that no doubt saw itself as a champion of virtue. "Fairbanks represents the establishment in this state," says Tim McDiffett, UAA's sports information director. "Anchorage is where the new money is." As the Fairbanks players warmed up, however, Anchorage didn't appear to be where any competition was. The other end of the court stayed empty until two young giants, their muscles encased in three-piece suits, rolled out a red carpet. The band struck up "Sweet Georgia Brown" and the Anchorage team thundered into the spotlight. Then, and only then, did Bob Rachal grace the scene with his presence. He was wearing a black swallow-tail tuxedo and a stovepipe top hat. Fairbanks didn't have a prayer.

And still that wasn't enough. Bob Rachal needed more, and he found the inspiration for it, oddly enough, in a place he would eventually get in trouble for ignoring—the NCAA rule book. But that is not to suggest his discovery didn't suit him perfectly. It did. It was a loophole.

Quite simply, the rules stated that a team couldn't have a regular-season schedule of more than 28 games within the 48 contiguous states. Fine. Rachal could live with that, particularly since Alaska isn't contiguous to anything except the top of the world. And he figured rightly that a lot of coaches would share his sentiments if they could come to a tournament over the Thanksgiving weekend and have three more shots at 20 victories and three more chances to study their talent without having it count against them.

There were skeptics, of course. "When I heard what they were talking about," recalls McDiffett, who was then sports editor of the *Anchorage Times*, "I said, 'right. A basketball tournament in Alaska.'" But Rachal just kept plugging dimes into that pet pay phone of his at ungodly hours and waiting for athletic directors to call him back.

They did, too. Look at the field he put together for the tournament's 1978 debut—North Carolina State, Louisville, Indiana, Texas A&M, Pepperdine, Penn State and Lamar. The tournament was a thing of beauty except for Rachal's insistence on calling it the Seawolf Classic. Billy Packer, college basketball's TV mouthpiece, would change that a year later by coming up with the Great Alaska Shootout, but Rachal had to get the news long-distance. He had been fired.

The ax fell right after Rachal's first season, long before the first game in the first tournament was played. It had been coming since the day Rachal's two gigantic prize recruits—one from New York, the other from Detroit—hit town and immediately made the front page by getting arrested for stealing a pistol.

"Pretty soon, there were all kinds of other problems," Lee Piccard says. "Kids started talking about promises Bob had made and wasn't keeping. Money? I'm not sure whether anybody was promised any money, but I know they got very upset."

So did the NCAA, and Rachal was history. The bulk of his legacy consisted of the idea for the tournament, though his foul-tempered successor, Gary Bliss, often got credit for it. But students of the Shootout will tell you there was something that stamped it as undeniably Rachal's and, perhaps, quintessentially Alaskan.

"People up here always want to see what's up the hill, they're willing to take an extra step," Piccard says. "You take a $300,000 deal like a concert or a tournament anywhere else and people want the money in the bank first. In Alaska they just say, 'Let's put it on and see if we can make the $300,000.' Well, that was Bob Rachal with this Shootout. He had contracts with all the schools before we even had a gym for them to play in."

Piccard can't stop himself from laughing at the memory, but in the laughter is a heart-felt sentiment.

"God, I loved that guy."

★   ★   ★

They wound up playing the first five Shootouts in a gym on an Army base, and it was wonderful. So wonderful, in fact, that when you hear them reminisce about humble beginnings in Fort Richardson's Buckner Fieldhouse, you get the feeling they might march this year's teams over there for a look at the sweet used-to-be.

There were backboards hanging on both sides of the court, the swing-up kind you find at the YMCA. You can see them in the scrapbook pictures. Look, there's Patrick Ewing going to block a shot and you can't tell which basket the poor devil he's about to stuff is aiming for.

But there were other things it was better to experience for yourself, like all those lines on the court and the splintered wooden bleachers they pulled out of the walls so they could seat 3,200 paying customers. And the smell. Don't forget the smell.

"It was perfect for a 1925 gym," says Harry Larrabee, who is entering his fifth season as UAA's head basketball coach. "It was like they mixed sweat with popcorn."

That funky ambiance carried all the way to the locker rooms, where there were sometimes no chalkboards but always two teams. "One of them would be getting a halftime talk and the other one would be putting on their socks and jocks," Larrabee says. "I think some of the coaches liked that. It was like they were telling the players, 'These are your roots.' "

In that case, maybe they told their players, "This is reality" when the Shootout moved downtown to the freshly constructed Sullivan Arena two years ago. For reality it surely was. Every gaudy show needs a gaudy showplace, and now the Shootout had one.

The problem was, you might find only 75 percent of the seats filled for a championship game, and not even half that many when seventh and eighth place were at stake. The lack of local interest sends tournament boosters scurrying for explanations about how Alaska is for doing, not watching, and about how the lack of dormitories on campus—a short-coming that will be corrected come January—cuts deeply into attendance. Every once in a while, you will even find someone wiping his brow and saying he's glad the Shootout got started when it did, because money's getting too tight to spend it on a bauble like this.

Still, the Shootout lives and, in the eyes of the Lower 48, thrives. There is no more need for money from the Alaska legislature, the way there was in the beginning. "With ESPN, we'll even make a dollar or two," Lee Piccard says. And now the state's politicians and businessmen can profit from the tournament's high visibility. "Remember those advertising spots Alaska bought during the Super Bowl?" Tim McDiffett asks. "I'll bet the Shootout has done more for the state than that."

But the man who dreamed up this world-class promotional gimmick died without ever having seen it. The cancer Bob Rachal thought he had beaten chased him from Alaska to an assistant coach's job at the University of Massachusetts, then to a recreation department job down home in Alexandria, La. When he left there to resume coaching, this time at Eastern Wyoming College, the cancer followed. And it ate away at him until it was all he could do to drag himself to his wife's Alabama home and die last March at age 43.

You can only hope someone took the time to tell him what he had accomplished in Anchorage. "If he hadn't found that NCAA rule," Harry Larrabee says, "there wouldn't be a Shootout, there wouldn't even be a basketball program here."

And you can only wish the powers that be at UAA had summoned the courage to invite him back to take a bow just once. "I mentioned it a couple times," Piccard says, "and all I heard was, 'Nah, not a good idea.' "

But there is a story that Ron Petro, UAA's new athletic director, tells that makes you wonder whether Rachal's spirit hasn't always been hovering over the Shootout. The story begins with Petro making his pitch to the ESPN people in a fancy-schmancy New York restaurant. In the middle of it, a waiter noticed that he was wearing a Shootout blazer. "The kid asked me if that was who I was really with," Petro says, "and when I told him yes, he went crazy. He wouldn't stop talking about how he went to Fordham, and how Fordham played up here, and how he loved the Shootout. So I just sat there and let him sell the tournament to ESPN for me."

Even if it wasn't a hustle, let's call it one. In honor of Bob Rachal.

North Wins U.S. Open

GOLF

By *GARY NUHN*

From the Dayton Daily News
Copyright © 1985, Dayton Newspapers Inc.

They hit every kind of lousy golf shot imaginable Sunday.

They hit shanks; they hit toppers; they hit into trees and shrubs. They hit sidewinders, worm-burners, duck hooks and pop flies. Tze-Chung Chen even made a particularly wretched swing during which he hit the ball twice.

Given all that, you have to know it was the final round of the U.S. Open.

Sunday, as usual, no one won the Open. The Open won.

For the second time in his career, Andy North was handed the silver chalice symbolic of the Open champion, but the best thing that can be said of North is that he finished standing up with his shoes still tied.

He shot 74 on this windy, chilly day, winning by default when the leader, Chen, rummaged around to a 77, and when the man closest to him, Dave Barr, bogeyed the final two holes, including an incredible ground ball out of a fairway bunker on the 18th.

North himself came in with a bogey on the final hole, symbolic of a round in which he hit just four of 14 fairways and eight times landed in bunkers. On a positive note, he missed 110 bunkers. He did make a birdie. One. And he won by a shot. One.

That the leaders weren't immediately invited to Wednesday's showdown for Golf Digest's "Worst Avid Golfer" was merely an oversight.

The whole scenario was nothing new for North, a 35-year-old from Madison, Wis., (or "Mad-City," as he calls it). In 1978, North shot a similar final-day 74 with a similar bogey on the final hole to win the Open at Cherry Hills Country Club in Denver.

This 74 gave him a total of 1-under-par 279. He had gone 70-65-70 before his Sunday wanderings. Added together, it was worth $103,000.

All three of the men who tied for second, foreigners every one—Chen of Taiwan, Barr of Canada and Denis Watson of South Africa—missed tying North by the faintest of margins on the 18th.

Watson was first. Playing three groups ahead of North, Watson had a 10-foot birdie putt, but misread it. He thought it swung right, but it swung not at all.

Watson had been penalized two strokes Thursday when he let a putt sit on the edge of a cup for 38 seconds. The rule allows 10 seconds. Sans penalty, Watson would have won by one, but he chose not to make an issue of it. "That happened Thursday. I put it out of my mind Thursday," he said.

Barr had the next chance to get to 1-under and tie North on 18. After his grounder out of the bunker, he hit a wedge to the back fringe where he faced a 15-foot downhill chip. He popped a beauty that ran dead at the cup until one foot away it took an almost imperceptible left turn and missed by the width of a ballpoint pen.

Finally came Chen, the little man who had led this tournament from Day One and had charmed an entire country as he did. Chen bunkered his approach shot to 18, but he is a master in the sand. His explosion flew across the terrace in mid-green, landed lightly and slithered down the slope, breaking left to right as it went. It had a chance all the way, but died two inches on the high side.

The foreign invasion quelled, North took a nice leisurely two-putt bogey and threw his arms in the air in triumph.

Better he should have copied Hale Irwin's act from Inverness in 1979. After Hale had tapped in for a double bogey there to close a torturous final round, he staggered back from the hole like a boxer on rubbery knees.

So what happened on Sunday after the sharply dressed men took liberties with Oakland Hills for three straight days?

"The Monster bit back," said Barr.

The most vicious bite, and the one that opened this Open, came at the fifth hole. Chen, who had led by two when the day began and by four when he and North arrived at the fifth tee, hit a perfect drive.

On Chen's hat all week was the brand name ThreeBond, a Japanese glue used in the manufacture of automobiles.

In the middle of the fifth fairway, Chen came unglued.

He blocked out a 4-iron behind two trees. Instead of just winging it on the back of the green and accepting a two-putt bogey, he made the mistake of trying to save par. He thus hit it too fine and was still short of the green in lush, wet, jungle rough.

That's when Chen made his double-hit. He hit behind the ball first, popping it straight in the air and, on his follow through, hit the ball again, knocking it left.

This counted as one stroke, plus a penalty stroke. So he was lying five and still not on the green. A chip and two putts gave him an eight on the par-4. Some people call that a "quadruple bogey." On the Tour, it's called a "snowman" because of the shape of an eight. Chen called it a "double-par."

By any name, it smelled not sweet.

In a five-minute period, his four-shot lead, built over three days, had vanished.

Chen called his first pitch shot from behind the trees, the one with which he tried to save par, "a stupid thing, you know."

"I like to say, I just play bad," the sad Chen said. "I just play pitiful golf today. But I finish second. That not too bad first-time U.S. Open."

He left the media tent to an ovation from men who applaud once a decade.

The "double-hit" allowed all manner of men back in the tournament. Barr led for a time, North for a time and Chen actually regained the co-lead for a time.

Finally, North made the fewest mistakes.

He had not won since that '78 Open, suffering through back problems, a bone spur on his elbow and a shoulder injury.

"This is the first year I've played without pain for eight or nine years," he said. "When you struggle as long as I have, it's hard to make yourself believe you can hit good shots again."

He was asked to characterize his final round.

"Guts," he said. "Determination. Just finishing."

Those are the codewords of every Open champion since 1895. The Open wins. The winner merely survives.

Ty Cobb, Here I Come

BASEBALL

By *RICK REILLY*

From Sports Illustrated
The following article, "Ty Cobb, Here I Come" by Rick Reilly, is reprinted
from the August 19, 1985 issue of Sports Illustrated. Copyright © Time Inc.

FIVE A.M.—The Big Clock

What you see before you could be any 44-year-old man slurping
any bowl of cereal and watching any baseball game on TV, except
that the man is a millionaire, his picture is on the cereal box and it's a
little early for breakfast. What might also be worth mentioning is
that this is Pete Rose, one of baseball's living icons, and he should
damn well be asleep considering the kind of day he has in front of
him. But he's not.

Rose doesn't care how much sleep he gets this night. Rose doesn't
care how much sleep he gets any night. He doesn't care that he has
The MacNeil-Lehrer Report at 3, *P.M. Magazine* at 4 and Nolan
Ryan at 7:30. Rose doesn't sweat time. This is because Rose and time
have an understanding. Neither believes the other is for real. Rose
has put the aging process on permanent call waiting.

How Rose fits more into a day than any three other people is a
secret he learned from his father, which is not unusual, because Rose
learned all things from his father. What is unusual is that this secret
his father taught him *after* he died.

It was at the funeral in December 1970. Rose was still seeing
everything through Plexiglas then. Walking but not going anywhere. Eating but not tasting. His father had dropped dead of a heart
attack two steps up the stairs at home, and nothing had seemed real
since. The preacher got up and one of the things he said was, "You
know, ladies and gentlemen, from the day we're born we start to
die." "And it hit me," Rose says. "He was right, you know? Just like
my father. You got to make the most of what time you got."

Peter Edward Rose has not been prodigal with his allotment. He has married two women, disappointed God knows how many others, kibitzed with three presidents (Reagan rang him up from Air Force One), toured the world, owned a Rolls-Royce, a BMW M-1, a 1933 three-window Ford coupe, half a dozen or so Porsches, had his name on any number of restaurants, and will soon have his portrait hanging in the Cincinnati Art Museum. Painted by Andy Warhol himself. Is that a pair? Warhol dyed his hair gray at 23 so he wouldn't have to bother with "the responsibility of acting young." Rose used to stump for Grecian Formula. Go figure.

Anyway, all these things came to Rose for his uncanny ability to get hits. Celebrity arrived for what he did between them—sliding molars first, running even when he walked, bouncing baseballs off AstroTurf to punctuate the end of an inning. That is the rice pudding. The prime cuts he made with his bat.

Twenty-one to go. Twenty-one hits and Rose becomes the most prolific amasser of hits in history, whistling by Ty Cobb's 4,191 as if Cobb were standing still, which he is. Just about every honor and thrill baseball can dole out has been Rose's. He has played in 3,455 regular-season games, 1,916 of them wins, both all-time records. Those winning games are more than 47 Hall of Famers, including Joe DiMaggio, ever played in, making him, as Pete likes to say, "the biggest winner in history." He was The Sporting News N.L. Player of the Decade for the '70s; the Hickok Belt winner in 1975 as pro athlete of the year; and Sports Illustrated's Sportsman of the Year in 1975. He has played in 16 All-Star Games and 34 World Series games. "Peter is baseball," Sparky Anderson, his old manager, says. "He's the best thing to happen to the game since . . . well . . . the game."

But 4,192 . . . 4,192 will be the rarest acquisition of all. It should be. Rose paid plenty for it.

Still, for now, as dawn breaks on his five-acre, four-bedroom, two-car-garage, chalet-style house, Rose is most concerned with tuning in Westar V on his souped-up satellite dish. He is in search of the replay of the Kansas City-Detroit game, much of which he saw the night before. So why are you up, Pete?

"I was hungry," he says. Funny how Rose's stomach growls him awake precisely when a ball game comes on. Yes, even Pete's innards love baseball.

TEN A.M.—The Big Knock

Time was when Rose would sleep till noon, have breakfast and get to the ball park by 1, but these are the days of The Big Knock (a "knock," in Rose lingo, being a hit, and The Big Knock No. 4,192), and there's much too much to be done. So here is Rose, resplendent in his maroon bathrobe, Prince Valiant haircut and legs that Reds right fielder Dave Parker describes as "vanilla milk shakes."

While Pete feeds his four horses, Carol Rose, 31 and divinely favored, readies to feed Pete. How many former Playboy bunnies and ex-Philadelphia Eagle cheerleaders can whip up pancakes that don't have the relative density of manhole covers? Pete will make the coffee. No French maids *chez* Rose. Carol outpoints a French maid any day.

Last night Rose went to bed at 2:30, was up at 5, as we have noticed, retired again at 6 and is up again. This is what's known as sleeping like a baby. Rose should know. He has one—10-month-old Tyler Edward Rose, who is named in honor of The Big Knock. Rose says everything he has comes from baseball, so it's fitting he offer up his offspring.

These are remarkable days. Knock talk has gone beyond sports into real life. In the last two months, Rose has glibbed it up for *Life, Time, People, Newsweek, U.S. News & World Report, Boy's Life,* just about every network morning and evening news show, newspapers of all shapes and sizes and even *Face the Nation. Face the Nation?* Cobb just did a 360 in his grave. In Anaheim, Rod Carew, in search of 3,000, wasn't doing interviews. In Chicago, Tom Seaver, stalking 300, pulled a little Garbo. But the Reds' player-manager makes like Pia Zadora for every mike. It has hurt his hitting, but Rose says it's part of the job. Besides, who is better on Rose than Rose?

ELEVEN A.M.—Big Talk

As Rose drives south along I-75 to the ball park in his black Porsche, he passes two billboards adorned with his considerable countenance. In Cincinnati these days, Rose's mug is plastered everywhere. And what a face. It prompts Parker to remark, "If I had his head, I'd make a butcher-block coffee table out of it." Says Rose, "Your face would look old, too, if you'd been sliding on it for 23 years."

Rose looks right at his billboards as we pass. No feigned indifference. *Ohhhh, that ol' thing.* Not Rose. He stares up and then stares at you, grinning that dulcet grin, as if to say, "I guess it's big enough."

Rose, as egotist, is sufferable. He rolls out his stardom, like a rug he has just woven. *It's pretty. Have a look. We'll both get a kick out of it.* For example, when Rose says, "I've doffed my cap so many times I'm losing my hair," you think, "funny," but you get the point, too. Some people feel queasy about hanging honors. Rose has a room full of plaques, paintings, trophies, urns, belts, baseballs and bats, plus a storage closet containing more that he'd love to find room to display.

Rose isn't apologetic about being rich, either. Nor about being proud, which gives him the reputation of a statistics monger. Wrong, Decimal Breath. Rose is a baseball monger. Any number that can be associated with baseball, Rose can spit out as if he were a dot-matrix printer. Rose knows the 34 major and National League records he holds. And, yes, he might refresh you as to which 40-year-old led the N.L. in hits in 1981 (Pete, with the Phillies); who played 23 years with only one ride on the disabled list (Pete, 21 days); which singles hitter took Tom Seaver, Jim Palmer and Catfish Hunter over the wall in postseason games (Pete). But he can also recite how White Sox righties do against Red Sox lefties.

You think he's up at 5 a.m. to watch the sunrise?

TWELVE NOON—The Old Block

Face the Nation: "Pete, this record must be pretty important to you. You named your son after Ty Cobb, didn't you?"

Rose: "Well, I named him Tyler Edward Rose. My name is Peter Edward Rose. I can honestly say if I was chasing some guy named Harry, I wouldn't have named him Harry, I can say that."

Actually, Rose *is* chasing some guy named Harry. Rose's father was Harry, but he didn't like the name, either. Growing up in Cincinnati, Harry was fond of a vegetable-cart horse named Pete. Each day when that horse came around, Harry would climb on and refuse to climb off, so they called him Pete.

By day, Rose's father was a farsighted bank employee who suffered headaches after long hours adding figures. But when he got off the bus at night and swept up his son, Harry Rose went through a metamorphosis. Bartleby became Achilles. As an amateur boxer, he fought as a flyweight under the name Pee Wee Sams. As a sturdy semipro halfback and defensive back, he played until he was 42. He was a member of the original Cincinnati Bengals, who played against teams like the Chicago Bears. When *Cincinnati Post* columnist Pat Harmon retired in August after more than 34 years on the job, he named Rose's father the most remarkable athlete he had seen. "He was," says Rose. "I've seen a lot of football, but my father was the best player I ever saw."

Once, Harry Rose broke his hip on a kickoff, then crawled downfield to try to make a tackle. Another night he came off the field with a knot on his arm the size of a softball. He took a handkerchief, filled it with ice, wrapped it around his arm, went back into the game and made an interception on the next play. After the games, win or lose, he would run hills while young Peter watched. "I didn't need to read about dedication," Rose once wrote. "I lived with it."

No wonder Harry Rose became his son's idol—and then some. "He took me to *all* the games," says Pete. Says Rose's mother, LaVerne, "Pete would be in the car before his father could say, 'Pete, you want to go?' "

When Pete became an athlete, his father rarely gave praise. "My dad never talked in terms of individuals," Rose says. "He always talked about teams." But when Pete was not around, Harry talked about one individual—Pete. "Once, when Peter was about 4, he and his father were playing baseball in the backyard," Pete's mother recalls. "Peter hit a ball that cracked a window. I tried to get it fixed one day, but big Pete says to me, 'Don't you dare!' He wouldn't let me fix it. He wanted to show people how far Peter could hit a ball."

Fifteen years after his father's death, Pete is still trying to break windows. "What he instilled in me—pride, the will to succeed—that's what drives me."

Of course, the difference between chasing Ty Cobb and chasing Harry Rose is that Cobb can be caught.

ONE P.M.—The Modern Jock

Rose arrives at the ball park 6½ hours before the game. First one here. Again.

On off days, Rose is the only one here besides Billy DeMars, the Reds hitting coach. They meet at 11, take two buckets of baseballs to the net batting cage rigged under the bleachers and DeMars throws to him for 45 minutes. This has been Rose's off-day routine for 23 years. "It amazes me," says DeMars. "Here's the guy who will go down as one of the greatest hitters of all time and he works harder than anybody. And we got guys hitting .136 who wonder what's wrong."

Rose is obsessive about preparation. Name an umpire and Rose can describe the nuances of his strike zone. If an outfielder strikes out with men on base to end the inning, Rose knows that player's mind will be elsewhere. If Rose singles his way, he'll look for two bases. Rose even knows which grounds crews leave a field ripe for bunts and which don't. So who needs a fancy computer system? The Reds have Rose.

Because Rose lives inside the game, he is disappointed by players who don't live anywhere in the neighborhood. Consider bats. Rose doesn't go anywhere without his bats. Whether he's up next or ninth, he is fondling a bat at all times. He cleans them with alcohol before every trip to the plate—practice or otherwise—so that afterward he can see where cowhide met wood. Then he cleans them again. On road trips, he broods over them until Bernie Stowe, the clubhouse man, has safely stashed them aboard the truck. "And then," Rose says, wincing, "I see guys get to a ball park on the road and they're screaming, 'Hey, Bernie! Where's my bats? I can't believe you didn't pack my bats!' And this is how the guy makes a living! Or, like the other night, I put a guy in and now he can't find his glove. 'Where's my glove? Damn! It's around here somewhere.' He has to run back to his locker to get it. *His glove!"*

Still, Rose has turned one of baseball's habitual underachievers—last, last and fifth in the N.L. West from 1982 through 1984—into a contender six games over .500. And it wasn't by trading for Schottzie, either. Rose has done it with will, inspiration and respect for players as (gasp) people. "Pete has two rules," says Parker, who is second in the league in RBIs. "Be on time and give 110 percent. Everything else is irrelevant."

Irrelevance was Job One under Vern Rapp, the manager before Rose. Under Rapp there were no TV sets in the players' lounge, no children in the clubhouse and no smiling after losses. Worst of all, no beer was allowed on plane flights. "What's wrong with two cases of beer for 40 guys?" says Rose, who doesn't drink. When Rapp's Reds began a road trip, they wouldn't fly until the morning of the first game. "You'd get to the park and you'd be drained, man," Rose says.

"Just to save a night in a hotel."

Enter Rose, who turned the franchise's losing attitude around, from laundry boy to owner. There's a TV in the lounge, fruit on the tables, enough beer on the trips, smiles on faces (even after losses), card games on the flights and a decent day's rest on the day of road games. There are also 12 fewer losses in the scorebook, and 313,000 more fans in the seats than this time last year.

"I want nice things at the ball park," Rose says. "Who wants to come to the park if you can't stand it there?"

FOUR P.M.—Holy Wedlock

For the MacNeil-Lehrer interview, Rose is wearing a fire-red PETE ROSE: HUSTLING FOR THE RECORD T-shirt. Rose doesn't catch much MacNeil-Lehrer, but he knows businessmen do, so he wears the shirt. Never know who might want a piece of the action. Rose never took Accounting 101, but he carries a mean calculator in his head. "I'd have made a damn good promotions guy," he says.

For the Cobb chase, you can buy T-shirts, key chains, hats, posters, original Rose/Cobb lithographs, limited-edition silver ($20) and gold ($1,000) coins, and, coming soon, Pete Rose's diary of the chase, written by Hal Bodley, a sportswriter whose best man was Rose. All of the projects are approved by Rose, some started by him. Why should he apologize? Money makes him feel young. Rose likes to feel young.

Rose has sometimes been called a baseball mercenary, which is balderdash. When he came back to the Reds, his salary was pruned to less than $250,000 per year, a cut so fat that it had to be approved by the Players' Association. With attendance incentives, he will probably make at least $500,000 in '85.

Not that Rose won't turn another dollar now and then. He has plugged Aqua Velva, Jockey, Geritol, Wheaties, Swanson's TV dinners, Gekimen noodles, Zenith, Mountain Dew and even his own soda pop, a chocolate-flavored concoction called Pete. Like Rose, it had lots of fizz. He is also a chief spokesman for Mizuno sporting goods, a deal that earns him about $100,000 per year.

All that money makes Rose attractive, not just to three-piece suiters, but to two-piece bikiniers, which gives him a reputation as a ladies' man, which is not exactly true, either. "Not a *lot* of ladies," he says. "It was always just one at a time."

Well, that's not exactly true, either. His first wife, Karolyn, filed for divorce in 1979 because, she says, he was seeing Carol Woilung in public. Carol, 5-7 and dripping blonde, was tending bar at a place called Sleep Out Louie's, only a stand-up double from the stadium. "The clubhouse man said, 'If you want to see the prettiest butt in Cincinnati, go to Sleep Out Louie's,' " Rose told *Cincinnati* magazine. "I had to take him up on it." Says Carol, "I had no idea who this guy was when he walked in. He'd come in and we'd just talk. He found out I wasn't easy like all the other girls. We'd talk about things. He was funny. And such a gentleman. He made me happy." Says Rose, "She made me feel young. . . . I like to live like that. Fast cars, fast horses, a young wife. That keeps you young."

Women grow fond of Rose and seem especially unwilling to give him up. Karolyn once ripped a diamond necklace off Carol at Riverfront Stadium. She was still married to Pete at the time. Twice, Karolyn tattooed Carol's face. "Split my lip," she says. This is life in the big leagues.

Rose was not amused about the way the divorce was handled in the papers. "You'd think I was the only guy in America to ever get a divorce," he says. Still, Rose is not likely to follow Alan Alda onto the cover of *Ms.* magazine. For instance, when Rose became a manager, he was asked if he could handle his players' personal problems. No sweat, he said, especially if it involved the marital sacrament. "Hey, just give her a million and tell her to hit the road," he was quoted as saying. Says Karolyn, "I don't think women mean anything to Pete." This is not exactly true. Baseball just means more.

"You got to spend some time with Pete," says Sparky Anderson. "He's not like the rest of us. Nobody will ever know him completely. Can't know him. He thinks about baseball day and night. He can't sit five minutes in a chair and talk to you about something else. He'll get up. Baseball is all he thinks about. He'll never leave the game. He'd die first."

Rose's affair with baseball has meant that he hasn't had much time to spend with his daughter, Fawn, 20. His son, Petey, 15, had the good sense to be a boy and thus has spent much of his life with his father in clubhouses. But, as Rose says, it was harder with Fawn. "I couldn't bring her to the ball park at 2 o'clock. What's she going to do all by herself at the ball park at 2?"

Though Fawn believes she and her father have become closer in the last year, she wonders what price he paid to become baseball's most durable player. "That's why I'll be so happy for him when he breaks this record and becomes the best of all time," she says. "Because he sure had to give up a lot to get it."

SEVEN P.M.—The Big Shock

MacNeil-Lehrer: "You've often been called Johnny Hustle. Are you proud of that?"

Rose: "*Johnny* Hustle?"

Nolan Ryan is throwing for the Astros and, because Ryan is a righthander, Rose will start at first base. Against lefthanders, Rose, although a switch hitter, yields to youth—Tony Perez, 43. Perez is hitting .320. This is the happiest coupling of senior citizens since *On Golden Pond.*

If you wonder if Rose should be given a contract for 1986, consider this: When Rose has written his own name on the lineup card in '85, the Reds have gone 42-34. Although he's hitting only .266, 39 points below his career average, he ranks third in the league in on-base percentage and eighth in walks. He is the quintessential No. 2

hitter. (For moving the runners up, nobody beats the manager.) And guess who leads the club in hit-by-pitches?

Still, when Rose's average sagged to .236 in late April, *Cincinnati Enquirer* columnist Tim Sullivan suggested that he might help the team if he forgot to pencil his name in the lineup more often. Rose politely disagreed. He attributed his low average to the revolving door full of press that had descended upon his home. And it was true. Rose was going home at 1 a.m., rising at 8 for photo shoots, posing and interviewing until 1, then hurrying to the ball park.

To prove Sullivan wrong, he raised his average to, at one point, .301. "Pitchers think they can blow the fastball by me and they can't," Rose says. "But they're trying, just like when I was coming up."

Still, it is a wonder Rose ever gets a hit. So far today, he's done interviews in his office, around the batting cage, in the dugout, in the tunnel to the clubhouse, in the clubhouse and in his office again. The last reporter leaves at 7:10 p.m., 25 minutes before the first pitch. But when Rose steps in against Ryan at 7:45, that hunch looks as foreboding as ever. Not a bad moment in baseball history. How many times does a guy with 4,000 strikeouts face a guy with 4,000 hits?

With one ball and one strike, Ryan, the ultimate speed freak, throws a straight changeup that dupes Rose so badly he resembles a glazed twist.

"Where'd you get that?" he hollers at Ryan, who shrugs. They both smile.

"He doesn't have enough stuff that he has to learn to throw a straight change?" Rose asks his unoffical assistant manager, George Scherger, after missing another for strike three. "Can you believe that? The Express? With a straight change?"

Carol and Ty arrive in the fourth inning and Rose makes note of it. They always sit in the same seats—four rows back of home plate. Rose's father was not that easy to track. Superstitious, he'd sit down and if Pete didn't get a knock, he'd move. Pete would always find him again, but it took some doing. After the game, Carol and Ty will come down to the family lounge just outside the clubhouse, but Rose's father would rarely visit. "Only twice did he ever come in the clubhouse," Rose says. "Once was the day we won the 1970 pennant, and the other time was for a Sports Illustrated picture. Otherwise, he'd always go home."

Just as in the old days, Harry Rose was not easily swayed to show approval of his son. "If I'd go 3 for 4, he'd say, 'Did you have something on your mind that third time up? You didn't run to first very hard.' And, you know, he'd be right. I'd think back on it and usually I did have something else on my mind."

Tonight, Rose goes 1 for 4. Ryan strikes him out twice, but Rose dumps a bunt down third in the seventh inning off Jeff Calhoun, and while the Astros are deciding who should have the honor of playing it, Rose hustles it out for a hit.

Signs and lights and tote boards and typewriters and Magic Markers start a symphony of Cincinnati celebration as all across the city, 28s become 27s. One of the bat boys asks the umpire for the ball and squirrels it away. The Reds have been keeping every ball since 4,107. Won't be long now till The Big Knock.

In the clubhouse, though, Rose is not smiling. The Reds beat Ryan, 4-1, to keep the Dodgers' lead at 5½ games, but now Rose must do the only thing at a ball park he dreads.

Alan Knicely, his backup catcher, has to be shipped to Denver to make room for pitcher Jay Tibbs. Rose hates this one more than most because Knicely is the second hardest-working player on the team. How can he, the Dead End Kid, give up on a guy who is trying, as Rose would put it, "like hell?" Besides, Knicely makes only $45,000—not bad for most people, but Knicely has extra expenses because his son, Brad, has cerebral palsy. "Knicely *lost* money playing baseball last year," Rose says. Rose is so ill at ease with failure that he always requests that Reds General Manager Bill Bergesch be in the office with him when he breaks bad news. "Otherwise," says Rose, "I'd be in here talking to the kid all night."

TEN P.M.—The Last Stalk

Media Type: "Do you think Ty Cobb is up there looking down at you as you chase his record?"

Rose: "From what I know about the guy, he may not be up there. He may be *down there.*"

In Rose's office, it's a return engagement of the same questions, answers and subject as the night before. And the night before that.

What do you say to people who think you're playing just to break the record? . . . . Do you think it's fair that you'll do it with 2,000 more at-bats than Cobb? . . . How do you think he'd do today? . . . Do you think you'd like each other?

Often, Rose pretends to know less about Cobb than he does. Yet he used to pick the brain of the late Hall of Fame pitcher and long-time Reds broadcaster, Waite Hoyt, about Cobb. "Sometimes I feel like I *know* Ruth and Cobb," Rose once told a writer. Of course, until four years ago, Rose told writers that Cobb's record was out of reach. Maybe the closer you get to a legend, the more human he looks.

The highlight reel: "I never said I was going to be the greatest hitter of all time, I just said I was going to have the most hits. . . . Cobb's .367 average, that's untouchable. That's great. But if he was playing today, he'd hit .315, no doubt in my mind. Think about it. They never had any relief pitching back then. We get a fresh arm throwing against us every two innings sometimes. How tough could the pitching have been? You tell me how a guy is going to win 511 games. And did you ever see those gloves they used? They were about the size of a guy's hand. They had no padding at all. How many diving catches you think they made? . . . I'm not saying Cobb wasn't a great player, I just think you're better off when you don't compare eras, OK?"

Finally, the office is clear and Rose can leave. As he starts walking out, he notices Knicely's wife sitting glumly in the corner of the lounge and Brad in his wheelchair. Rose's eyes meet hers for an instant, then he turns away and sees a friendlier face.

"Smooooooooogie!" he says.

Ty Rose, answering to Dad's pet name for him, comes a-waddling.

The Porsche hums for home now, and inside we have open lines.

"Yes, I'm a first-time caller."

"Turn your radio down."

"Oh, OK. Just a sec. OK. Yes?"

"Yes. Go ahead."

"Yes, I'm a first-time caller, and I'd like to know why Pete didn't pinch-hit for that catcher, Bilardello, in the sixth, when it was 2-1 and we had guys on. I think he should have pinch-hit for that catcher."

Rose is unruffled. "I like to hear what the fans think," he says. "I like it when they say good things about my players. Sometimes, they don't know all the circumstances in a situation, but I still like to hear.

"For instance, I'm not going to pinch-hit for Bilardello there, because if I pinch-hit for Bilardello then I have to use Krenchicki and if I bring in Krenchicki, they're going to bring in that lefthander, and then I'd have to use Doggie (Perez), and then I'd have gone through two of my best pinch-hitters and it's only the sixth inning, and besides, I'm ahead and I need Bilardello for defense and besides, Soto is going good. You understand what I'm saying?"

Is the caller there?

At home, it's another cheeseburger midnight. This is also the hour when Rose can be reached by phone. As such, the Rose end of a lot of conversations is "Gmmphmph." Most people want tickets. Between bites and calls, he digests the Dodger game; Jim Davenport's Giants blow it in the ninth. As the Giants unravel, Rose finds himself pacing. "Jeez!" he screeches. "I'm more worried about this game than Davenport!"

It is not until after 3, after all the Orioles and Blue Jays and White Sox and Red Sox have gone to bed, that Rose capitulates.

"Good night," he says.

But we know better....

FIVE A.M.—The Long Walk

Could Rose be happier? Wheaties still crunchy, White and Red Sox dancing on the dish, history knocking on the door. He is content. Some might find Rose extravagantly one-dimensional, but Rose does all right. He never pretended to attend Swarthmore, anyhow. He grew up on the wrong side of Cincinnati, never went to college, rarely reads a novel and zaps public broadcasting as fast as it comes on. "And he has the most street sense of anybody I know," says his attorney, Reuven Katz. "He knows who he is."

Indeed, Rose will be a first-ballot inductee into the Hall of Fame, and possibly the first unanimous choice, because he followed his one simple motto: "Be yourself." And what Rose is, above all things, is his father's son.

"All I am," he says, "is a young American boy who knew what he could do and what he couldn't do and did it for a long, long period of time. I did the dos more often than I did the don'ts and I didn't mind the dedication. . . . I'm the next generation of my father with an opportunity to show what he could've done."

Forget cash or clout or Cobb or cars. What drives Pete is Harry. "I was in the barbershop, getting my hair cut," Rose says. "I remember getting the call, but I can't remember who was on the other end of the line. Whoever it was said, 'Your dad died.' And I said, 'No, you mean my mom.' My mom had just about everything wrong with her. Her heart was real bad. But the person said, 'No, your dad.' And I couldn't believe it. I don't know why, but I finished getting my haircut. It didn't hit me until I saw him in the funeral home. That's when it hit me, that he was gone."

At the end of every season, Rose drives to the cemetery and makes the walk to his father's grave.

"He took me once," Carol says. "He gets to talking about him and sometimes I see tears come up in his eyes. That's the only time he ever gets very emotional. I think he misses his father very much. He goes there every year just to say thanks."

The minute you're born, you start to die.

Pete will get his Big Knock, but he doesn't even need it. We appreciate Pete Rose because Pete Rose politely declined to grow up. Rose still plays a child's game and plays it as though any minute he'll get that dreaded call for supper.

What was it Satchel Paige said? "How old would you be if you didn't know how old you were?" Rose knows his age. He's 13 and the summer never ends.

The Down Cycle

by Adrian Keating of the Journal Inquirer. Alan Bates of Adams, Mass., learned a hard lesson when he went head over heals on the second turn of the Manchester, Conn., Labor Day bicycle race. Copyright © 1985, Journal Publishing Co. Inc.

Down Under

by Jay Koelzer of the Rocky Mountain News. This is what you call really being on top of the action. Denver Nuggets forward Bill Hanzlik hits the floor after being outmuscled for a rebound during action in a Denver-Utah National Basketball Association game. The interesting camera angle gives the viewer a distorted sense of distance. Copyright © 1985, Denver Publishing Company.

Straub's Team Learns What 'Heart' Means

FOOTBALL

By JOHN ED BRADLEY

From the Washington Post
Copyright © 1985, the Washington Post

Of course, it was always important to remember that he was a football coach and could not be defeated, at least not without a struggle.

And who could help but picture him walking through the glass doors of Holy Cross Hospital as if it were a stadium filled with enormous possibility? Or wearing that funny porcupine flattop as if determined to hang on to what simple prettiness he could of the old days? Oh, what a haircut! And now some of his boys at John F. Kennedy High School in Silver Spring are paying money to try to get their hair fashioned that way, in the good but archaic style of Brady Straub.

You might imagine what happened in his home June 19, the day school let out for the teachers in Montgomery County.

He was in his bedroom, lying on his side, almost asleep, when the phone rang. He could hear his wife say "OK" a couple of times. And he could feel the sting in his side where the doctors, doing a liver biopsy, had stuck needles the day before, long, impossible needles that seemed to reach clear across to the other side. Then she was coming up the stairs, and he was remembering how he used to take her to those dances at the student union, back when they were just kids in school. And how he'd take her out for a pizza afterward and they'd talk for hours, and laugh, and then he'd walk her to the door. Those walks, those good long walks.

She sat on the edge of the bed. And she told him what it was. He knew she wanted to cry. So he said right away, "We're gonna beat this thing. I'm telling you, Janie. We're going to beat it."

And he was glad that he knew, bad as it was. He was glad, all right, even if it was cancer. Cancer, of all things, and of both the colon and the liver. Brady Straub, who is only 37 and the best and toughest coach you'd ever want to meet, had cancer.

"As you know," he told his boys last Saturday morning, the first day of football practice, "I've been ill. There'll be times when you see me sitting down or lying down or even leaving the field to go inside and rest up. This is because I'm like a Cadillac running with an engine the size of a lawn mower. I'm sick, boys. But I guarantee you, I'll give this team 110 percent all the time, no matter what."

Then he told the 48 assembled what he expected of them. Although coaches generally are pretty lousy at giving speeches, Brady Straub has a way of letting you know that he's read a poem or two in his time. He's read them through, start to finish, and come away somehow different, changed in a way that will make him a "better human being," as coaches are known to call people looking to do the right thing.

This one poet, football Coach Grant Teaff of Baylor University, once said, "I am only one, but I am one. What I do can and does make a difference. So let me do it to my God-given ability," and Brady Straub never forgot it. He took it to heart. And this is what Brady Straub told his boys about heart:

"Heart is something you've got to bring with you. But what is heart? Heart is something we can't give you. But heart makes up for a lot of things. Maybe you don't have the size or the speed or the strength, but you were born blessed with the ability to hit. You've got to look and find something within you, and it all comes from heart. You can't go to the store and buy it. We can't order it for you. There's nothing we can do about it, but if you look real hard, maybe you'll find it.

"Heart, like I said, makes up for a lot of things."

★   ★   ★

He knew he was really sick over the Easter break, when he and Janie and the kids, Amy and Katie, were visiting family in Knoxville.

For some reason, he couldn't eat. Everything seemed to sit on his sternum and he was nauseated. Then about a week later, after they'd returned from Tennessee to Maryland, he was cutting the grass out in the yard and started feeling it again. He came inside and sat on the steps leading up to the kitchen.

"I don't feel well," he told his wife. "Something's wrong."

She said, "I'll call the doctor and make an appointment."

And he told her something she already knew: Brady Straub was never one for doctors.

The way he always dealt with his players, he'd say right off the bat, "Don't lie to me; tell me the truth," because that was how he liked to be treated. If he thought a kid wasn't talented enough to play, he'd pull the kid aside after practice and say so. He never made any guarantees. And he never pretended to be anything he wasn't.

Back when he was in college at Middle Tennessee State, where he'd been a baseball star, Straub had talked to several scouts about playing in the big leagues and said he wouldn't sign for nothing, and one had told him they could pick up 50 really poor kids with equal or better talent for what he was asking. He never forgot that. It was hard, but it was honest.

His father had driven a milk truck in Maryland before retiring and moving to Dalmatia, Pa. Brady always said his father had a tough life, getting out of bed every night at 12:30 and hitting the streets. Bob Straub delivered milk to giant supermarkets and little quick shops. He'd get home at about 3 o'clock in the afternoon, take a shower, eat a little something, then head out to the ball park. Almost every day, Brady could count on his father giving him a ride home after practice. They were close in a way you really couldn't put into words, close enough for Brady to remember his father as being a great teacher and coach who happened to drive a milk truck for a living.

When Brady Straub was a boy, it seemed playing games meant a whole lot more than it does today. There were only a couple of decent movie theaters and no MTV. Back then, you found an open field or went to the ball park when the day slowed down. His mother might have gone so far as to inquire about his health if he moped around the house for more than a half-hour. Who ever thought kids would find transport in shopping malls? Hell, who'd ever heard of a shopping mall?

There was baseball and there was football and there was basketball and there was wrestling. And that's all there was. At Northwood High School in Silver Spring, where he later would coach for 15 years, he lettered in three sports and won the county wrestling championship against Larry (Thunder) Thornton, a 145-pounder who'd won the title the two previous years. Thornton would have won the match had he not heaved Straub off the mat and slammed him home, knocking him unconscious. Robert (Dr. Mac) McNelis, the Kennedy assistant principal who then was Straub's wrestling coach, said the official disqualified Thornton for not returning his opponent safely to the mat. Brady woke up in the ambulance on the way to the hospital, the champion by default.

"That was the first time I'd ever been knocked out," he said. "The second time was when they put me under for surgery."

★   ★   ★

Brady Straub took over as football coach at Kennedy one year before the Montgomery County school board closed Northwood's doors forever. Some people accused him of "being just like Benedict Arnold," leaving his alma mater at its time of need to work at its biggest rival. He took their criticism pretty hard, remembering the 15 years of coaching he'd put in at the school and how he and his staff had turned a losing program into a winner. While at Kennedy, he oftentimes slipped and called it Northwood. He told his close friend and assistant, Ken Rippetoe, that his love for the old place was something he could never give up.

"It was home," he said, "a part of me."

When Kennedy played Northwood in 1984 for the last time ever, Brady Straub watched the game from a chair on the sideline. He'd missed almost two weeks of school with a virus so bad many of his colleagues, including Dr. Mac, wondered if maybe it was something worse than an intestinal bug. With the new job, Straub had been under a tremendous amount of pressure, and several friends suggested he get tests to see if he had stomach ulcers. Shortly after watching his team slip by Northwood, he started to come around and eventually felt strong enough to guide Kennedy to the state championship.

Last March, shortly before Easter vacation, Straub had a complete physical examination and received, he says, "flying colors. My doctor's only comment was that I was in good enough shape to get in even better shape.

"Then, out of nowhere, it hit."

Over the following three-month period, during which he had countless blood tests, a gastrointestinal exam, a CAT scan and a nuclear scan, Straub lost almost 50 pounds, dropping from 195 to 146. The examination of his colon and liver biopsy he had in June both proved cancerous, but he said he was prepared to do "anything it takes to get well. I was ready to take a year away and relax."

On July 17, he said, "I was supposed to have surgery at 7:45 in the morning. They were going to insert a pump that would send small doses of chemotherapy to my liver. It was one of three choices my doctor said I had.

"I could have done nothing and let the doctors sit back and observe me. I could have treated it with straight chemotherapy, which gives you about a 20 percent success rate. Or I could have the operation and have the pump put in, giving me an 80 percent chance of success. It took me only about 10 minutes to decide. There was really no decision to make. I wanted the surgery."

He said he came to in the recovery room and asked the nurse, "Did they get the pump in?" When she told him no, the pain seemed even worse.

"They went inside," he said, "and looked around. Then they stitched me right back up. They found more cancer in my colon than they'd anticipated. Now I'm taking chemotherapy once a week, and I've got this scar forming that's shaped like a question mark, just like a question mark etched right across my lower belly. It runs right around the navel and then comes straight down."

★   ★   ★

Brady Straub wore his favorite coaching outfit to practice the other day: Kelly green shorts, a white shirt and white athletic socks dressed with a clover leaf on each ankle. There were only four players wearing flattops, but Shawn Crawford, a junior linebacker and the first to cut his hair that way, figured it wouldn't be long before some of the other guys started looking for an old-time barber. Crawford had been on vacation when he heard about Brady Straub. The mother of one of his teammates had called him out in Ocean City with the news; she'd said that Coach Straub had inoperable cancer and was dying.

As soon as he returned home, Crawford went to the hospital with a box of saltwater taffy, a gift for Straub. He said he felt good knowing that his taffy was the first "real food" Brady had eaten in three days. Later that night, his mother told him not to worry. She said Coach Straub would pick up, she could tell, and that was when he decided to get the flattop. He figured he had to do it.

A few weeks later, Crawford went by Straub's office to see how he was doing. This was on a Friday noon, less than 24 hours before August two-a-days began. Straub was sitting at his old metal desk, telling the story again.

"Every doctor I've been to," he was saying, "and I mean every one—the internist, the gastroenterologist, the surgeon, the oncologist and my family doctor—my first question after they finished testing me was: Am I going to be able to coach football this year?"

A Champion's Heart

HORSE RACING

By *STAN HOCHMAN*

From the Philadelphia Daily News
Copyright © 1985, Philadelphia Daily News

Spend A Buck won the Kentucky Derby by five lengths, in the third fastest time in the whole cockeyed history of the race, by the biggest margin in 30 years, after the swiftest mile in 111 runnings.

After the race was over, after jockey Angel Cordero punched a joyous hole in the Kentucky sunshine with his fist, trainer Cam Gambolati saw something more remarkable.

"I didn't see it until I looked at the replays," Gambolati gurgled yesterday. "At the press conference to announce the decision to skip the Preakness and come to the Jersey Derby.

"They were showing the Derby over and over again and I saw it. The gameness everybody wondered about.

"After the race, Cordero is trying to pull him up. He's galloping out, his ears are pricked. Two horses come alongside. It took 'em a half-mile to catch up.

"And now, the reins went from dangling to tough, and Angel couldn't pull him up. The outrider with the microphone came alongside to get some quotes and Angel waves her away, because he can't pull the horse up. He wasn't going to let anyone pass him, even then.

"I wanted Lafitt (Pincay) to see that. So, this afternoon, we went into the publicity office and looked at the tapes of his last three races. I showed Pincay what happened after the Derby and I told him, 'There's gameness there everybody don't know about.' "

Everybody knows about it now. Everybody knows that Spend A Buck has a heart as big as Mount Everest and just as rugged.

"They hooked him early, they hooked him late," owner Dennis Diaz said, after the screech of the Jersey Derby finally had faded into history.

"They ran at him inside, they ran at him outside. And he wouldn't quit."

Spend A Buck earned $2.6 million for Diaz yesterday, and the agonizing dramatics of the mile-and-a-quarter race should have left the owner drained and speechless.

Instead, he gives us eloquence, he gives us poetry, he gives us truth.

Indeed, they hooked Spend A Buck early, with a swift, untested colt named Huddle Up. Huddle Up would finish a curled-up sixth.

And they hooked him late, when Creme Fraiche swaggered alongside him, after six furlongs in a throat-parching 1:09.

Spend A Buck looked him in the eye, and Creme Fraiche blinked. But first, they leaned into the turn for home, matching strides, matching heartbeats the way Marty Liquori and Jim Ryun once did, turning for home at Franklin Field one afternoon in an unforgettable mile race.

And if that wasn't enough, here came El Basco on the outside, the centrifugal force of his late rush spinning him out to the middle of the race track.

Pincay stung Spend A Buck three times, with the whip in his right hand. Then he switched the whip, slick as a Bill Mazeroski double-play pivot, and he whacked him once lefthanded.

And then he grabbed another handful of rein and he buried his Inca solemn face in Spend A Buck's braided mane and he goaded him to the finish line, a neck in front of Creme Fraiche, with El Basco another nose back.

"It was," Pincay said later, "the toughest race I can remember for a long, long time. Go the first part so fast, and then one horse comes at you inside, another one outside."

"It was," Gamolati said with a sigh, "the longest two minutes and two seconds of my life."

"It was," Diaz said, running out of poetry, "a great, great race."

It was a magnificent race, to be cherished for years and years and years, because it symbolized and summarized and shouted from the neon-trimmed rooftops of this gaudy new race track what is best about this sport.

All in 2:02 3/5.

The gates clanged open and Spend A Buck toppled out, awkward, off-balance, the ground turning to crumbly dust beneath his front feet.

Purple Mountain, thrashing out of the gate to his left, careened into Spend A Buck's left hip, jolting him off stride, putting a gash above his left rear ankle.

Spend A Buck, startled, put his head down. Pincay yanked it up. The horse would return from this incredible journey with his tongue cut and bleeding. It probably happened just a few strides out of the gate.

Pincay, a replacement for Cordero, who chose to ride Track Barron in New York, gathered his horse quickly and urged him into the lead.

There was no point in adding confusion to the early chaos by allowing Spend A Buck to get shuffled behind two or three horses. Not when the charts of his last three races look like a picket fence, with all those 1-1-1-1-1s.

"He had to go with him," Gambolati said. "He'd never been behind horses early. He had to send him."

Spend A Buck rippled through the first turn, with Huddle Up at his flank. D. Wayne Lukas trains Huddle Up, who never had won past six furlongs.

"If he wins today, Spend A Buck is a great horse," Gambolati said earlier, "because there are horses in here today, just out to cook me.

"Lafitt rode him (Huddle Up) when he broke his maiden. He said he didn't think Huddle Up could go a mile and a quarter. Lukas just wants to burn me, because he's got Tank's Prospect (the Preakness winner)."

"Ridiculous," snorted Lukas before the race. "The thought never crossed my mind.

"I'm in here because I think we can win the race. I've said it before and I'll say it again—champions are determined in the fall, not the spring."

There will be time for Spend A Buck and Tank's Prospect to meet, perhaps in the Travers at Saratoga on August 17.

"First, the doc will X-ray him from stem to stern on Wednesday," Gambolati said. "Then we'll Federal Express the X-rays to the doctor who did the knee surgery on him in November. And then we'll decide on when and where he'll race next.

"I know why Huddle Up was in the race. And I know why Woody Sedlacek put that other horse (Purple Mountain) in there. But I've said all along, you try and run with him, you're going to finish behind him."

We found out Spend A Buck had speed in those earlier romps at Garden State. We discovered he had stamina in the mile-and-a-quarter scorcher at Churchill Downs.

Yesterday, they poked around inside him with a sharp stick and found out what he was made of.

William Farish wants to buy a large piece of Spend A Buck and organize his syndication as a stallion. Mr. Farish is an established Kentucky breeder, an officer of the Jockey Club, and was host to the Queen of England, when Her Majesty visited the Kentucky horse farms recently.

Had Mr. Farish seen a new dimension of Spend A Buck scuffling across Jersey's muggy landscape?

"Guts," said Mr. Farish, Kentucky breeder, Jockey Club official and host to the Queen of England.

The Wright Stuff

BASEBALL

By *DON BELL*

From MVP Magazine
Copyright © 1985, Don Bell

I figure it'll be a piece of cake, this story on Johnny Wright. An obscure baseball hero. The Forgotten Black. Mark the cabby, who looks like a toad with a baked potato sticking out of his head, which is his nose, still can't figure out why I've hired him to drive me to Carlton, normally about 20 minutes from the French Quarter of New Orleans.

"Who do you know *there?*" he asks for the umpteenth time. The "there" has a sinister that-isn't-the-kind-of-neighborhood-for-white-folk-to-go-roamin'-around-in ring to it. Either Mark isn't listening when I try explaining, or he's hard of hearing.

"Just a friend. A guy I know."

"You have a friend *there?*"

Mark's driving around in circles because he doesn't know the streets. He has to phone the dispatcher for directions. At the hotel, they phoned for a white cabbie. "If you have a black driver he'll take you for a tour of the city and it will cost a fortune."

They called United, the white taxi company that services most of the small hotels in the French Quarter. So now Mark's taking me for a tour that will cost a fortune.

And besides, his conversation is irritating. "Who'd you say you were seeing?" he asks again.

Listen Marky, I'll tell you the story from the beginning if you keep your mouth shut and your eyes on the road. Your meter is up to nine bucks and we've hardly left the French Quarter.

Mark, what's happening is that you and I are on our way to score a big journalistic coup, a story that will win us prizes and international recognition. How would you like to be standing by my side, Mark, as we're handed a Pulitzer Prize? We may even go to Stockholm with this one for the biggie.

I'll let you in on a secret. Everyone thinks that John Roosevelt

(Jackie) Robinson was the first black man to play in organized baseball. But *two* blacks broke in simultaneously with the Montreal Royals—the Brooklyn Dodgers' farm team in the old International League—in 1946. The other, Johnny Wright, is from right here in New Orleans and we're on our way to see him. I can see that, as a liberal thinker who champions racial equality, you're quite impressed by this news.

Almost 40 years after the fact, we're going to set history right, Mark. Johnny Wright has never been recognized properly. He was always in Jackie's shadow. We're going to give Johnny Wright his proper due, rescue him from obscurity. Are you up for it?

I can see you're thirsty for more details. I'll try to fill you in.

At the time Wright was brought up to the Royals as part of Branch Rickey's "noble experiment," most observers thought his role was mainly to be Jackie's companion ("Robinson would be a lonely boy without a member of his race around," Harold C. Burr wrote in *The Sporting News*). Yet, several major leaguers who played against both in exhibition games thought that quiet-spoken Wright, rather than Robinson, was the better prospect. With the Homestead Grays of the Negro League, he won 25 and lost only four in 1943, and performed peerlessly for the all-black Great Lakes Naval Station during the war, posting the lowest earned-run average of any pitcher in the armed forces. Scouts described him as "a willowy right-handed pitcher" with good control, a live fastball and a wide variety of curves, knucklers and sinkers in his repertoire.

He went to spring training with the Royals in 1946 and endured the same pressures as Robinson in Florida (a padlocked ball park in Jacksonville, a daytime game in Deland called off on the pretext that the stadium lights weren't functioning, a policeman in Sanford walking on the field in the middle of a game and ordering that play be stopped unless Robinson and Wright were removed, citing a local ordinance that banned interracial sporting events).

The stress multiplied as regular-season play began; vicious racial insults were hurled at both players. Wright was the target of the same abuse, the same bench-jockeying as Robinson.

He made two official appearances in relief, the first in Syracuse during the series in which a Syracuse player threw a black cat out of the dugout while Robinson was at bat, yelling "Hey, Jackie, there's your cousin!" Robinson promptly belted a double and, when he later scored, passed by the Chiefs' dugout and shouted: "I guess my cousin's pretty happy now!"

In one of the games, Wright pitched 3⅓ innings of relief, giving up four runs and five hits. Control, always his strongest suit, was a problem for him, possibly because he was so much in the spotlight and couldn't concentrate. But he fared better in his second outing in Baltimore. Inserted in the sixth inning with the bases loaded and the Royals behind five runs, he pitched out of the jam and finished the game without allowing a run.

But it was his last appearance in a Royals uniform. Mississippi-bred Manager Clay Hopper sat him on the bench the following three weeks. Robinson, by this time, had proven himself and had settled in with the team. Then, in May, Wright was sent down to Trois Rivières, Quebec, in the Class C Border League, where he pitched the rest of 1946. The following year he returned to the Grays.

So that, Mark, sums up John Wright's short career in so-called Organized Baseball. The point is that, technically, he was—with Robinson—the first of *two* black players who broke the color barrier. (There were a few who played with white teams in the 19th century, but that was before official records were kept.)

That's why you're driving me to Carlton. We're going to meet this 68-year-old former pitcher—*the man nobody knows!* This is a historic ride, Mark. If you play your cards right, you have much to gain. You'll be able to exchange this old United cab for a limousine and start your own all-white taxi company!

★   ★   ★

I can see you're curious and want to know how I traced Wright. It was a stroke of luck. Like you, Mark, I'd also thought that Jackie Robinson was the trailblazer, that he alone opened the gates for Don Newcombe, Roy Campanella, Larry Doby, Willie Mays, Hank Aaron—all the others—making democracy in baseball possible. Even when rooting for Robinson as a kid in Montreal's old Delormier Stadium, I didn't realize there was a Johnny Wright as well. It wasn't until researching a magazine story on Robinson three years ago, while riffling through some old *Montreal Heralds,* that I spotted the name of the man who is now the Forgotten Black.

The first step was to find out, if Wright was still alive, where he lived. I phoned the Expos. Somebody in the front office suggested trying the Los Angeles Dodgers—they might have addresses of players once in their organization (The L.A. Dodgers, of course, were formerly the Brooklyn Dodgers.)

Fred Claire, the Dodgers' vice-president, replied to my letter that he didn't have any background on Wright and I should try the Hall of Fame in Cooperstown, N.Y. No luck there either. I wrote to Mayme Clayton, director of the Western States Black Research Centre in Los Angeles, but the letter was returned unopened, stamped by the U.S. Post Office: "Return to Writer."

How did they know I was a writer? Was the U.S. government on my case? Why wasn't it stamped: "Return to Policeman" or "Return to Golfer?" Would there be visits in the middle of the night by FBI agents?

Then, finally, Mark, a lead. The National Association of Professional Baseball Leagues in St. Petersburg replied to my letter with a "last known address" for Wright in New Orleans. It was probably decades old. I phoned New Orleans information: they did have a Hazel Wright at that address—probably Johnny's daughter, I figured. I phoned. A man answered. A soft, pleasant voice. "Which

Johnny Wright do you want?" he asked.

"The former baseball player."

"Who'd you say you were?"

"A Canadian journalist."

"What do you want to talk to me about, man?"

Bingo! I'd found the Forgotten Black. I told him about wanting to write a story about him, and asked how he'd been occupying himself since retiring from baseball. He said he'd been employed at National Gypsum in New Orleans as a driver and janitor, but was now retired. Sure, he had a *box* of clippings about his baseball days, but they were falling apart. He couldn't send them, but if I came down, I could go through his box. And that was about it.

I kept in touch with Johnny, phoning him every now and then, sending him the Jackie Robinson article when it came out and a photocopy of some pages where he's mentioned in Jules Tygiel's superb book, *Baseball's Great Experiment: Jackie Robinson and His Legacy.* I encouraged him to "drop me a short line just to have an idea of what kind of life you've been living since retiring from baseball," but never heard from him.

But this winter, Mark-o, as you can see, I finally made it down. You know, as a cabbie, you have all sorts of fares, don't you? It's similar in my profession. There are many different stories to write. Some, technically, are more difficult than others. But this one, Mark, is already writing itself in my mind. I can't wait until the interview is over and the challenge of the writing begins.

Listen, what we'll do is we'll start with a *National Geographic*-style lead with a bit of *The Old Man and the Sea* thrown in. We'll set up the scene, this lethargic old man, now living in total obscurity, not even his neighbors knowing who he is, fishing on the Louisiana bayous. . . .

"The morning sun rose higher and the chorus of whistles and chirps became louder as John Wright, the Forgotten Black, threw his line into the murky waters of the Atchafalaya swamp. A fat brown cottontail slithered away from us into the cypress forest. Before us, hundreds of dazzling white egrets regurgitated their catches of crawfish into the mouths of their young. . . .

"How did baseball treat you?" I asked Johnny, swatting away the mosquitoes as they flew around our heads in the excruciating heat.

Wright's line suddenly snapped and trembled. "I got something," he said. "It's a big mother."

And then, as this monster of a fish towed our boat through the bayous, Johnny would begin his tales about the old Negro Leagues: stories about Jelly Gardner, Jew Baby Bennette, Mule Suttles, Goo Goo Livingston, Moocha Harris and, of course, his old teammate with the Homestead Grays, the fastest man ever to put on a pair of baseball cleats, Cool Papa Bell.

It's said of Cool Papa that the infielders had to catch the ball on the first bounce to throw him out. He bunted for *doubles,* legged out ground balls to the pitcher and went from first to third on sacrifices. When he rounded second base, it looked like his feet weren't touching the ground. When he was planning to steal a base, he told the hitter to stand deep in the box, forcing the catcher back a few inches and giving him an added jump. At 40, playing on the Homestead Grays with Johnny Wright, he led the league in steals.

Before leaving for New Orleans, I tried finding people who remembered Wright. I reached Jackie's widow, Rachel Robinson. She said she knew Johnny but didn't recall too much about him except that he was "a very soft-spoken, gentle, clean-cut, friendly person, somebody we got to know and like very quickly." During the short period when her late husband and Wright were together on the Royals, "they felt very paired. They knew that they were in the struggle together. They had the same concerns and anxieties about performing well."

Robinson implied in his autobiography that Wright had caved in, couldn't stand the pressures, that it was particularly tough for him because he was a pitcher. "Things that went on up there were too much for him," Robinson has been quoted as saying. It would be interesting to ask Johnny how he felt about Robinson's choke-up charges, and did he think that Jackie spoke out of turn?

I tried tracing Frenchy Bordagaray, a former member of the St. Louis Cardinals' Gas House Gang, who was Wright's manager in Trois Rivières, and Roy Partlow, a fellow black pitcher who was called up to the Royals after Wright left and, like him, was also shipped to Trois Rivières after Hopper sat him on the bench. Partlow had an unlisted number in Philadelphia and Bordagaray had left instructions with the Cooperstown Hall of Fame not to give out his address.

I did reach Herb Trawick, the first black player in Canadian football who broke in the same year as Robinson. Trawick now runs a courier service in Montreal. He said he came to Montreal from Pittsburgh only in August of 1946, after Wright had left, so didn't meet him, but he and Robinson became friends.

"It was easier for a football player," Trawick remembers. "You could fight back. If an opponent made a racial slur, you would change your position on the line and give him a little tap with your elbow at the appropriate time. The elbow was the great equalizer in race relations." Trawick recalls the climate was such at the time, even in Canada, that both Ottawa and Toronto threatened to quit the Canadian Football League when the Alouettes signed him.

But this is all peripheral, Mark. The core of the story is to meet our man, Johnny Wright, and ask him directly what it was like. It's taking a long time, Mark. Do you know where we are? Are you sure this isn't the road to Baton Rouge? I saw a sign back there saying "This way to San Francisco."

I arrived last night and phoned Johnny from the airport. "I bet you thought I'd never make it down here, John." It sounded like a party was in progress. Music, voices, tinkling of glasses. "Listen, man," Johnny said, "if you don't like the hotel you're staying at, you phone me back, will you? I have just a small humble abode here, but if you have any problems, just let me know, man. I woulda picked you up at the airport, but I'm having some motor problems with my vehicle. . . ."

Here we are, Mark. That must be the house there, and I think that's Johnny waiting for us in front. Thank you for the tour of New Orleans. You better get out of this neighborhood quickly before they steal your hubcaps or slash your tires. Luckily, I'm not judging all of Louisiana by you. Your nose is so long, it must grow an inch every time you take a customer for a long ride.

★   ★   ★

Lionel Irons, you're looking at a very confused fare. I think I just blew it. Perhaps you'd have some advice for me. I need somebody to talk to.

I'm glad you came so fast. We've been phoning United Cab for an hour but I guess they don't service this neighborhood. Mr. Horse, Johnny Wright's friend across the way, swears he has the right number. Mr. Horse says he phoned United six times and each time they said they'd be sending a cab right over, but we're still waiting. As soon as Johnny phoned the all-black Elks cab company, you came promptly.

Thank you, man, and take me to the Andrew Jackson Hotel in the French Quarter. Royal Street. By the way, is it all right if I call you "man?"

As I was saying, man, I have a problem. Flew all the way from Canada to interview Johnny Wright. You say you know him? Former ball player. A star in the Negro Leagues. Did you know that he broke the color bar in Organized Baseball with Jackie Robinson?

When I stepped out of Mark's United cab earlier this evening, Johnny was waiting in front of his bungalow. Nice place, a little garden in front. For some reason, I half-hoped to find a lame-looking, grizzled old man who had been fishing on the bayous all day. He'd be sitting in a rocker on the porch and there'd be flies buzzing around his head.

But Johnny was anything but that. He was tall, slim, fit-looking, suave. Looked like he could step on the mound and still go nine innings.

Mark was still hovering in his cab.

"Are you waiting for this fella?" he asked Johnny.

"It's all right, Marky, you can go."

I remember Jackie Robinson's first meeting with the Royals' Mississippi-born manager, Clay Hopper:

"I was relieved to see him stick out his hand," said Robinson, "for even in those days a great number of southerners would under no circumstances shake hands with a Negro."

"Johnny, it's good to meet you at last," I said, sticking out my hand.

Johnny apologized again for his car troubles. "I'm really sorry, man. I woulda picked you up at the hotel, but, man, you know the way it is."

We went inside. A cozy home with comfortable furniture, a bar counter separating the kitchen from the bright living room, shelves full of knickknacks; but no trophies or baseball mementoes were readily visible.

Johnny still had that loose, *willowy* look. Long arms and knuckly fingers that had clenched thousands of baseballs and struck out hundreds of batters, including some of the legendary hitters in the Negro Leagues.

We sat on a sofa in the front room. There was a large box on the floor filled with clippings and photos.

"If you had told me exactly when you were coming in, like I say, man, I woulda asked Mr. Horse to pick you up," Johnny said.

"Mr. Horse?"

★   ★   ★

"That's what I call my friends. Mr. Horse. Mr. Chicken. If you stay around long enough, I'll start calling you Mr. Horse."

We talked about the weather in "Big Easy," as Johnny calls New Orleans, and the snow and cold in Canada, and then, perhaps too hurriedly, I started taking out the large tape recorder that I'd brought along.

"Listen, man, I know you're doing your job," Johnny said, "but I've been thinking about this and I don't know how to put it, man. I know you came all the way down here to see me. I shoulda told you this, man, before you came, but this magazine you're working for, they're gonna sell a lot of copies, man, if my life story is in there. Like I say, I don't know how to put it, but what will I get in return, man?"

Oh oh.

"Uh . . . there's recognition, John. Here's . . . uh . . . a chance for you to tell your life story and see it in print."

"I know, man, that's why I can't give it away for nuthin'."

"Uh . . . nothing much has been written about you since you retired from baseball. . . ."

"Hey, man, look at this box. It's full, man. *Sports Illustrated* wrote about me." He pulled out copies of two June 1983 issues with excerpts from Jules Tygiel's book *Baseball's Great Experiment*. Johnny is mentioned, but the excerpts really focus on Robinson; it was the same material that I'd photocopied and mailed to him.

"But this will be something different, Johnny. It will be about *only* you. It'll be a sympathetic story. I think you'll really like it."

"I know, man, that's why you'll sell a lot of magazines."

"Well, uh, how much would you want, John?"

"Hey, man, if you have my story between those covers, that's worth a lot of money."

"Well, it's a new magazine you know, John, and it sells only in Canada. Would you accept . . . uh . . . a hundred bucks?"

"Hey, man, you gotta be kidding. My life story for a hundred bucks?"

"If you can give me an idea of how much you'd like, I can phone the editor and discuss it with him."

"Would you sell *your* life for a hundred bucks? I'd rather pay your flight and all your expenses in New Orleans than give away my life for a hundred bucks."

I phoned Toronto but the editor wasn't there.

"If we can get this straightened out, man, you can come here and spend as much time as you need going through this box." Johnny began pulling out tattered old clippings from *The Sporting News* and black newspapers.

"Do you read Spanish, man?"

He yanked out stories and photos from newspapers in Cuba, the Dominican Republic, Venezuela, Mexico. (After his fling with Trois Rivières, Johnny played for a year with his old team, the Homestead Grays, then continued playing another 10 years, both summer and winter ball, in Latin America.)

"Here's Mexico. When I was down there, man, I asked them to let me pitch always on Saturdays so I could be off on Sundays and go to the bullfights. They used to call me conejo—rabbit—because I was so fidgety, not just when I was pitching, but all the time."

★   ★   ★

Johnny pulled out a photo showing him and Sam Bankhead with the Zulu Cannibals—baseball's answer to the Harlem Globetrotters. The Zulus wore grass skirts, played in their bare feet and splashed their faces with war paint. It was burlesque rather than baseball, in the tradition of the Tennessee Rats, the Miami Clowns and the all-bearded House of David team. In one of their funniest routines, a batter would take off and run toward third on a ground ball instead of first, creating traffic jams and confusion on the base paths.

"Man, it'll take you a week to go through this box. This is my whole life in here, man. A hundred bucks? I know what my life is worth." He thrashed around in the box for more clippings, pulling them out at random. "Man, we weren't pampered in those days. We'd be barnstorming for two weeks in those old Mack buses without ever seeing a bed. It was fun. We were like a family. Now, a player has a sore little finger and he's out of action for a month."

I tried steering the conversation toward breaking in with Jackie with the Montreal Royals.

"Yeah, sure, I felt all the pressures. Man, my own catcher was tipping off the batters about what pitches I'd be throwing."

This was a new twist, something that hadn't been mentioned in any of the literature on Jackie Robinson.

"Sure, man. It was Herman Franks," Johnny told me. "We were

playing an exhibition game in Buffalo and the umpire called a conference out on the mound and told Franks to stop announcing the
pitches. They were doing everything to make it difficult for us."

"Did Jackie know about this?"

"Sure. He was out on the mound when the umpire called us together. Man, you'll have a lot to write about. I'll bring you fishing
with me on the bayous with Mr. Horse and I'll tell you everything,
man."

"Do you live here alone, John?"

"I'm shacked, just as of this week, man. My wife is still in New
Orleans. We're on good terms."

"Kids?"

"Kids? Hey, man, I got four kids, 18 grandchildren and four
great-grandchildren. I told my kids it looks like they ain't got time
for nuthin' else."

"You ever still throw a ball around, John?"

"I'd like to, man, but my cousin Arthur won't let me."

"Arthur?"

"Arthritis," Johnny laughed, rubbing his pitching arm.

He brought a Coke in from the kitchen. "Sorry I don't have any
beer left, man. We had a party last night." He called Mr. Horse. Mr.
Horse tried phoning United Cabs. United didn't come. We chatted
about this and that. Johnny paced nervously. Then Johnny phoned
Elks and within two minutes, Lionel Irons, you were here.

This is the hotel. What am I going to do now, Lionel? Came all the
way down to New Orleans and no story. Anyway, thanks for lending
me your ear. I feel better now. How much is the fare? . . . hey, man,
that's three bucks *less* than what it came to with the white driver.

"Take it easy, man."

"You too, man."

★   ★   ★

"Smoking or non-smoking?" asked the maitre d' at An Oyster
Bar Named Desire on Bourbon Street.

I decided to sit at the counter. The waitress came over.

"We have a special today on crab balls," she chirped.

I ordered the special, a beer and half a dozen raw oysters.

"One Bud, six nude oysters and an order of crab balls coming
up!" she shrilled all over the restaurant.

Waiting for the food, I asked myself what the next step would be.
Was there some way Johnny Wright could be persuaded to cooper-
ate? Suppose I offered him 15 percent across the board of everything
I earned, including TV and film rights?

I gobbled down the last of the crab balls. Should I just scrap the
whole story? New Orleans had its literary traditions. I couldn't just
give up. What would Tennessee Williams have done in similar circumstances?

My train of thought was interrupted by the waitress.

"Would you like a Sweet Desire?" she asked.

I was about to bound over the counter and claw off her "I Eat Lobster" apron, but she threw up her hands.

"I'm referring to dessert," she said. "You should try our black bottom pie."

It was all I could do to get out of An Oyster Bar Named Desire as fast as I could.

★　　★　　★

For the next two days, there was a series of telephone negotiations between Johnny and myself. Confident that it would work out, I even bought a small cassette recorder, thinking we'd go fishing on the bayous with Mr. Horse and I'd install the recorder on the dashboard of Mr. Horse's pickup to record the dialogue as we drove along the dusty Cajun backroads. These tapes would become historical documents.

But the miniature recorder had the flaw of picking up the sound of its own whirring reels as well as the voices that were being recorded. When I went back to the Canal Camera Center less than an hour after making the purchase and asked for a refund, there was no way the manager would hear of it. He just stared blank-faced and said "No."

"But I just bought it from you."

"No."

"I couldn't test it properly in the store because of the background noises."

"No."

"It's still in the box. It hasn't been touched."

"No."

"It's defective. It's a lemon."

"No."

"Can't you do anything?"

"No."

"It was my last 40 dollars."

"No."

"I'm a tourist. Is this the impression you want tourists to have of New Orleans?"

"No."

I was in an ugly mood. I threw the tape recorder at him. But he just stood there.

I thought I'd return later and hurl a rock through the window, or rent a car and drive it into the shop and ask for a pizza to go. It was muggy in New Orleans and there was violence in the air. Perhaps I should buy a pistol and run amok in the streets? Or molest a few people or hijack a plane?

★　　★　　★

MVP Magazine authorized me to offer Johnny $400 for the rights to his story.

"Hey, I don't want to be mean, man," Johnny said over the phone, "but I'm not stupid, man. That's an insult, man. If your dude makes me a reasonable offer, I'll listen, man. But I'm not going to sell my life story for $400, man. Hey, man, I'll take you fishing with Mr. Horse on the bayous if you stay around the Big Easy and I'll pay for your hotel, man. But I'm not gonna surrender my life to anybody for that price, man. As far as this article is concerned, shove it."

A few hours later, Johnny phoned back.

"I'm serious, man, about taking you fishing on the bayous. I just want to let you know I have a heart. I shoulda discussed this with you before you came all the way down here to see me, man."

"I've booked a flight home for tomorrow, man," I told him.

"You have a safe trip back home now, man."

★   ★   ★

I'm drinking a Jewish coffee—sabra liqueur with coffee and whipped cream—in the Pontalba Cafe on Jackson Square. A man in dark sunglasses and a black suit comes in, rants about corruption and sin in the world and grovelling in the darkness, and hands out a printed leaflet called "Your Destiny," which says: "The Light could not and cannot be put out."

I know now where the answer lies.

I have to find Cool Papa Bell.

James Bell isn't listed in the St. Louis phone directory, but his wife Clarabelle Bell is. If he were still alive, the fastest man ever to put on baseball shoes would be 81. I phoned. Clarabelle answered. The connection was bad. She couldn't hear too well. I explained I was a Canadian writer. I told her I was embarrassed but didn't know whether Cool Papa was still alive or not.

"He's right here," she said. "Do you want to speak to him?"

Cool Papa still had the rich accent of his native Starkville, Miss. I told him I wanted to come down and do a story on him, but I was curious if he knew Johnny Wright.

He said I had phoned him at a bad time. He had a hospital appointment. He was blind in one eye and had glaucoma in the other. Also, he couldn't hear too well. And there was a journalist from *St. Louis Magazine* in the house interviewing him at that very moment.

I asked again if he knew Johnny. Yes, he knew Johnny Wright, he said. He played with him for a couple of years with the Grays. "He was a pitcher. Yeah. I remember him. He had no change-up and not much of a curve."

"How did he get batters out?" I asked.

"Satchel Paige didn't have much more than a fastball either, but he threw them so fast nobody could see them."

"Did you know Johnny well?"

"Yeah, sure, Johnny was a nice fella. He had a clean life and everything. Johnny wasn't no rough guy. A lot of players in the old days, both black and white, had a rough style both on the field and off. Not Johnny. He was very gracious. A good man. He wasn't a troublemaker."

In recent years, Cool Papa has been much in demand by modern baseball historians, and has been accessible to anyone curious about what it was like during his 30 years in Negro baseball. Many of his valuable clippings and photos were loaned out to researchers, and not all of them were sent back. Although he doesn't resent it, he has never received anything in return for his availability.

Perhaps what Johnny Wright was doing, protecting himself, made sense. Was a life worth $400? Was a life worth a million? I think Johnny just wasn't in the mood to think back. Perhaps it was the *pressure* that inconvenienced him. Perhaps he would, after all, prefer fishing on the bayous, or enjoying the good laid-back life in Big Easy.

Georgia Tech Has A Night To Remember

COLLEGE BASKETBALL

By *MARK BRADLEY*

From the Atlanta Journal
Copyright © 1985, The Atlanta Journal-Constitution

It was December. Bobby Cremins was speaking of his team, and why Georgia Tech couldn't win its conference. "You don't win the ACC," he said, his voice awash with reverence, "with three recruiting classes."

Two months later, in joyous victory, the Yellow Jackets coach was reminded of those words. "I was wrong," he said Wednesday. Then, shaking the head that still reeled from the audacity of this achievement: "But I don't believe it. I don't believe we held it together."

Believe it. Believe that Tech, in as grand a night as its basketball program has known, defeated North Carolina, 67-62, before 15,501 at the Omni and bought itself a share of the hallowed ACC regular-season championship. Believe what the Jackets themselves were afraid to believe, lest the knowledge shake their very souls.

One by one, Tech's players and coaches heard the final from Raleigh—Maryland 71, North Carolina State 70—knowing that State's loss was the sliver of daylight they needed. Still, the Jackets had to beat North Carolina, and to beat lordly Carolina a second time in a season a team must concentrate, and who can concentrate when you're worrying about the out-of-town scores?

Common sense told those Jackets who'd heard State lost to keep it to themselves. Alas, human nature dictated otherwise.

Craig Neal, the injured guard, found out first. "I heard it at halftime," he said. "I wasn't going to tell, but I couldn't stand it. So when we went up by eight in the second half, I told Mark (Price), "Man, you won't believe this, but State lost.' "

Price: "Quit lying. You're always joking."

Neal: "I'm *serious.*"

Finally convinced, Price bore his burden in silence. For two minutes. Then he told forward Scott Petway. Petway told somebody else, and somebody else told Antoine Ford, who told all the guys on the bench. By the shank of the ballgame, Cremins was wielding the State score like a whip.

"We'd stayed away from the championship thing," Cremins said, "and I think it worked. But the last couple minutes, every time somebody made a turnover, I'd call 'em over and say, 'Hey, State lost. We can win the ACC *championship.*' "

Ultimately, every Jacket got the word, save Yvon Joseph. "No telling what he'd have done if he'd heard," Cremins said. And it was Joseph, standing at the foul line on wart-ravaged feet in blissful ignorance, who made the free throws that ended the last Tar Heels thrust.

Tech hadn't scored in nearly five minutes, and a three-point play by Carolina's Joe Wolf and a Brad Daugherty foul shot had sliced the Jackets' lead from 60-54 to 60-58. Thirty-seven seconds remained when Heels forward Dave Popson whacked Joseph at midcourt. As his mother, who'd flown from Haiti to Miami and driven the rest of the way, watched from the seats, Joseph made both shots. Nineteen seconds later, he made two more. Then, with one second to play, Cremins told Joseph of State's fate.

Instant lunacy.

"Yvon started screaming in the huddle," said forward John Salley. "I said, 'Relax, man.' Me, I wasn't celebrating until I saw three zeros."

But the Jackets had known before the scoreboard struck 0:00 that the night was theirs. They suspected in the first half when Bruce Dalrymple played as if shot from a cannon, grabbed every rebound and loose ball in sight, when the patchwork ensemble consisting of Ford, Petway and Jack Mansell astonishingly built upon Tech's lead.

They sensed the kill in the second half, as Price made basket upon basket to expand the margin to 50-42 and freshman Duane Ferrell scored eight points in three minutes to fend off the surging Heels. And then, after Joseph's first two foul shots, came the moment where everyone positively *knew.*

With 30 seconds left and Tech up by four, Dalrymple, the best player on the floor all game, flung himself in front of a Kenny Smith pass and fled for the basket. As he went, Dalrymple threw back his head and howled. It was a night for howling.

That Tech can do no better than tie for the championship meant nothing. Their league game done, the Jackets will learn Saturday with whom they'll share the title—definitely either Carolina or Duke, who play each other, and possibly State, which meets Wake Forest. What mattered Wednesday was that Tech can do no worse than split a title and seldom has the thought of sharing pleased a team more.

Seven hours before tipoff, Salley and Price had come to the Omni to shoot around, just the two of them, one to a basket. Together, they'd formed the nucleus of Cremins' first recruiting class, the first of the three that Cremins said weren't quite enough. Then Salley and Price had looked upon the ACC championship as a distant light—visible, but so very far away. Little did they know.

"I remember thinking, 'Maybe my senior year, we'll contend for it,'" Salley said. "But I always hoped, and hope is the beginning of faith."

Grambling Coach Nears Win Record—Unknown

FOOTBALL

By *MITCH ALBOM*

From the Detroit Free Press
Copyright © 1985, the Detroit Free Press

Midnight. Forty young black men get on a bus in Mississippi. Their coaches follow. Then the assistants. The trainer. They are all black. Eddie Robinson, the head coach, gets on last, still in the suit he wore on the football field hours earlier.

The air is cold and still. You can hear crickets. Robinson nods, and the bus rolls. Seven hours and 400 miles will pass before the team gets home to Grambling, La. This is how they travel.

Robinson leans against the window, his forehead creased with age lines, and holds out a roll of mints. "Want one?" he asks. Then he begins to reminisce, his voice a whisper over the engine.

The stories. Fascinating. Horrible. Of the 1940s, and the lunch-meat sandwiches he used to prepare for his players because blacks were not allowed in the restaurants.

Of the 1950s, and how they broke down somewhere in the Deep South, and the nearest mechanic picked up a wrench and yelled, "Don't bring that nigger bus in here."

Of the 1960s, and how some players came from such poor backgrounds, "they did not know how to use a knife and fork."

Eddie Robinson took them all. Taught them all.

Where you expect anger in his voice, there is none. Where you expect resentment, there is none.

I took this bus ride with him two years ago, a year after he won his 300th game. Now, in his 44th season, his foot is in the door of history again.

He is about to pass Bear Bryant as the most victorious college football coach *of all time.*

And where you expect recognition, there is none. Not the kind

Eddie Robinson deserves.

★   ★   ★

Remember that when Bear Bryant was starting out at Maryland, Eddie Robinson was already at Grambling, coaching football. A one-man staff.

And when Bear Bryant was making a name for himself at Kentucky, Robinson was at Grambling, coaching football. And hosing off the field, and directing the girls drill team.

And when Bear Bryant was turning into a legend at Alabama, Robinson was still at Grambling, coaching football. And writing the game stories for newspapers that generally didn't print them.

And when Bear Bryant passed Amos Alonzo Stagg in all-time victories among college coaches, Robinson was still at Grambling, coaching football. And sending his 200th player to the pros—though his quarterbacks were almost always given new positions. "Not smart enough," the pros said.

For decades, black athletes in the South came to Robinson, for they had no choice. If they wanted to play college football, it had to be at a "black" college; a Grambling, an Alcorn State, a Southern.

Eddie Robinson took them, molded them, won with them, made sure they graduated.

And when, in the 1960s, the previously all-white schools were integrated, the black schools were suddenly shunted aside. Their programs sank as their would-be players were wooed away by promises of network TV and fancy stadiums.

Robinson would not complain. "I watched black kids risk their lives to integrate society," he says. So he settled for the also-rans. The leftovers.

And he taught them. And he won with them.

Time magazine once asked him about the irony of it, and he shrugged. "Some build the roads, some drive over them," he said. "We're getting there."

★   ★   ★

Well, maybe and maybe not. Saturday marks the start of Grambling's 1985 season, with Robinson only four wins from breaking Bryant's career mark of 323 victories. And I don't hear much fuss, much Pete Rose-type hoopla.

Oh, there's an article here and there. But you can bet if he were white and at a major school you'd know Eddie Robinson's name backward by now.

And meanwhile, he goes on, still on a tiny budget, still making the midnight bus rides, still driving the Louisiana backroads to recruit players.

He is 66 now, and how many men owe him their football careers? Tank Younger, Willie Davis, Ernie Ladd, Buck Buchanan, Doug Williams. And how many less famous others owe him their diplomas, their manners, their pride?

Remember Ralph Ellison, the brilliant black writer who called himself an Invisible Man because people refused to see him?

Eddie Robinson has been invisible. Too long.

No doubt there are some who don't want Bryant's legend eclipsed—and particularly by a black man. Tough. It's going to happen.

And when it does, it might be worth noting that Bryant did not have a black athlete in his program until 1970. The same year Grambling finally got a sprinkler for its football field.

Some build the roads, some drive over them.

This college year belongs to Eddie Robinson. And sadly, too few of us know it.

Head Fake

by Bill Frakes of the Miami Herald. Is that the Invisible Man running through a hole in the New York Jets line? No, it's simply perfect timing on a picture that captures a Jets helmet en route to the turf during a National Football League game against Miami. Copyright © 1985, William Frakes, Miami Herald.

PRIZE-WINNING WRITERS IN BEST SPORTS STORIES 1986

Phil Hersh (Baseball Is a Dream That Can't Go Away) handles special assignments for the *Chicago Tribune,* which in 1985 presented him an Outstanding Professional Performance award for "his compelling writing in regularly bringing to life the fascinating characters and personalities that lurk behind the box scores in sports." Hersh, a 1968 graduate of Yale University, previously worked for the *Gloucester (Mass.) Daily Times, Baltimore Evening Sun, Chicago Daily News* and the *Chicago Sun-Times.* Hersh, who is making his fourth appearance in *Best Sports Stories,* is a first-time winner.

Jeffrey Marx (co-author of Boosters' Gifts Lined Kentucky Players' Pockets) is a sportswriter for the *Lexington Herald-Leader* in Lexington, Ky. The 23-year-old Marx, a graduate of Northwestern University's Medill School of Journalism, joined the paper in June 1984 after serving two sports and news internships in Lexington. Marx, who was born in New York City, first reported on sports while working as a summer assistant with the Baltimore Colts of the National Football League. Marx is making his first appearance in *Best Sports Stories.*

Mike McKenzie (Eddie Robinson) is a special assignments sportswriter for the *Kansas City Star and Times.* His first-person account of witnessing the Hyatt Regency skywalks collapse in Kansas City in 1981 contributed to coverage that earned the papers a Pulitzer Prize. He also was voted winner of the best sports-event story in the 1983 Associated Press Sports Editors contest. The 44-year-old McKenzie previously worked for the *Huntsville (Ala.) Times, Atlanta Journal, Ames (Ia.) Daily Tribune, Tuscaloosa (Ala.) News* and the *Baton Rouge Morning Advocate.* McKenzie, a first-time winner, is making his second appearance in *Best Sports Stories.*

Mike Trimble (Memoirs of a Miner) is an associate editor of *Arkansas Times* magazine in Little Rock, Ark. The 42-year-old Trimble is a native of Bauxite, Ark., a mining town that no longer exists. He formerly worked for the *Arkansas Gazette* in Little Rock. Trimble is making his first appearance in *Best Sports Stories.*

Michael York (co-author of Boosters' Gifts Lined Kentucky Players' Pockets) is the Washington Correspondent for the *Lexington Herald-Leader* in Lexington, Ky. The 32-year-old York is a graduate of the University of Kentucky and the University of North Carolina Law School. He joined the *Herald-Leader* in 1979 after working for newspapers in North Carolina and Florida. York, who is married and has two children, is making his first appearance in *Best Sports Stories.*

OTHER WRITERS IN BEST SPORTS STORIES 1986

Mitch Albom (Grambling Coach Nears Win Record—Unknown) writes a sports column for the *Detroit Free Press.* Albom, a former columnist and feature writer for the *Fort Lauderdale News* and *Sun Sentinel,* has had his work published in such magazines as *Sport* and *Sports Illustrated* and in such newspapers as the *Philadelphia Inquirer* and *The New York Times.* He is appearing in *Best Sports stories* for the first time.

Paul Attner (Tom's Still Terrific!) is a national correspondent for *The Sporting News.* The former *Washington Post* staff writer is a 1969 graduate of California State University at Fullerton, where he earned a Bachelor of Arts degree in Communications. Attner, the author of three books, has won numerous sportswriting awards, including three first places in the annual Pro Football Writers Association of America writing contests and a first-place award in the U.S. Pro Basketball Writers annual contest. He is an active member of the Society of Professional Journalists, Pro Football Writers Association of America and Pro Basketball writers of America.

Don Bell (The Wright Stuff) is a free-lance writer making his home in Sutton, Quebec. His offbeat sports stories appear regularly in *MVP,* a Canadian sports review. Bell is a former winner of Canada's prestigious Leacock Humor Award for his book *Saturday Night at the Bagel Factory and Other Stories.* Bell, who was born in Brooklyn, N.Y., but now is a naturalized Canadian, often writes under the pseudonym Joe Two Knockouts. A collection of his best sports pieces soon will appear in book form under the title *Frenchy's Hockey Fantasy and Other Stories.*

Ira Berkow (Age Hasn't Cooled the Fire Inside Ali) is a sports columnist and feature writer for *The New York Times.* Berkow, who holds degrees from Miami (Ohio) University and Northwestern, is a former sportswriter for the *Minneapolis Tribune* and a former sports editor and columnist for *Newspaper Enterprise Association.* He is the author of several books, the most recent of which is titled, *Red: A Biography of Red Smith.* Berkow has appeared in *Best Sports Stories* several times.

Ron Borges (The Hard Times of a Hard Hitter), a sportswriter for the *Boston Globe,* has spent the past 11 years chasing professional athletes from coast to coast. He began his career with a small Massachusetts weekly newspaper before heading for California and stints on the *Sacramento Union* and the *Oakland Tribune.* Borges left Oakland in 1982 for the *Baltimore News American,* where he covered the Baltimore Orioles for a season. He joined the Globe in 1983. Borges is making his third consecutive appearance in *Best Sports Stories.*

Thomas Boswell ('Best' Team Won, Even If It Wasn't Most Talented and Knight, Riggins Could Learn From Each Other) is a reporter for the *Washington Post.* The 1969 Amherst College graduate, who ranks as one of the most respected baseball writers in the country, contributes to such publications as *Golf Digest, Esquire* and *Playboy.* Boswell has written two baseball books, *How Life Imitates the World Series* and *Time Begins on Opening Day.* Boswell, a three-time winner in *Best Sports Stories* competition is making his eighth appearance in the anthology. He also is a former winner of the American Society of Newspaper Editors first prize for sportswriting.

John Ed Bradley (Straub's Team Learns What 'Heart' Means) is a sportswriter for the *Washington Post.* Before arriving in Washington, Bradley attended Louisiana State University, where he earned four letters as a center for the LSU football team. He was captain of the 1979 squad. Bradley, who contributes regularly to *Esquire* magazine, is making his second appearance in *Best Sports Stories.*

Mark Bradley (Georgia Tech Has a Night To Remember) is a sportswriter and columnist for the *Atlanta Journal and Constitution.* After graduation from the

University of Kentucky in 1977, Bradley began his career with the *Lexington (Ky.) Herald-Leader* before moving to Atlanta in 1984. That was the year he finished second in the Associated Press Sports Editors column-writing competition. He followed that up one year later with a first place in the U.S. Basketball Writers Association feature-writing competition.

Michael Davis (co-author of Mom, Apple Pie and Wrestling) is assistant managing editor for news at the *Baltimore EVening Sun*. Davis, who is married and has two children, previously was the national correspondent for sports and deputy sports editor at the *Chicago Sun-Times*. He also served as an adjunct professor of journalism at Northwestern University.

Michael Disend (King of the New York Athletic Club) is a novelist, free-lance writer and boxer. Disend, who lives in New York's Hell's Kitchen, contributes to such publications as *Gentlemen's Quarterly*, in which this story appeared, and *Penthouse*. He has written a book, *Stomping the Goyim*, and is making his first appearance in *Best Sports Stories*.

John Eisenberg (My Destiny Was Not To Be a Good Player) has been writing features and profiles for the *Baltimore Sun* since 1984. The University of Pennsylvania graduate previously worked five years for the *Dallas Times Herald*, the final two of which he covered the Dallas Mavericks of the National Basketball Association. The 29-year-old Eisenberg is making his first appearance in *Best Sports Stories*.

John Feinstein (Evert Wins Record Sixth French Open) grew up in New York City and received a history degree from Duke University in 1977. After working as a summer intern at the *Washington Post*, he was hired as a metro staff reporter before moving to the sports department. During his nine years in Washington, he has covered police, courts and state politics on the news side and pro soccer, college football and basketball, major league baseball and tennis on the sports side. He currently covers college basketball and tennis. Feinstein, who is making his third appearance in *Best Sports Stories*, has contributed to such publications as *Sports Illustrated, The Sporting News, Inside Sports, the Washington Post Sunday Magazine* and *Outlook*. His first book, the story of one season with Indiana basketball Coach Bobby Knight, is scheduled to be published in November 1986.

Joe Hamelin (Wildcats Pitch a Perfect Game) has been sports editor and columnist for the *Sacramento Bee* since 1981. The 43-year-old Utica, N.Y., native began his career with the *Utica Daily Press* before spending three years with the *Indianapolis Star* and 11 with the *San Diego Union*, where he covered professional basketball. Hamelin lives with his wife and three sons in Auburn, Calif.

Sam Heys (Former Player Cleans Up the Gym) has been writing sports and general-assignment feature stories for the *Atlanta Journal and Constitution* for the past eight years. The 35-year-old Heys, a native of Chattanooga, Tenn., is making his first appearance in *Best Sports Stories*. He has a wife and three children.

Stan Hochman (Mays, Mantle Should Still Be Out) has worked as a baseball writer, sports editor and columnist during his 26 years with the *Philadelphia Daily News*. Before going to Philadelphia, Hochman worked for newspapers in Georgia, Texas and California. The Brooklyn native, who holds a master's degree from New York University, is not the only member of the Hochman family with a flair for journalism. His wife, Gloria, is an award-winning medical writer and his daughter, Anndee, is a reporter for the *Washington Post*.

Richard Hoffer (Hagler Puts End to Brawl and to Hearns in Third) has been writing features and covering boxing and a variety of other sports for the *Los Angeles Times* for the last six years. The Miami (Ohio) University graduate previously wrote for the *Massillon (Ohio) Evening Independent, Riverside (Calif.) Press-Enterprise* and the *Cincinnati Post*. Hoffer, who also holds a master's degree from Stanford University, was a 1985 winner in the *Best Sports Stories* reporting category and is appearing in the anthology for the fourth time.

Curt Holbreich (The Clemson Nightmare) covers University of Pittsburgh sports for the *Pittsburgh Press*. The 27-year-old Holbreich, a graduate of Wesleyan University and the Columbia University School of Journalism, joined the Press in December 1984 after stints at *USA Today* and the *Camden (N.J.) Courier-Post*. He is making his first appearance in *Best Sports Stories*.

Buck Johnson (Steps of True Grit) is the sports editor of the *Chattanooga (Tenn.) Times*. Johnson is a former junior high school coach who began working for the Times in 1952 on a part-time basis and finally retired from his coaching job in 1979 to devote full attention to journalism. He has been recognized many times, both for his coaching abilities and feature-writing skills. Johnson was cited 12 times as coach of the year on a local basis and was cited nationally as the Amateur Athletic Union's Media Man of the Year. He also received national recognition for a series he wrote on water pollution in the Chattanooga area.

Bruce Keidan (Players Betrayed Tanner's Trust in Them) has served as sports editor of the *Pittsburgh Post-Gazette* since 1980. He came to Pittsburgh after 11 years with the *Philadelphia Inquirer*. The University of Washington graduate also spent some time with the *Seattle Times* and the *Associated Press* before making the move to Pennsylvania. The 42-year-old Keidan is making his second appearance in *Best Sports Stories*.

Mike Klingaman (co-author of Mom, Apple Pie and Wrestling) has been a reporter for the *Baltimore Evening Sun* for 15 years. The West Virginia University graduate was a finalist in specialized reporting for a Pulitzer Prize in 1985 and captured a first place in the 1985 Associated Press Sports Editors competition for newspaper enterprise reporting. Klingaman, who also writes a weekly garden column, is making his first appearance in *Best Sports Stories*.

Tony Kornheiser (In the World Series, Any Buddy Can Be a Hero) is a columnist for the *Washington Post*. He previously was a staff reporter for *Newsday* and *The New York Times*. His work has been published in such publications as *Sports Illustrated, The New York Times Magazine, New York, Rolling Stone, People* and *Esquire*. Kornheiser won the feature-writing competition sponsored by the *Associated Press* in 1977 and 1981 and was the news-feature winner in *Best Sports Stories* in 1979. He is the author of *The Baby Chase*, a non-fiction book about adoption.

Kevin Lamb (Please Don't Feed the Bears) has covered the Chicago Bears and the National Football League since 1975 for the *Chicago Daily News* and the *Chicago Sun-Times*. He is a frequent contributor to magazines and has written three books, one of which was titled, *Quarterbacks, Nickelbacks & Other Loose Change: A Fan's Guide to the Changing Game of Pro Football*. The 34-year-old Lamb also has worked at the *Milwaukee Journal* and *Newsday* and has covered major league baseball and pro and college basketball as well as football. He is a 1973 graduate of Northwestern University.

Mike Littwin (Valvano Should Think This One Over) is a sports columnist for the *Baltimore Sun*. The University of Virginia graduate moved to Baltimore last August after working for seven years as a feature writer and occasional columnist for the *Los Angeles Times*, the publication in which his *Best Sports Stories* entry appeared. Before moving to Los Angeles in 1978, Littwin worked for the

Newport News Times-Herald and the *Virginian-Pilot* in Norfolk, Va. Littwin, who is making his fifth appearance in the anthology, wrote a biography of Dodgers pitcher Fernando Valenzuela that was published in 1981.

Roy McHugh (John Galbreath) is a former sports editor and columnist for the *Pittsburgh Press*. The 69-year-old McHugh retired in 1983, but continues to contribute stories on a periodic basis. A graduate of Coe College in Cedar Rapids, Ia., McHugh began his newspaper career with the *Cedar Rapids Gazette* in 1940. After rejoining the Gazette following service in World War II, McHugh moved to the Press in 1947 before taking the sports editor's job with the *Evansville (Ind.) Courier and Press*. McHugh, who was named Pennsylvania Sports Writer of the Year three times by the National Association of Sportscasters and Sportswriters, returned to Pittsburgh in 1969 as sports editor and added the column to his duties three years later. This is his sixth appearance in *Best Sports Stories*.

Sam McManis (Pure Kareem) has been a sportswriter with the *Los Angeles Times* since 1980. Since coming to Los Angeles, the 25-year-old California State-Fullerton graduate has covered a variety of sports, ranging from horse racing to Olympic track and field. He has spent the last two years covering professional basketball. McManis, who is making his debut in *Best Sports Stories,* is an occasional contributor to *The Sporting News* and *Sport* magazine.

Gary Nuhn (North Wins U.S. Open) covers golf and college sports for *Dayton Newspapers Inc.* and is a frequent contributor to *Golf* magazine. Nuhn, a Geneva, N.Y., native and Ohio State University graduate, has earned more than 20 national writing awards. He is making his fourth appearance in *Best Sports Stories*.

Bill Pennington (Hometown Bids Maris Farewell) covers baseball and writes feature stories for *The Record* in Hackensack, N.J. Before moving to The Record in 1984, the 29-year-old Pennington was sports editor of *The Advocate* in Stamford, Conn. The Boston University graduate won three national writing awards at the Associated Press Sports Editors conventions in 1983 and 1984 and two of his stories were selected New England's best by sports editors in his region. Pennington is making his second appearance in *Best Sports Stories*.

Ron Rapoport (Veeck Death Symbolizes End of an Era) has been a sports columnist for the *Chicago Sun-Times* since 1977. He was the 1984 winner of the National Headliner Award for "consistently outstanding sports columns." Before moving to Chicago, Rapoport worked for the *Los Angeles Times, Associated Press* and *Sport* magazine. He has been named top sports columnist in Chicago twice and is making his sixth consecutive appearance in *Best Sports Stories*. Rapoport has a degree from Stanford University and did his graduate work at the Columbia University School of Journalism.

Rick Reilly (Ty Cobb, Here I Come) has written features and covered college football for *Sports Illustrated* since April 1985. The Boulder, Colo., native began his career in 1981 with the *Boulder Daily Camera* after graduation from the University of Colorado and later worked for the *Denver Post* and *Los Angeles Times*. Reilly won two national awards at the Associated Press Sports Editors convention in 1984 and won the top feature award at the Associated Press Editors convention the same year. He is making his second appearance in *Best Sports Stories*.

Randy Rieland (co-author with George Starke of My Life With the Redskins) is a senior editor at *The Washingtonian*. He is former editor of *Pittsburgh Magazine* and *Regardie's*, a business magazine in Washington, D.C. Before that, Rieland worked as a reporter with the *Baltimore Sun* and the *Pittsburgh Press*.

Dick Schaap (The Gold That Tarnished) has been the sports editor for *Parade* magazine since 1983. Born in Brooklyn in 1934, Schaap graduated from Cornell University and then attended the Columbia University Graduate School of Journalism on a Grantland Memorial Fellowship. The versatile Schaap has been the city editor of the *New York Herald Tribune*, senior editor of Newsweek and the author of numerous books, including one of the best-selling sports publications of all time, *Instant Replay*. Schaap also has been a sports reporter for *NBC-TV's Nightly News, ABC-TV's World News Weekend Report* and *Today*.

John Schulian (Northern Star: The Great Alaska Shootout) is a syndicated columnist for the *Philadelphia Daily News* and a regular sports commentator for National Public Radio's *Weekend Edition*. Schulian, who moved to Philadelphia in 1984 after six years with the *Chicago Sun-Times*, also contributes to such magazines as *Playboy* and *Gentlemen's Quarterly*. He is a two-time winner of both the *Best Sports Stories* commentary award and the Associated Press Editors column-writing competition. Schulian also has received a National Headliner Award, an Emmy, the Nat Fleischer Award for excellence in boxing journalism and two nominations for a Pulitzer Prize. His 1983 book, *Writers, Fighters and other Sweet Scientists*, brought him favorable comparison with Red Smith and A.J. Liebling. Schulian is making his 10th appearance in the *Best Sports Stories* anthology.

Ross Wetzsteon (Dick Young's America) has been a writer and editor at the *Village Voice* for 20 years. He has written numerous free-lance stories on theater and sports for such publications as *Playboy, Rolling Stone, Sport* and *Tennis* magazines. His books include *The Obie Winners* and *Fool for Love and Other Plays (Sam Shepard)*.

Steven Will (After the Fall) is a free-lance writer and ice climber based in Auke Bay, Alaska. Will became a close friend of Kate Bull, the protagonist in his story, and became her climbing partner after her return to health. The story, which is based on conversations with her in the years following the accident on Old Snowy, appeared in *Women's Sports* and *Fitness* magazine.

PRIZE-WINNING PHOTOGRAPHERS IN BEST SPORTS STORIES 1986

Louis DeLuca (Loose-Ball Scramble) is a staff photographer for the *Dallas Times Herald*. He began his career with the *Shreveport (La.) Journal*, moved to the *Chicago Sun-Times* in 1983 and to Dallas a year later. The 29-year-old DeLuca was named 1982 Photographer of the Year in Louisiana, Texas and New Mexico and has won numerous other awards. He also captured first prize in the 1984 *Best Sports Stories* black-and-white action category.

Jeff Shaw (Devastated) began working as a staff photographer for the *Dallas Times Herald* in May 1984 after graduation from the University of Missouri at Columbia. The 26-year-old Shaw, who was born in Ann Arbor, Mich., and grew up in Ames, Ia., is making his first appearance in *Best Sports Stories*.

Gary Weber (Andujar's Rage) is a contract photographer for *Agence France Presse (AFP Photo)* and runs the photo service's Houston bureau. Weber, who graduated from the University of Wisconsin in 1982 with a degree in mass communications, moved to Houston after serving as *United Press International's* bureau manager in Des Moines, Ia. The 25-year-old Weber, a native of Milwaukee, previously worked part time at the *Milwaukee Journal* and served as a team photographer for the Milwaukee Brewers and Bucks.

OTHER PHOTOGRAPHERS IN BEST SPORTS STORIES 1986

Mike Adaskaveg (Soccer Somersault) is a staff photographer for the *Journal Inquirer* in Manchester, Conn. After graduation from Central Connecticut State University in 1975, Adaskaveg began his photojournalism career at the *Meriden (Conn.) Record-Journal.* He moved to Manchester a year later and covers both general assignments and sports for the publication. One of Adaskaveg's hobbies is photographing auto races. He is making his first appearance in *Best Sports Stories.*

Terry Bochatey (4192: The Emotion) has worked for *United Press International Newspictures* since his graduation from Colorado State University in 1972. He began his career in New York and was transferred to Columbus, O., a year later to take over as bureau manager. He moved to Cincinnati in 1980 to become Newspictures manager for the Ohio-Kentucky region. Bochatey is making his third appearance in *Best Sports Stories.*

Bernard Brault (Always Look Up! and What's Up Mr. McEnroe?) is a free-lance photographer who works out of Canada. Brault, who lives in Longueuil, Quebec, began his career in 1976 as a staff photographer for a local newspaper before taking the free-lance trail four years later. His work has appeared in several Quebec sports magazines and he has contributed to such wire services as *United Press Canada, Reuters* and *Canadian Press.* Brault, who recently began contributing to *La Presse* newspaper, earned second-place honors in the 1984 Baseball Hall of Fame photo contest. He is making his first appearance in *Best Sports Stories.*

Bill Frakes (Head Fake) has been a staff photographer at the *Miami Herald* for six years. Frakes has won numerous honors, including 1982 Newspaper Photographer of the Year, an award presented annually by the University of Missouri, an R.F. Kennedy Award and recognition from both World Press Photo and Overseas Press Photographers. Frakes, who is making his first appearance in *Best Sports Stories,* also free-lances for several other publications.

Adrian Keating (The Down Cycle) is a staff photographer for the *Journal Inquirer* in Manchester, Conn. Keating began his professional career as an English teacher in the Connecticut public school system before deciding that a change was in order. He hit the free-lance photography trail in 1977, doing work for both the *Associated Press* and *United Press International.* He became a staff photographer for the *Bristol Press* in 1983 but was part of a company-wide layoff that resulted in his move to Manchester. Keating won first place in the 1985 *Best Sports Stories* black-and-white action category.

John Keating (Float Like a Butterfly) is a staff photographer for the *Dallas Times Herald.* Before moving to Dallas, Keating worked as a staff photographer for the *Chicago Sun-Times.* He is married to Toni Giovanetti, a writer for the Times Herald.

Ted Kirk (Hold on There) is a staff photographer at the *Lincoln (Neb.) Journal and Star.* After attending the University of Nebraska, Kirk began his photography career with the *Daily Nebraskan,* a student newspaper. In 1976 he became a stringer for *United Press International* and took his current job in 1978. Kirk was named the Nebraska Newspaper Photographer of the Year for 1984-85.

Jay Koelzer (Down Under) has been a staff photographer for the *Rocky Mountain News* since July 1982. Koelzer, a 1977 graduate of the University of Kansas, began his career with the *Jackson (Miss.) Clarion-Ledger* before moving to Denver. While in Jackson, he was part of a team that won a 1981 Meeman Award for an investigative report on the waste-disposal policies of a major corporation. Koelzer has won two National Headliner awards, one in 1984 for sports and another in 1985 for feature photography.

Dave Kraus (Concentration and Heave Hay) is a staff photographer for the *Tulsa Tribune*. After graduating from the University of Kansas in May 1981, Kraus worked at the Tribune as an intern over the summer and joined the staff full-time in August of that year. He has since been named Oklahoma News Photographer of the Year three times.

Matthew McVay (Caught in the Act) is a staff photographer for the *Seattle Times*. He has photographed a wide variety of sports, ranging from the National Basketball Association championship series to major league baseball's All-Star Game. His photographs have appeared in such publications as *National Geographic, Time, Life, Newsweek, Ms., The New York Times* and the *Los Angeles Times*.

Odell Mitchell Jr. (Proud Moment) is a staff photographer for the *St. Louis Post-Dispatch*. Mitchell, a St. Louis native who received a journalism and mass communications degree in 1979 from Iowa State University, began his photography career for the *Iowa State Daily*, the student newspaper. After graduation, he spent two years as a staff photographer for the *Florida Times-Union/Jacksonville Journal* before moving to St. Louis. The 31-year-old Mitchell is married and has a 22-month-old daughter.

John Sheckler (Read My Lips) is a staff photographer for *The Standard-Times* in New Bedford, Mass. The 39-year-old Sheckler began his career as a newspaper photographer in Frankfort, Ky., moved to the *Middletown (O.) Journal* for eight years and finally to New Bedford. Sheckler has received awards from the National Press Photographers Association and the *Associated Press* in both Ohio and New England.

Paul A. Souders (Splash, Crash!) is a staff photographer for the *Montgomery County Journal* in Rockville, Md., a suburb of Washington, D.C. Souders, who specializes in shooting college and high school sports, has been working professionally for 3½ years. He also attends the University of Maryland and is slowly working his way toward a journalism degree. His only previous experience came for the Maryland student daily, the *Diamondback*.

The Panel of Judges for Best Sports Stories 1986

Brian Brooks is the *St. Louis Post-Dispatch* Distinguished Professor of Journalism at the University of Missouri and managing editor of the *Columbia Missourian*. The former reporter and editor at the *Memphis Press-Scimitar* is co-author of *News Reporting and Writing* and *The Art of Editing*, best-selling textbooks in their fields.

George Kennedy is an associate dean at the University of Missouri and an associate professor in the university's School of Journalism. Before moving to Columbia, Kennedy spent 7½ years as a reporter and editor with the *Miami Herald* and two summers as a writing coach for the *San Jose Mercury*. He is co-author of *News Reporting and Writing* and *The Writing Book*, two college and professional textbooks.

Ken Kobre is an associate professor in the photojournalism sequence at the University of Missouri. The former *St. Petersburg Times* and *Boston Phoenix* staff photographer is the author of two leading books on photography and has been director of the national Pictures of the Year competition for the last three years.

Daryl Moen is a professor at the University of Missouri and director of mid-career programs in the university's School of Journalism. He is the former managing editor of the *Columbia Missourian* and two other dailies. Moen also is co-author of *News Reporting and Writing* and *The Writing Book* and author of *Newspaper Layout and Design*.

George Pica is an assistant professor at the University of Missouri and director of the J. C. Penney-Missouri Awards Program. He is a former prize-winning editor of the feature and magazine sections of the *Eugene (Ore.) Register-Guard* and assistant managing editor of the *Seattle Post-Intelligencer*. Pica is a regular judge for other national writing competitions.